T0274096

THE
Witch's
BOOK OF
Spellcraft

About the Authors

Jason Mankey is a third-degree Gardnerian High Priest and helps run two Witchcraft covens in the San Francisco Bay Area with his wife, Ari. He is a popular speaker at Pagan and Witchcraft events across North America and Great Britain and has been recognized by his peers as an authority on the Horned God, Wiccan history, and occult influences in rock and roll. Jason writes online at *Raise the Horns* on Patheos Pagan and for the print magazine *Witches & Pagans*. You can follow him on Instagram and Twitter @panmankey.

Matt Cavalli has been a practitioner of the magical arts for over twenty-five years. He is an initiated Gardnerian Witch, a ritualistic and magickal teacher, and an accomplished drag performer. Matt has an unhealthy obsession with 1980s horror films and most days can be found haunting the Serpent's Kiss magic and ritual supply shop in Santa Cruz, CA.

Amanda Lynn has been dedicated to Witchcraft since childhood. For thirteen years she was a priestess in her local community, where she developed a penchant for ritual creation and spellcraft. These days, when she's not taking long walks in cemeteries or circling with one of her covens, she studies aromatherapy, esoterica, and intuitive magic. You can often find her checking out new music and wearing lots of glitter.

Ari Mankey has been practicing Witchcraft and creating spells for over twenty years. Away from the Craft, she has devoted her life to medical science and developing the perfect whisky ice cream. With her husband, Jason, she runs two covens in the San Francisco Bay Area.

THE
Witch's
BOOK OF
Spellcraft

A Practical Guide to Connecting with the Magick of Candles, Crystals, Plants & Herbs

JASON MANKEY
Matt Cavalli • Amanda Lynn • Ari Mankey

Llewellyn Publications • Woodbury, Minnesota

The Witch's Book of Spellcraft: A Practical Guide to Connecting with the Magick of Candles, Crystals, Plants & Herbs © 2022 by Jason Mankey, Matt Cavalli, Amanda Lynn, and Ari Mankey. All rights reserved. No part of this book may be used or reproduced in any manner whatsoever, including internet usage, without written permission from Llewellyn Publications, except in the case of brief quotations embodied in critical articles and reviews.

FIRST EDITION
Third Printing, 2024

Book design by Donna Burch-Brown
Cover design by Kevin R. Brown
Interior art by the Llewellyn Art Department

Llewellyn Publishing is a registered trademark of Llewellyn Worldwide Ltd.

The recipes, suggestions, and ideas in this book are based on the authors' personal experience and are not meant to constitute medical advice. For illnesses, consult a healthcare professional.

Library of Congress Cataloging-in-Publication Data
Names: Mankey, Jason, author.
Title: The witch's book of spellcraft : a practical guide to connecting
   with the magick of candles, crystals, plants & herbs / by Jason Mankey,
   Matt Cavalli, Amanda Lynn, and Ari Mankey.
Description: First edition. | Woodbury, Minnesota : Llewellyn Worldwide,
   Ltd, 2022. | Includes bibliographical references and index. | Summary:
   "This book explains how magick works and then describes the various
   types of magick that Witches use. Includes 15–20 spells of each type"—
   Provided by publisher.
Identifiers: LCCN 2021047184 (print) | LCCN 2021047185 (ebook) | ISBN
   9780738768748 (paperback) | ISBN 9780738769363 (ebook)
Subjects: LCSH: Magic. | Witchcraft.
Classification: LCC BF1611 .M3745 2022 (print) | LCC BF1611 (ebook) | DDC
   133.4/3—dc23
LC record available at https://lccn.loc.gov/2021047184
LC ebook record available at https://lccn.loc.gov/2021047185

Llewellyn Worldwide Ltd. does not participate in, endorse, or have any authority or responsibility concerning private business transactions between our authors and the public.

All mail addressed to the author is forwarded, but the publisher cannot, unless specifically instructed by the author, give out an address or phone number.

Any internet references contained in this work are current at publication time, but the publisher cannot guarantee that a specific location will continue to be maintained. Please refer to the publisher's website for links to authors' websites and other sources.

Llewellyn Publications
A Division of Llewellyn Worldwide Ltd.
2143 Wooddale Drive
Woodbury, MN 55125-2989
www.llewellyn.com

Printed in the United States of America

Other Books by Jason Mankey

The Horned God of the Witches
(Llewellyn, 2021)

Llewellyn's Little Book of Yule
(Llewellyn, 2020)

Witch's Wheel of the Year
(Llewellyn, 2019)

Transformative Witchcraft
(Llewellyn, 2019)

The Witch's Altar
(cowritten with Laura Tempest Zakroff, Llewellyn, 2018)

The Witch's Book of Shadows
(Llewellyn, 2017)

The Witch's Athame
(Llewellyn, 2016)

Forthcoming Books by Jason Mankey

Modern Witchcraft with the Greek Gods:
History, Insights & Magickal Practice
(cowritten with Astrea Taylor, Llewellyn, 2022)

Disclaimer

This book is not intended to provide medical advice or to take the place of medical advice and treatment from your personal physician. Readers are advised to consult their doctors or other qualified healthcare professionals regarding the treatment of their medical problems. Neither the publisher nor the author take any responsibility for any possible consequences from any treatment, action, or application of medicine, supplement, herb, or preparation to any person reading or following the information in this book.

*In memory of Michael Harris (1942–2021),
mentor, elder, dear friend, and
brother in the Craft*

Contents

Introduction
𝕸hat 𝕴s 𝕸agick?

It was a Friday night in mid-May and our coven was especially focused. For the first time ever we were all participating together in a large jobs spell. Several of us needed a change from our current circumstances, and a jobs spell seemed like the best place to start. Not all of us were looking to start completely over. Ari, for example, was simply looking for a little nudge that might advance her career. No matter the exact reason for each participant's involvement in the spell, we were all restless and seeking new opportunities.

Our spell involved a variety of disciplines. There were tokens representing wealth and prosperity, and a collection of stones and herbs had been laid out, all associated with growth and new beginnings. We wrapped all of these materials into small squares of cloth, saying incantations as we tied cords around our sachets and secured them with knots. Our bags now bound tightly, we anointed them with oils for success and sealed everything with a few drops of candle wax. We finished our work by chanting together, infusing our bags with extra energy. Every bag that night was unique, in a way every spell was different, but because of our shared energies, each bag was also a part of a greater whole.

The results trickled in over the next few weeks. Matt took a new job managing a local metaphysical bookstore. Amanda left behind the life of a barista and began managing a fleet of food trucks in Silicon Valley. Ari got that promotion she was looking for and was now the unquestioned leader of her department at work. Jason received an email from Llewellyn Publications (the publishers of this book), asking if he'd be interested in writing a book for them. The results from that night were real and tangible, and we've all had other successes when utilizing the power of magick.

It's not fair to say that magick was the only reason these things happened. Matt had to apply for the job he got and have the skills to succeed in it. Amanda worked hard to obtain her college degree and then had to seek a new employer. Spellwork didn't suddenly make Ari a stellar employee; she already was that. Jason had been writing online and teaching at Pagan festivals for years before he was asked to write a book. We were already in a position for these things to happen, but all of us believe that magick played a part in our subsequent successes. It was the little "push" that brought what we were looking for into our lives.

There are many who think that magick is not real, and that at most it's a trick of the mind. While we do not share this view, it's worth exploring for a moment. What if magickal success simply comes from a belief that we can change our own circumstances? What would be wrong with that? If the end result is the same, who cares how we get there? But because we've all experienced magick working in our lives, we ignore those who go out of their way to discredit it.

If you've spent a lot of time reading about magick over the years, you've probably read several different explanations for magick. Some of them sound quite scientific, while others are sweet and fluffy. What all of those sources suggest is that there is no real agreement as to just what magick is. The most notable definition of magick belongs to the English occultist Aleister Crowley, who wrote in his 1929 book *Magick in Theory and Practice* that magick is "the science and art of causing change to occur in conformity with Will." While there's a lot to like about that definition, it's far from complete.

Magick is both a science and an art. A well-organized Witch will keep track of the spells they cast and record the results of those spells. Over time, patterns generally emerge, allowing us to better examine our successes and failures. In a way, spells are like laboratory experiments, where certain actions consistently produce certain results. We can then choose to utilize what works best and discard the rest.

Spells are also like art. Ask a great painter just *how* to paint and it's likely that you won't get a satisfactory answer. Certainly practice and hard work contribute to greatness, but sometimes people are just born with certain skills that others don't possess. There are often people who are simply *very good* at working magick and do it almost unconsciously. Our intuition often serves as a powerful magickal guide.

Most of us probably use a combination of science and art when performing spellwork. We might look up the phase of the moon, consult a few books to find the best herbs and stones, and burn a particular incense while crafting a spell to obtain a certain result. While doing a spell, we might say a few poetic lines that feel appropriate to add to the magick we are creating. Whether your spellcraft is an art or a science is immaterial. What matters most is the results.

Crowley's definition of magick mentions "Will," a term that comes up frequently when discussing magick.[1] There are several competing ideas as to just what constitutes our will, but the simplest definition can be summed up as "our truest intent." When our will is guiding our magick, we are looking to manifest what we most desire. Sometimes our will disagrees with our conscious mind about what it is that we really want. You might think a promotion at work will make your life better, but your will might be pushing for a change in career instead.

When our waking mind is aligned with our true will, our magick becomes that much stronger. This is why an oft-repeated adage in magick is "Magician, know thyself." If you don't truly know yourself, it will be that much harder to manifest the changes you want in life. Effective magick requires more than just the knowledge of spellcraft; it requires us to truly know ourselves.

In the rawest sense, magick is simply energy. Energy is often something we can feel, though sometimes it can't be measured by conventional means. Energy on its own is neutral; it exists but often has no specific purpose. When we infuse energy with our intent (or will), it becomes magick. After we've filled that energy with our intent, we send it out into the universe to work for us.

Most everything in the world contains at least a little bit of energy. Stones and herbs can be used for magickal ends because they contain energy, and that energy generally affects most people in a certain way. Aventurine (a type of green quartz) emits an energy that tends to attract money and prosperity. Carrying a piece of aventurine in your pocket will make you the beneficiary of that energy.

The average person often suffers from the delusion that magick is "supernatural." Magick is not supernatural; it's the force that powers the universe. Sometimes we can explain the magick, such as a seed becoming a seedling and rising up from the ground, but it's still magickal. Just because something can be explained doesn't make it any less magickal. Magick is more than spells by candlelight; it can be found in the awe, wonder, and joy of existence.

There are many who argue that science and magick exist in opposition to each other, but nothing could be further from the truth. Science itself is magickal. That we live in a universe where new stars, galaxies, and planets are continually born is an example of magick in action. Energy exists everywhere throughout the universe.

---

1. To say Aleister Crowley was problematic is an understatement. He's had an enormous impact on the practice of modern magick, but many of his writings are sexist, racist, and anti-Semitic. It's hard to write about magickal philosophy without mentioning Crowley, but by no means are we endorsing all of his work.

It's the glue that holds everything together. We can explain a whole host of things through science, but the fact that complex systems of life and death were created from dust and gas is magickal, and it's magick that keeps everything humming along and moving together.

Using magick is empowering. Knowing that we can change our circumstances provides us with a certain amount of confidence and swagger. Magick has changed our lives on the outside, but it has also changed our lives internally. It allows us to better deal with what the world throws at us. Magick is not a crutch we use to get by; it's a force that strengthens instead of weakens.

Magick requires confidence on the part of the Witch. If you doubt your ability to work magick, then your magick will most likely fail. Instead of being infused with your magickal intent, it will contain nothing but doubt and misgivings. Magick requires us to *know* that it will be effective to have any sort of impact on our own lives.

Magick allows us to manifest change for ourselves and others. It turns thought into action. While many people sit around daydreaming about what they would like their lives to be like, Witches actively work to make their dreams a reality. Magick is not a passive activity; it's an active process and requires both our own contributions and our attention. If we aren't actively contributing to the spells we've cast, we aren't helping them manifest, and if we stop paying attention, we will fail to notice when we obtain the results we are seeking. The successful Witch is one who knows their purest intentions and powerfully acts to create them.

What Magick Can and Can't Do

Because magick and energy are natural parts of the universe, they behave in certain ways. Magick can't alter the course of a river or violate universal laws, but it can and does nudge things forward in our favor. Magick is a way to improve the odds of something happening, whether it's getting a new car or finding a suitable place to live.

Magick skeptics will often say things like, "If magick is real, why aren't you rich?" Magick is not going to manifest seven winning lottery numbers out of the blue. Instead, magick creates opportunities for us to get and keep a job. If you are looking for a new place to live, a prospective landlord isn't going to call you, but magick very well might result in you coming across their phone number.

Magick cannot rewrite the rules of biology. It does not have the power to cure cancer. However, when we do healing magick for our friends who are sick, we are sending them energy that makes them feel better and gives them the power to fight their own infections. A friend of ours was dying of lymphoma several years ago, and the night our coven sent him energy, he could both see and feel it arrive at his bedside. We didn't tell him we were doing a working for him. He simply felt it and told us about it the next day. Our coven didn't cure anything, but we did give him a bit of energy and strength to fight (and eventually win) his battle.

A love spell will not suddenly result in the person of your dreams knocking on your front door the next day. What a love spell will do is put you in a position where you might find a new lover or partner. When we work on a love spell, we are more aware of what we are searching for and pay more attention to what's going on around us. When we pay attention, good things happen.

Magick will make your life better, but it's not a cure-all. If you are sick, see a doctor. If your life is threatened, go to the police. But after doing those things in the mundane world, magick can help you feel better, and magick can help provide security where you live.

Magick works best when it's directed at very specific goals and problems. Wanting a million dollars sounds like a specific problem, but it's not. No one *needs* to be a millionaire. However, finding yourself without a home is a real problem, and the goal when dealing with such a problem is "a place to live NOW!" This is when magick is at its best: when it's used to find a solution to a real problem with a specific end goal.

Magick is also a long game. While sometimes the results can be quite quick, other times it can take years. Do you want to visit a foreign country? The magick used to create such an opportunity will manifest itself slowly over time. You'll have to start with a passport, and then enough money for an airline flight, and then money for a hotel. Periodically you may have to reinforce the magick you've put out into the universe with more magick.

There will also be times when your magick simply doesn't work. There are a variety of reasons for magickal failure. It's possible that your spell was too specific. Magick can't move a mountain in a week or even a lifetime. Or perhaps your magick wasn't in alignment with what you most truly desired. It's also possible that your heart was simply not in your work, or you were filled with doubt, or you were focused on something outside of your spell. Failure is a part of life, and that applies even to magick. When something doesn't work, the productive Witch works on figuring out why and then, most importantly, tries again.

Four Witches, Four Mostly Different Practices

Hi, my name is Jason, and I'll be your guide as we move through this book. Since elementary school, I've been fascinated with ancient paganisms, magick, and the unexplained. As a young adult, I made the conscious decision to live my life as a Witch, and I've been doing so ever since. My first few years as a Witch were solitary ones, but eventually I met other Witches (and Pagans) and began doing rituals with them. Over time I ended up leading and writing a lot of those rituals, which led me to do workshops on a variety of subjects at various magickal gatherings. Eventually I began writing books. This particular volume is the eighth to have my name on it.

For most of my life as a Witch, my practice has not been my own; it's been one I've shared with my wife, Ari. She discovered Witchcraft while in high school and then practiced magick in secret, away from the prying eyes of a fervently Catholic mother and stepfather. I struggled with the Craft (an abbreviation for Witchcraft) when I began practicing. Ari, on the other hand, is a natural-born Witch. She's never spent much time looking up correspondences for stones and oils in books but instead can simply hold such items in her hand and tell you their magickal properties. She was eighteen when I met her, and already one of the most gifted Witches I'd ever met.

Over the years, Ari and I have been in a number of Witchcraft groups and have maintained both our individual practices, along with rites and rituals that we share only with one another. We learned to write and lead rituals while in a Pagan student group at Michigan State University. When I first began doing workshops and leading rituals publicly, Ari was right there helping to guide, shape, and direct me. After many years of eclectic Witchcraft practice together, we were initiated into a British Traditional Witchcraft coven, which has been a part of our lives ever since.

In 2011 Ari and I moved to California's Bay Area and began visiting all of the local Witch and Pagan groups that would have us. Two of the first Witches we met during that time were Amanda Lynn and Matt Cavalli. When Ari and I started hosting rituals at our house a year later, Amanda and Matt were two of the first people we invited. By the end of the year, our rituals had turned into a full-fledged coven practice, and we've been doing it now for ten years.

When I put the first outline of this book together, I reached out to Matt for his opinion. I found Matt's comments on that outline so spot-on that I asked him if he would help me write this book! Like the rest of us, Matt began his love affair with Witchcraft and magick at a young age. At the local library he haunted the occult/

paranormal section of the stacks, enthralled by books on ghosts, hauntings, Halloween, and, of course, Witchcraft and magick..

At the age of twelve, Matt stole his mother's copy of *The Spiral Dance* by Starhawk, one of the essential Witchcraft books since its publication in 1979, and the seed was planted. When he read Laurie Cabot's *Power of the Witch* (1989) shortly thereafter, there was no turning back. Matt embraced the path of the Witch and began studying and practicing in earnest.

Matt's magickal interests extend far beyond Witchcraft. He's been enormously influenced by folk magick. In 2009 he started formally studying Conjure through the Lucky Mojo Curio Company and finds that this practice is the perfect complement to his Witchcraft. A warm and gregarious people person, Matt is an accomplished drag performer and is a mainstay at our most fabulous local Witch shop, Serpent's Kiss, in Santa Cruz, California.

At this shop, Matt guides Witches old and new through the ins and outs of creating powerful and effective spells. Whether he's simply offering advice to shoppers or conducting the most thorough magickal workshops in Northern California, Matt's magickal acumen is nearly legendary in our neck of the woods. Matt relies on both his intuition and his ongoing magickal studies to craft the most effective spells possible. I can say without hyperbole that Matt is one of the most formidable and talented Witches I've ever met. To both practice with him and have him as a part of this book has been one of the most rewarding experiences of my life.

As Matt and I discussed the contents of this book, we realized that we needed a couple more voices to make things as complete as possible. There were really only two choices: Amanda and Ari. While we all have very different personal practices and foundations, when we work magick and ritual together, it's like poetry. Not only did we know that Ari and Amanda would be great to work with, but we also knew we'd be getting a little extra Witchcraft education when they shared their practices with us!

Amanda began walking the path of the Witch early on. She was performing full moon rituals, studying astrology, and reading tarot cards while still a teenager. At the age of nineteen she attended the Spiral Dance, an annual Samhain ritual in California's Bay Area organized by the Reclaiming tradition of Witchcraft. That night, alongside two thousand other Witches, Amanda fell in love with group rituals and large Pagan gatherings. By her early twenties she had joined a public Pagan group in Santa Cruz, California, and found herself creating rituals and acknowledged as a High Priestess.

One of the most inspiring things about Amanda is how immersed she is in magick and Witchcraft. She truly loves the practice of the Craft and is involved in a variety of circles and covens, including an initiate-only tradition and an LGBTQ+ affirming women-only coven. As her practice has continued to grow, she has begun reconnecting to her ancestry through studying Jewish mysticism and has led rituals and workshops honoring Santa Muerte (a passion she shares with Matt and me). Amanda is one of the most accomplished Witches I know, and it's a privilege to share her point of view in this book.

Having four voices in one book means a lot of different perspectives, but as we started to put this book together, we began to wonder, "Is four really enough?" Because magick is so intensely personal and there are so many different ways to practice it, we asked some of our friends to contribute some spells and formulas. Sometimes their processes are radically different from ours, and that's great! We hope that by including other voices, we can paint a bigger picture of how today's Witches practice magick. The work of our friends is included in the "Shared Spell-craft" sections scattered throughout the spell chapters in this book, and they are some of the best things in these pages!

Because there are a variety of different perspectives in this book, you might occasionally come across bits of information that seem contradictory. We've tried to minimize such confusing moments, but magick is a very personal practice. Witches have all different kinds of worldviews and approaches to their Craft, so they often disagree on things related to magickal practice. The ideas expressed in this book are starting points, and we don't expect everything in these pages to resonate with you. In both our individual and our group practices, we use what works and discard the rest. We urge you to do the same.

How to Use This Book

If this is your first book about Witchcraft and/or magick, it might be tempting to just skip immediately to the spells and begin your work as a Witch. There's nothing wrong with doing that. The spells in this book are easy to do and rarely require very much in the way of exotic materials. But to get the most out of this book, you'll want to start at the beginning and build your spellcraft knowledge step-by-step.

This book is designed so that every chapter builds on what has come before it. We start at the beginning, with how magick works and a few magickal philosophies that have proven beneficial to Modern Witches. From there we move on to more advanced techniques, continually referencing previous material. You can go straight for the candle magick if you want, but your candle magick will be stronger and more effective if you master a few basics first.

Many of the chapters in this book contain long lists describing the magickal qualities of a variety of herbs, stones, trees, oils, and incenses. Those kinds of lists are often tedious, but we tried to do ours differently. Instead of just listing a few key words suggesting what a certain item can be used for in magick, we've included small bits of related spellwork from our own practices to make them more interesting.

This book concludes with four appendices designed to make it as easy as possible to find specific spells and the magickal qualities of the stones, oils, herbs, incenses, and colors written about in this book. The first part of appendix I lists twenty-two different categories of spells and their potential uses. No matter what type of magickal work you find yourself needing to do, it will likely fall into one of the categories included in this section. If you aren't sure about what type of spell you need to do, the explanations of the twenty-two spell categories included here will help you out.

The second part of appendix I takes those twenty-two different spell categories and provides a list of correspondences for each spell goal. If you need to work on a love spell, for example, you'll find over thirty different ingredients associated with love that are all profiled in this book. With the list of items and correspondences found under "love," you can easily create your own love spell or find a substitute for an item you don't have in one of the spells we've written.

Appendix II is a list of every herb, stone, crystal, oil, incense, and color written about in this book, and the magickal associations of each. Most stones and herbs have a variety of uses, and this appendix is a quick way to see the magickal properties of those items you do have. Want to burn some incense while doing a spell to banish a bad behavior? Use this appendix to see which incense you have on hand that will work best.

There are over a hundred spells scattered throughout this book. Most of those spells appear in the chapters dedicated entirely to spellwork, but there are many smaller spells included in the how-to chapters. Appendix III, our "Master List of Spells," includes every spell, oil blend, and magickal technique in this book, including those that aren't specifically called out by a heading in the text.

Appendix IV is a list of every spell in this book by category. If you need to work some magick to banish something or someone, you can flip to "banishing" in appendix IV and get the names and page numbers of over thirty banishing spells. This last appendix will help you find specific types of spells in a hurry.

The study of spellcraft doesn't require learning an entirely new lexicon, but there are a few terms out there used almost exclusively in Modern Witchcraft. If you are new to "the Craft" (short for Witchcraft), you might stumble across an unfamiliar word or two in this book. There's a glossary in the back of these pages that should answer any questions you have about particular Witch words.

Most bibliographies contain only the source materials used to put together a particular book, but ours is different. In addition to the sources that have informed the text, our bibliography is also a "further reading" list. We cover a lot of magickal topics in this book, and many of those specific topics have been the subject of entire books! We dedicate a few pages here to sigil magick, while our friend Laura Tempest Zakroff wrote a 250-page book about it! If you find a particular type of magick really resonating with you and want to learn more about that practice, you'll find something well worth reading in our bibliography.

We hope that you find the magick you are searching for in these pages and that the practice of the Craft improves and strengthens your life. And now, let the magickal journey begin!

Amanda, Ari, Matt, and Jason
July 2020

Chapter One
Magickal Philosophies and Ethics

Are there specific rules that must be followed when practicing Witchcraft? We are of the opinion that there are not. However, there are certain magickal philosophies that we find beneficial. These philosophies are ideas we return to again and again when writing spells or deciding what magickal tools to work with. These ideas are used by many, but certainly not all, Witches today.

Whether you choose to apply the philosophies in this chapter to your own Craft is entirely up to you. However, we will return to many of these philosophies several times throughout this book. We believe there are certain magickal adages that will make your spellwork more effective and more powerful. Many of the ideas expressed in this chapter have been a part of magick for thousands of years, while others are of a more recent vintage. Being familiar with a few of the more common and popular magickal philosophies in today's Witchcraft, no matter their age, will inform your own magickal practice.

Many of the most popular magickal philosophies tie directly into magickal ethics. There have always been fierce debates in the Witchcraft world about whether it is "proper" to curse or hex another person or even a fellow Witch. Ultimately, how you choose to wield magick is a personal choice.

Like Attracts Like

Perhaps the most frequently recited rule in magickal practice is "like attracts like." At its core, "like attracts like" is an example of sympathetic magick. While the ideas behind sympathetic magick most likely go back to our earliest human ancestors, the term itself was coined by folklorist James Frazer (1854–1941) and can be found in his seminal work *The Golden Bough*, which was published in over a dozen volumes across several decades. According to Frazer's description of sympathetic magick, "any effect may be produced by imitating it."[2]

In *The Golden Bough*, Frazer gives several different examples of this theory. In one of them, Frazer writes of a man carrying a bag of flaxseed that reaches from his shoulders to his knees. As the man sows the flaxseed, he walks with long strides, which makes the bag sway upon his back. This swaying is thought to imitate the waving in the wind of the eventual flax crop.[3]

Frazer, who wasn't a magician or a Witch, only scratches at the surface of sympathetic magick, which goes far beyond mere mimicry. It's probably more accurate to say that sympathetic magick simply involves any two (or more) things that might be related. For example, in the United States, where our money is green, a Witch would use items such as green candles or stones to work a money spell. Green candles are related to money because money is also green.

Money is an especially good example here because "like attracts like" and sympathetic magick are also related to the old adage "it takes money to make money." In the mundane world, it's difficult to start a business without at least a little bit of capital. In a similar fashion, many of us who work job or money spells actively include real money in those magickal workings. This doesn't mean that Witches burn twenty-dollar bills to find a new job; it means that we most likely use a couple of coins or a one-dollar bill as a symbol of money.

Using actual money in a money spell is beneficial for a couple of reasons. The first is that money has the energy of what we are looking for: more money. Both bills and coins have very real energies attached to them because of what they have been used for and what they are designed for.

Using money in a money spell serves another purpose, and this one might be even more important: it serves as a focus. If you are seeking more money and you are constantly looking at money, it's likely that you aren't going to lose your focus while working your spell. Magick requires focus, and "like attracts like" keeps our end goals in constant focus.

"Like attracts like" is such a powerful magickal adage that its end results can be seen in the real world. If someone is completely miserable all the time, it's likely that the people they associate with are also constantly miserable. On the opposite end of the spectrum, positive people tend to find positive people to hang out with.

---

2. James G. Frazer, *The Golden Bough: The Roots of Religion and Folklore* (1890; reprint, New York: Crown, 1981), 9.

3. Frazer, *The Golden Bough*, 10.

This idea also manifests in Witchcraft. If we seek out other Witches to work with who share our practices, we will most likely find them because they will be attracted to us. "Like attracts like" is often called the *law of attraction* and can be found outside of Witchcraft and other magickal traditions. It shows up often in self-help books and New Age materials and even among people who solicit business advice.

"Like attracts like" is one of the guiding principles in our magickal practices. If we were performing a love spell, for instance, we might use a piece of rose quartz as a focal point and then surround that rose quartz with paper hearts and rose petals. This would be done on an altar with a red altar cloth, after invoking the goddess of love, Aphrodite. There would also be rose incense and some pink (or red) candles burning on the altar. If the ritual was being done alone, we might play a love song suggestive of the type of love we desire. This would all be in addition to the words used in our spell, which would most likely be syrupy and poetic.

Everything added to the altar in this case would be something associated with love, and all of those objects would add their own energy to our magickal work, making it more potent. All of the items would keep our focus on the spell's intent as well. While burning frankincense will not doom anyone's love spell, the smell of that type of incense reminds some of us of (Christian) church. So the smell of frankincense might bring back unwanted memories and disrupt the focus of the spell. A better choice of incense would be anything associated with love, lust, or passion, such as cinnamon or rose. The more things you use in your spell to remind you of your end goal, the stronger your magick and spellwork will be.

When using the principle of "like attracts like" in your own magickal work, always trust your intuition. If you are doing a money spell, use what you think is a good representation of what you are trying to achieve. Books like this one really only offer suggestions and not absolutes. In the end, you have to use what makes the most sense to you. The connections between objects and ideas should be clear to you in order to create the most effective spellwork.

As Above, So Below

"As above, so below" is a magickal maxim that comes to us from the legendary *Emerald Tablet*. The Emerald Tablet is a brief list of magickal ideas that is generally thought to be quite ancient, though the earliest source of the tablet can only be traced to 800 CE. Although the Emerald Tablet is attributed to the supernatural figure Hermes Trismegistus, its true author is unknown. Scholars are not even sure exactly where the advice on the tablet comes from, with some thinking its origins lie in China and others Arabia (where our earliest copies come from). There are some who also think the tablet might represent Christian principles. No matter its origins, the Emerald Tablet has been a staple of magickal practice in the Western world for over eight hundred years; the tablet first showed up in Europe around the year 1200 CE.[4]

In most translations of the Emerald Tablet, there are only fourteen lines. While the most famous excerpt from the tablet is "as above, so below," the line itself is part of a much longer sentence: "That which is above is from that which is below, and that which is below is from that which is above, working the miracles of one."[5] As you can see, "as above, so below" is a pretty good abbreviation and is easier to say and remember during ritual or when performing spellwork.

"As above, so below" can mean a variety of different things. Some Witches link it to astrology, suggesting that the movements of the stars and planets are reflected here on Earth by our own actions. In an even more cosmic sense, "as above, so below" can refer to the mysteries of the universe, the belief here being that within ourselves we can see the wonder of the entire universe, and, conversely, we can see the individual human spirit in the grander, more cosmic scheme of things. If we are going to understand the universe or even just our world, we must first understand ourselves.

Perhaps most importantly in a book on magick, "as above, so below" is illustrative of how magick works. It's not enough to just live in the magickal world and cast spells to solve our every problem. What we do magickally must be acted upon in the mundane world. If we are doing magick to secure our financial future, we also have to do things in the everyday world to secure that future. Lighting candles and chanting to solve our money woes is not enough. The magick we cast on our altars has to be followed up by our own actions.

Magick doesn't exist in a vacuum; it's connected to the earth and to the greater universe. While we often work on our spellcraft in places set aside for magickal work, the energy we create there remains a part of something bigger than just our circles and altars. We enact magick in these smaller places to enact change in larger spaces. What we do in the microcosm is eventually reflected in the macrocosm.

---

4. Christopher Drysdale, in Jason Mankey's *The Witch's Book of Shadows* (Woodbury, MN: Llewellyn, 2017), 85–88.

5. Drysdale, in Mankey's *The Witch's Book of Shadows*, 85–88.

Another way of looking at "as above, so below" is to use the phrase "as within, so without." What exists inside of us will also show on the outside. If a person is looking for love, they must first learn to love themselves before they will be capable of loving another. If we want to be successful, we have to feel the potential for success in our heart and mind, even if we haven't quite achieved it yet.

What we do and how we feel will be reflected back to us. In a sense, "as above, so below" is tied directly to "like attracts like," but it's also a reminder of our responsibilities after working magick. What we do magickally has to then become a part of our mundane life. It's not enough to simply cast a spell; the spell must be acted upon. Our mundane self has to be in sync with our magickal self to get the results we want.

The Wiccan Rede: An It Harm None, Do What Ye Will

Mention the Wiccan Rede online today and you are likely to hear a whole bunch of complaints from people who are adamant that the Rede doesn't apply to them. And those people are right, of course: the Rede only applies to Witches (Wiccan or otherwise) who choose to follow it. Despite sounding rather grandiose, *rede* simply means "advice or counsel."[6] The Wiccan Rede is not a rule or a law, and like all pieces of advice, people are free to heed it or to disregard it entirely.

Though the Wiccan Rede sounds a bit archaic, it's actually a rather modern creation. It was first publicly uttered in its current form of "an it harm none, do what you will" by Doreen Valiente (1922–99) in 1964 at a dinner for the Witchcraft Research Association.[7] It's likely that the Rede predates its appearance in 1964, as a version of it appears in the 1959 book *The Meaning of Witchcraft* by Gerald Gardner (1884–1964).[8] In that particular book, Gardner states that the morality of Witches is similar to that of the "Good King Pausol," whose philosophy was "do what you like as long as you harm no one." Gerald Gardner is an important figure in the history of Modern Witchcraft. He was the first self-identifying public Witch, which was a pretty big deal back in 1951.

Good King Pausol sounds like a fine fellow, but he wasn't a historical personage; he was a twentieth-century French literary creation. Gardner also got his name wrong: Pausol should be spelled Pausole. If there was a real person other than

6. Lexico, powered by the *Oxford English Dictionary*, s.v. "rede," accessed October 1, 2021, https://www.lexico.com/en/definition/rede.

7. Sorita d'Este, and David Rankine. *Wicca: Magickal Beginnings* (London: Avalonia, 2008), 64.

8. Gerald Gardner, *The Meaning of Witchcraft* (London: Aquarian Press, 1959), 93.

Gardner lurking behind the Wiccan Rede, it was probably Aleister Crowley, whose magickal philosophy "do what thou wilt shall be the whole of the Law" sounds similar to the Rede.

Many of the bad feelings toward the Rede today arose from Witches proclaiming it as a philosophy or rule for the entire Witchcraft world. Back in the 1990s, it was common to write about Pagan practices as being nearly identical to Wiccan ones, all while Wicca was the only large Witchcraft tradition being actively written about. This led to blanket statements such as "all Witches practice the Rede," when such a thing was never true. Even many Wiccan-Witches don't have much use for the Rede, which is fine!

Throughout the late 1970s and into the early 1990s, people in many parts of the world (especially the United States) were gripped by "Satanic panic." People who promoted the theory of Satanic panic claimed that a worldwide network of Satanists were abducting children and sacrificing them to the Christian devil. There has never been any evidence for this, but people were sent to jail for decades, in some cases on bogus charges. Witches, even though they didn't worship the Christian devil, were also accused of being involved in this conspiracy. Because of this, it became more and more commonplace in the books of the period to talk glowingly about the Wiccan Rede as a crafty public relations move. The Rede probably means more to people outside the Craft than to people in it.

When thinking about the Wiccan Rede, we are often reminded of "like attracts like." While there are most certainly times when aggressive forms of spellcraft are called for, if that was the only type of magick a Witch practiced, they'd probably run into some problems. If like attracts like, and a Witch only throws curses at people, it seems likely that some of those curses will be lobbed back at them. Surround yourself with negativity and you'll attract even more negativity.

In the end, the Wiccan Rede is a piece of advice that the individual Witch is free to use or ignore. If the Rede makes sense to you, then by all means embrace it. There's plenty of magickal work that can be done that does not actively seek to hurt others. Spells for protection and justice can act as a deterrent to bad behavior and result in punishment for those guilty of bad behavior. If, on the other hand, you want to conjure up some curses to direct at your awful neighbors, have at it. We're guessing that most of you will probably find the middle ground that we all use in our own practices. We are generally nice and good to most people, but there are simply times when something a little more aggressive is called for.

The Threefold Law

An oft-repeated "rule" of Witchcraft is what has come to be known as the *Threefold Law* or the *Threefold Law of Return*. This idea basically states that if a person does good in this world, then that good will return to them threefold. Conversely, if a person does bad, that bad will return to them threefold. Most people interpret this rule as happening in something close to real time, meaning that whatever good the person does will come back to them in this lifetime and not the next.

The idea behind the Threefold Law is related to the idea of karma as expressed in many forms of Buddhism and Hinduism. The difference is that in those traditions a person's actions determine their fate in their next incarnation. Those who write about the Threefold Law in Witchcraft generally suggest that its end results will be felt in this lifetime, which means bad people will be punished for their dire deeds before they die.

An alternative version of the Threefold Law shows up in Gerald Gardner's 1949 fiction book *High Magic's Aid*. In that novel, Gardner's High Priestess character says, "But mark well when thou receivist good, so equally art bound to return good threefold."[9] This statement is the likely origin of the Threefold Law in Modern Witchcraft, but Gardner's High Priestess is suggesting something very different from karmic retribution. All that's being suggested is that if good is visited upon a Witch, a Witch should return that good three times. In other words, if someone gives you a dollar, you should probably also give something equivalent to that in time or money to others. Many people would refer to this philosophy as simply "paying it forward."

Instead of relying on the universe to reward or punish, we advocate the "paying it forward" approach to Witchcraft. When good things happen to us, we share that good with others. And as Witches, we believe in being active when circumstances are challenging. Instead of waiting for the universe to administer justice, we take matters into our own hands, using magick to create a better way forward for ourselves.

On Baneful Magick: Hexes and Curses

The terms *hex* and *curse* occur with frequency in Witch circles. Generally both terms refer to a magickal act designed to result in harm or punishment. Often included with these two words is the term *binding spell*, though it should be noted

---

9. Gerald Gardner, *High Magic's Aid* (Hinton, WV: Godolphin House, 1996), 188.

that a binding spell is quite different from a hex or a curse. Binding spells are most often pieces of spellcraft designed to stop someone from performing a certain action. They aren't necessarily harmful, but they do interfere with an individual's free will. Because of this last bit, there are many Witches who are as uncomfortable with bindings as they are with hexes and curses.

Because of the influence of the Wiccan Rede on Witchcraft as a whole over the last fifty years, binding, cursing, and hexing are seen as nonstarters by many Witches. We don't share that opinion. While we don't recommend using aggressive forms of magick in an attempt to solve all of life's problems, we do believe that such actions are sometimes necessary.

That brings up the question: Just what justifies an aggressive magickal response?

We all have the right to protect ourselves and those we love and care about. If you are being threatened physically, emotionally, or verbally, you are certainly justified in using magick to help stop the abuse. You have the right to try to magickally silence someone if they are spreading malicious gossip and actively trying to ruin your life. If someone at work is a sexist creep, spellwork can help put an end to that bad behavior. But magick should never be used to completely take the place of law enforcement or the judicial system. If your life is truly being threatened, seek help immediately.

Is your magickal work just or is it petty? This is a pretty big question in our minds. We've all had poor bosses at work, but do poor management decisions justify a threatening magickal response? Every situation should be looked at with nuance and with an understanding of just what is at stake. To us, just cause is about stopping someone from hurting us or others. If someone is taking advantage of people in our community financially or sexually, a measured and aggressive magickal response might be necessary.

Witchcraft is an empowering practice, and empowered people are not submissive. As Witches, we can't imagine letting people walk all over us, especially if we have the ability to put a stop to such things or prevent them from happening. Witches exist on the periphery of society, and that status as outsiders has traditionally made us strong. Our neighbors know we are Witches, and while most of them like us and think we are nice people, it's probably advantageous that deep down some of them are just a little bit afraid of us!

Before you decide to pursue an aggressive course of magickal action, it might be wise to try a different approach: kill them with kindness. Sometimes an approach built on changing a behavior for the better can produce more beneficial results.

One of us once had a terrible boss, someone who took credit for work they didn't do and generally was a detriment to the work environment. Instead of casting a spell to get this person fired, a spell to sweeten their disposition was done instead, and the results were favorable. This person became much easier to deal with and actually came to the realization that they were doing more harm than good and left on their own accord.

But just because more aggressive forms of magick can be justified, that doesn't mean a young Witch should begin with curses and hexes. There is some real benefit to rules like the Wiccan Rede when starting down the magickal path. Magick is about self-responsibility, and while "bad" is not guaranteed to be returned to you (or anyone else) threefold, there are always consequences to your actions. Before trying to remove someone from your life, it would probably be best to see just what power magick holds in your life first, and what its repercussions are when you practice it. In the end, we are all ultimately responsible for our magickal work and the effects it has (or doesn't have) on others. Proceed with caution, but don't let anyone step on you.

Chapter Two
Preparing Magickal Space

Magick can be done at any time and in any place. There are no rules dictating when and where a Witch can work a spell. However, there are certain places that are more advantageous than others. The most natural place for a Witch to work their spellcraft is at a personal altar. Altars don't have to be elaborate and can be as simple as the top of a dresser or a bookshelf.

What makes an altar special is that it's a place where a Witch does their work and stores many of their magickal tools. A place that is frequently used for magickal work will resonate with energy, and when a place hums with magickal energy, it becomes that much easier to tap into your magickal self. If you use your altar with regularity, it's likely that you can feel its presence every time you walk by it. Another powerful reason for having an altar is that any "leftover" energy on it can be directed toward whatever spellcraft you might be working on.

Does a Witch need an altar or tools? Absolutely not. If neither of those things appeals to you, they don't have to be used. But altars and tools allow us to focus our own personal energies that much more easily. Think of magick like cooking. It's possible to cook with nothing more than a pot and a campfire, but it's easier to make a great meal with the help of several tools and kitchen appliances. Magickal tools and magickal spaces add to the energies we raise when casting a spell, and often help make them more powerful.

Tools and altars can help us feel more magickal, and the more magickal we feel when working magick, the stronger our magick will be. Tools and altars have an almost hypnotic effect. The more witchy you feel while working magick, the more effective your magick will be. Do you have to do all of your spells by candlelight while burning incense? Of course not, but oftentimes the results of your spellwork will be just a little bit stronger if you do.

There are many Witches who go beyond just using an altar during magickal work and choose to practice their spellcraft in sacred space. In Witchcraft, sacred space is an area specially prepared for magick and ritual. In sacred space, powers such as goddesses, gods, and the four elements of earth, air, fire, and water are invited into the area where the Witch is doing their work. (If the powers are invoked properly, it's likely that the individual Witch will feel and be very aware that they are present.) Sacred space allows both higher powers and our beloved dead to interact more easily with us.

Creating sacred space is usually not necessary when doing spellwork, but if you are seeking allies in your work (such as deities, elemental powers, ancestors, etc.), those powers are easier to connect with in sacred space. When properly created, sacred space is sometimes referred to as a place "between the worlds."

There are several different ways to create sacred space. In Wiccan-Witchcraft, casting a circle is the most common method of creating sacred space. A circle is a magickal boundary designed to keep unwanted entities out, to contain magickal energy until it's ready to be used, and to act as a gateway to worlds outside of this mundane one. In Traditional Witchcraft, the Witches' Compass fulfills a similar role. If you are unfamiliar with these techniques, they can easily be found online and in hundreds of various books.[10] You should always set up your sacred space in a way that makes sense to you. There are no right or wrong ways to go about it.

No matter how sacred space is set up, there tends to be one constant that occurs at the beginning of the process: cleansing. It is important to cleanse both the self and the space where the magickal work will take place. It's nearly impossible to set up effective sacred space without cleansing, and it's equally challenging to practice magick if we aren't personally cleansed and ready for it.

Cleansing and Purifying

Because magick is essentially energy, it's important to get rid of any negative or unwanted energy before beginning spellwork. When Witches talk about cleansing and purifying, they generally are referring to a physical/mundane space, the energy that fills a space, and the self. The easiest of these three things to clean up is physical space. Before performing magick, we like to make sure our altars are prepared and ready for magickal work and the space around us is clean and tidy. In group

---

10. Jason writes extensively about those techniques in his book *Transformative Witchcraft*, which has a long section on creating sacred space.

settings, this often means sweeping and mopping the ritual space before meeting. (Brooms, they are for more than just flying!)

Perhaps even more important than making sure the floor is not dirty is to remove any unwanted energy in the space where you will be working your magick. Despite our best efforts, it's nearly impossible to be happy and content all the time. We all have bad days, and part of life involves the inevitable sadness that comes with losing friends, family members, and animal companions. When we are met with stress, grief, anger, heartbreak, and other more negative emotions, those energies accumulate in the spaces where we live. Cleansing and purifying are how we get rid of them.

You might not think of negative energy in your magickal space as all that important—"My day wasn't *that* bad!" comes to mind—but negative energy can have a major impact on spellwork. Think of the energy used for a magickal spell as being like a glass of water. You've poured nothing but your pure intent into your working, and your focus is completely clear (like water). But let's just say that there's some bad energy in the space where you are working magick, and that negative energy mixes with your clear and pure energy. The end result is something like a drop of ink splashing into your clear water. That water, like the energy you've raised, is now polluted.

The most important part of any cleansing begins with the individual Witch. If you perform a cleansing with a lackadaisical or bad attitude, you'll probably make the condition of your magickal area worse than it was when you started. The best way to cleanse is with a clear and sincere intention. You have to want your space to be clear of negative energy. If you don't truly want to change the space around you, it can't be changed.

Articulating your intention when cleansing will help with your focus and make your work more productive. To that end, we begin any cleansing by saying something like "I cleanse and purify this space, that it might aid me in my magickal workings." No matter how you choose to cleanse your magickal space, remember that you are an integral part of the work!

Common Ways to Cleanse Space

There are lots of different ways to cleanse and purify a magickal space. The most common ones involve salted water, incense/smoke, and a broom. None of these methods are superior to the others, and it's up to you to decide what works best for you. You can also use all of them at once or rotate between the various methods. As always, what resonates most with you will be the most effective way to cleanse your space.

Salted Water

Salt has been used to cleanse magickal spaces and tools for centuries. Salt has several properties that make it an important tool in magickal work. The first is that salt is very good at absorbing negative energy. Simply leaving a bowl of salt on your altar, or even just in your regular living spaces, will keep a lot of negative energy at bay. The salt absorbs the negative energy and also dissolves it, eating away at the bad stuff until the unwanted energy no longer remains. In magickal work, salt is most often mixed with water, and then that water is scattered around the ritual space.

Smoke and Incense

Smoke works the same way as salt: it will eat away at negative energy and leave your space cleansed and refreshed. Both incense and bundles of herbs work equally well to cleanse a space, so pick the option that resonates most with you. An incense stick or herb bundle can be lit directly with the flick of a lighter, but we think it adds a little extra *oomph* to ceremonially light whatever you are going to produce smoke with.

A handy alternative to smoke is a spray bottle of water with a few drops of essential oil added to it. Many essential oils are great for cleansing, and a few drops of ylang-ylang or clary sage added to some water will produce results similar to those of salted water or smoke. This is especially useful if you are bothered by smoke or live in an apartment or dorm room where incense burning is not allowed.

Using a Broom

Using a broom (sometimes called a *besom*, especially when used only for magickal purposes) to sweep up negative energy is similar to how we use brooms in our mundane lives, and it's perfectly fine to use your house broom to cleanse your magickal space, too. To use a broom to sweep up negative energy, simply sweep around your space in a clockwise direction, stopping to sweep upward when you feel it's warranted. We'll often sweep around windows, too, and even up toward the ceiling if we feel there's negative energy there. Be sure to keep the negative energy in front of your broom so you can sweep it all out and away.

Unlike salted water or smoke, a broom won't dissolve negative energy, so you'll have to literally sweep the negative energy out of your magickal space and ideally out the front door and far away from you. A broom is an effective tool for cleansing, but simply leaving the bad energy in your living room will lead to issues down the road.

There are times when cleansing a room is not really necessary. Well-kept (and used) altars keep negative energy away all on their own, and wild outdoor spaces are generally cleansed by the natural powers of rain/dew, wind, earth, and heat. Even if you don't think a room needs to be cleansed, it never hurts to do so.

Cleansing the Self

Cleansing the self is even more important than purifying our physical spaces. If a Witch begins their magickal work full of anger, that anger will slip into their work. While a bit of simmering anger might help to power a protective spell, it would probably have a disastrous effect on a love or money spell. Cleansing the self allows us to focus on the spellwork at hand and helps us set aside the distractions that might negatively affect our work. If self-cleansing is required, it should be done before you cleanse your magickal space.

Self-cleansing begins within. No amount of salted water or smoke can clear away all the worries of work or a troubled relationship. We are our own best tools when it comes to self-cleansing! Lingering work stress is a great example of unneeded energy. If your thoughts during a magickal working continually drift back to a looming deadline, your magick will suffer for it.

The easiest way to cleanse yourself is with an exercise involving breath. Before beginning this exercise, think about all the unneeded and unwanted things currently coursing through your brain and body. Imagine those thoughts and feelings collecting in your lungs. When you feel those things enter your chest, take a deep breath, and then exhale slowly, picturing all of those unwanted emotions leaving your body as you exhale. You may need to repeat this process a few times to rid yourself of all that's unwanted. And because all that unwanted energy is now sitting in your magickal space, you should immediately cleanse that space to get rid of it.

Blessing Bowl

Another great way to get rid of negative energy is with a blessing bowl. You don't need much in the way of tools to create a blessing bowl, just a bowl of water with a few drops of essential oil added to it.[11] You should set up your blessing bowl in a

---

11. What type of essential oil you use depends on how you feel at the moment. If you need an intense cleaning, a cleansing oil such as ylang-ylang is recommended. If you are simply looking to remind yourself that you are a being who deserves to be happy and loved, then something like rose oil would be appropriate.

quiet place where you won't be disturbed. After you've done that, you are ready to begin.

Start this rite by reminding yourself that you are a magickal person who deserves to use the power of Witchcraft to better your life. Once you have affirmed your right to the powers of the Witch, anoint yourself with the water in the blessing bowl by touching each part of your body where the rite calls for it, as follows:

I deserve to walk the path of the Witch.	(Anoint feet.)
I deserve transformation and change.	(Anoint hands and/or knees.)
I deserve to feel pleasure.	(Anoint sexual organs.)
I deserve to feel love.	(Anoint heart.)
I deserve to speak with power.	(Anoint lips or right above lips.)
I deserve to hear truth.	(Anoint ears.)
By sea and sky, by earth and flame, I am a Witch!	(Anoint center of forehead.)

This part of the rite can be used any time before a magickal working, even if you don't feel the need for a traditional self-cleansing. The blessing bowl is an affirmation that we are sacred, holy, and deserving of Witchcraft.

After you have blessed yourself, take the index finger of your dominant hand and begin swirling it clockwise in the water in the blessing bowl. As you do so, imagine the unwanted energies and emotions inside of yourself moving through your body, into your finger, and out into the water. As the negative energies pour out of your body, imagine them moving as if they were circling down a drain, moving further and further away from you. Continue doing this until you feel fully cleansed.

One advantage of pouring your negative energies into a bowl of water is that they are contained. If your space doesn't need a full cleansing, you don't have to do one, because the energy you've expelled from yourself is not going to creep back into it. You are free to begin your magickal work if you so choose. Just be sure to get rid of your negative water when you are done with your working. The water can be either poured down a regular old drain or taken outside and given to the earth.

When we work as a group, we often use smoke and salted water to cleanse all the participants of our ritual. Using such tools can be a bit harder for solo Witches but can still be done if it appeals to you. As always, what's most important is that the cleansing method you use works for you!

The typical order for cleansing before beginning magickal work is to cleanse the mundane space, then cleanse the self, and then finally cleanse the magickal space of negative energy. The exact amount of cleansing needed will vary from Witch to Witch and situation to situation. Always try to do at least the minimum of what you think is needed, and if you can do even more, great! The better cleansed you and your space are, the better your magick will work!

Chapter Three
Creative Visualization and the Written Word

With magick, you'll find that you often get exactly what you ask for, which means you should really take some time before casting a spell to think about what you truly want. Let's imagine that you want to cast a love spell for yourself and decide the purpose of your spell is "to fall in love." On the surface that sounds completely reasonable. Who doesn't want to fall in love? But a spell designed to help someone "fall in love" can lead to unexpected problems or consequences.

If you are looking for romantic love, simply "falling in love" doesn't guarantee that. You could fall in love with a new restaurant or have your heart stolen by a kitten or puppy. Perhaps the spell manifests by helping you realize you truly love one of your best friends or a family member. Or, perhaps worst of all, the spell ends up with you in love with someone you'd like for a romantic partner, but that potential romantic partner doesn't love you back.

A much better and more precise way of using magick to find a romantic partner is to build a spell around the idea of "falling in romantic love and having that love reciprocated." This more precise wording tells the universe that you are looking for a lover who will love you in return. Magick rewards being specific, though being specific is often more challenging than it's made out to be. Knowing how to articulate what we truly want as Witches is a skill that takes time to develop.

There are two skills that are especially helpful when trying to come up with specifics in spellwork. The first is note-taking. Taking five or ten minutes to jot down the specifics of what you are seeking will give greater focus to your magickal endeavors. Taking magickal notes doesn't entail writing a novel or even a paragraph; it's just a way to clarify what's in your head. An example of this would be to write down the characteristics you are most looking for in a relationship so you can include those requests in your spellwork.

But perhaps even more important than note-taking is a process known as *creative visualization*. Creative visualization (or CV) is when we see things in our mind's eye, but it goes much deeper than that. If someone asks us to imagine a perfect summer day, that's usually easy enough. We picture blue skies and imagine that it's warm outside, and generally visualize green grass and perhaps some flowers or a tree full of leaves. That's a good start, but good CV will often take that image even further, to the point that it indulges all of the senses.

Now let's imagine our perfect summer day but with even more details. The blue sky and green grass remain, but now we can feel a light breeze blowing from the west on our skin. Picturing ourselves barefoot, we feel the earth beneath our feet, cool and slightly damp. Breathing deeply, we can smell grasses and perhaps catch the faint scent of a distant flower. In the background we hear birds singing and the steady rhythm of cicadas chirping in the distance. Effective CV indulges more than just our sense of sight; it incorporates all of our senses. When "visualizing" something, we are experiencing everything that might exist in the mental picture we are painting.

Creative Visualization in Magick

When we work magick, creative visualization is a vital first step. If you can't see what you are trying to manifest, it's unlikely that your magick will work. No matter what magick technique you ultimately choose to use, it will generally start with CV. If you need a new job, it's likely that long before you light a candle or use an essential oil, you'll picture yourself in a new job, but that's only the beginning in order to use CV effectively.

Creative visualization is about more than just visualizing one picture; it's about seeing everything in motion. For a job spell, you'd want to imagine yourself in the type of job you are looking for and making the type of salary you are seeking. But in addition to that, you'd also need to visualize the steps it would take to get to that point. So truly effective CV would involve steps such as seeking a job (sending in resumes, etc.) and then going through the interview process. You'd want to visualize yourself acing all of those steps in addition to your end goal.

Because magick is very specific, using creative visualization allows us to see the details we might not have considered otherwise. It's easy (and usually enjoyable) to think about a new job, but it's another thing entirely to remind ourselves of the drudgery that often accompanies such endeavors. It's also important to picture how you might react in the situation you are trying to create. What type of person would you be if you were in a certain situation?

There are also a lot of variables involved in just about every potential scenario, and CV is an opportunity to explore those variables. Maybe you prefer to work on your own and all of a sudden you realize that what you thought you wanted requires dealing with lots of folks. Uh-oh! Use CV to create clarity to get exactly what you want. If you visualize something happening to you in realistic detail, it will help you see any undesirable consequences and situations that you might want to avoid.

Creative visualization can also work as a very immediate form of magick. Imagine for a moment a menial yet often frustrating task, such as trying to thread the eye of a needle with a fine piece of thread. Sometimes this can take several attempts, with each subsequent attempt getting more and more difficult due to rising frustration levels. Instead of getting angry, stop for a moment, close your eyes, and take a deep centering breath. As you breathe in, imagine the thread moving easily and precisely through the needle's eye. If you were doing this in real life, then upon opening your eyes and resuming your task, the thread should now go easily through the needle's eye.

It's possible to explain away magick in this case by suggesting that the deep breath and momentary look inward simply quieted the nerves and the brain and made the task at hand much easier. We aren't going to dismiss this interpretation, but there's most certainly magick at play here. Even something as simple as visualizing a specific task requires energy, and when we add a mental picture to that imagining, we've filled that energy with intent (in this case, the energy and focus needed to thread a needle). When we open our eyes after the visualization, we are releasing that energy out into the universe to manifest. Because the operation is small, the magick works quickly and easily and our needle has been threaded.

Magick is not limited to big life-changing events. It can be used for small tasks, too. Before a trip to Glastonbury in the UK, Ari increased the incline on the elliptical machine at her local gym and visualized herself walking up Glastonbury Tor easily, with no shortness of breath. To some, this may not have felt like magick, but Ari was casting a spell with those steps and that focus. She was casting a spell not only for the fitness to walk up the Tor but also to arrive safe and sound in Glastonbury. She released her intent out into the universe by visualizing it, turning the slog of the gym into a magickal exercise.

Creative visualization is similar to the idea of a mantra. A mantra is generally a word or phrase repeated over and over again that is used to focus the mind or help manifest an idea, want, or need. If you are planning a big spell, frequently visualizing your end goal and the steps needed to get there will make your magick more powerful. With every visualization, you are creating energy and focusing your mind on the magickal task at hand. A spell doesn't begin only when we light a candle or say a collection of words; it begins when we form it in our mind's eye and dedicate energy and focus toward it.

Creative visualization sounds easy when it's being written about but is often more challenging in the real world. Visualizing something and then creating energy to support that visualization are two very different things. This is one of the reasons Witches often work with tools. Tools help us to focus our energy, so we don't have to simultaneously balance two different tasks. Putting all of our energy and intent into an object like a candle allows us to focus on our desire and need exclusively. We then let the candle (or other object) release the energy and magick we've built up. If creative visualization were easy, then there would be little need for other forms of magick. But because it can be challenging, we supplement this first step in magickal practice with additional objects and methods.

The Written Word

There are a whole host of ways the written word can be used in spellcraft. An obvious one is that we'll often write out a spell ahead of time, or at least an outline of one, to help keep us on track when doing magickal work. As you progress through this book, you'll find other examples of utilizing the written word, such as scratching an idea onto the surface of a candle or jotting down a name when using a charm bag. But a lot of effective magick can be done with just a pen and a piece of paper, and written magick is one of the easiest kinds of magick to start with.

What makes the written word so effective is that it's very precise. If you are doing magick for a specific person, writing that person's name down is a very clear and tangible link to them. However, the written word can be more difficult as a magickal tool when dealing with abstract concepts. Turning "I want a new job" into a written piece of magick is probably more complicated for some people than simply visualizing it.

There are a couple of different ways to use the written word in magickal practice. The easiest involves writing a name or an idea on a piece of paper and then doing something with that slip of paper. If you were trying to remove a troublesome person from your life, a simple operation would be to write their name down on a piece of paper and then light that paper on fire. On the opposite end of the spectrum is writing a name down and freezing the slip of paper in an ice cube tray to immobilize a destructive person. Other things you can do with a piece of paper include burying it, flushing it down the toilet, sleeping with it under your pillow, or simply throwing it in the trash.

The written word can also be used as an extension of creative visualization. Before beginning any spell, you can write down everything you are seeing in your mind's eye and use that as a way to generate magickal energy. The more time and focus you dedicate to spellwork, the stronger that work will be. Writing things down is yet another way to generate energy. Along with creative visualization, making a quick written inventory of what you are trying to accomplish with a spell can be very helpful.

All of this sounds very simple, but the four of us have very different opinions on the effectiveness of the written word in magick. Jason swears by it, seeing it as a way to take creative visualization to the next step. Since precision is important in magick, what could be more precise than words? But not all of us do well with words, and we've probably all found ourselves in circumstances where we have been unable to accurately put our thoughts down on paper. Just how someone uses the written word in magick, especially with larger workings, probably depends to some extent on how strong their writing skills are.

On the plus side, the act of writing reinforces ideas and concepts. This is why when we are in school, we are often required to write down the information we are trying to learn or memorize. Writing things down might also bring otherwise forgotten ideas and goals into focus. Writing things down can help you organize your thoughts and help you see what you've overlooked.

Words are also full of emotion. If you are working on a spell to heal a broken heart, it's likely that you are composing such a spell because your heart is hurting. As you write down the details of what the repairs to your psyche will look like, you'll probably be able to feel your own powerful emotions as you write.

The downside here is that sometimes it's simply impossible to write down everything we might be thinking. While some people find writing a way to clarify their ideas, others lose details of their visualization while doing so. Perhaps there are just no precise words that can convey exactly what you are trying to accomplish, or perhaps what you write down doesn't adequately describe your original intention.

How someone uses the written word in their magickal work is a very personal thing. However, we've found that a couple of simple tips can help make it more effective. The first is to *be as clear as you possibly can*. Writing "heal a broken heart" is not nearly precise enough. A better practice would be to write "heal my broken heart," and even better would be to include how you want that heart to be healed: "heal my broken heart with a new love."

The second tip is to *avoid negative words*. Write down what you want instead of what you are trying to avoid. "Like attracts like" applies to words, too, and writing down negative things makes the likelihood of those things entering your life much higher. If you are headed on vacation and are trying to avoid getting sick or injured while on that trip, it's more effective to write "safe and healthy" than "no disease or disaster." There are times when it's impossible to avoid the negative, but it can generally be avoided. Avoiding negatives will make your magickal wants and desires clearer to the universe.

The use of the written word in magickal practice is constantly changing and growing. The practice of writing phrases, words, and mantras on the body in the form of a tattoo is an example of this. Positive affirmations forever immortalized in ink on the human body are most certainly magickal. Putting a deceased loved one's name on your body is a magickal link to that person that can never be severed (unless it's covered up). Everything has the potential to be a vessel for magick, including tattoos.

Magickal Alphabets

The Witchcraft books we grew up with often mentioned writing in magickal alphabets. Magickal alphabets are similar to our Latin alphabet but use different symbols to represent those letters. One of the most popular Witchcraft primers of the 1980s and '90s suggested writing everything related to Witchcraft in magickal script, from words etched onto an athame to an entire Book of Shadows. The four of us don't utilize magickal alphabets very much in our practices, but that's just personal preference. There are many Witches who swear by magickal alphabets for reasons we'll get to.

The main benefits of using magickal alphabets are increased concentration and secrecy. Let's start with concentration. Since most of us are probably not going to memorize Theban script (the most common magickal alphabet in Witchcraft), utilizing it requires extra work and focus. Let's say you were trying to banish a bad habit such as sloth by writing the word *sloth* on a piece of paper and then burning it. Instead of writing *sloth*, you'd write ᛤᛉᛊᛇᛊᛤ, which is Theban for that word. (Since Theban is a font you can now easily download, using this magickal alphabet is far easier today than it was forty years ago!)

ᛤ	ᚴ	ᛤ	ᛊ	ᚲ	ᛤ	ᚢ	ᛤ	ᚢ	ᛡ	ᛉ	ᚾ
A	B	C	D	E	F	G	H	I/J	K	L	M

ᛞ	ᛊ	ᛥ	ᚴ	ᛊ	ᚧ	ᛉ	ᚱ	ᛥ	ᚢ	ᛈ	ᛞ	ᛯ
N	O	P	Q	R	S	T	U/V	W	X	Y	Z	• (end of sentence)

Theban Script

Because the use of Theban would require us to look up every letter in order to spell a word such as *sloth*, we would then be spending extra time thinking of sloth. For some people this would probably be the case, but for an equal number of us we'd probably lose track of banishing our bad habit and instead simply focus on looking up the Theban letters. Add in the difficulty and stress of successfully drawing a symbol we are not familiar with, such as ᚧ (that's an *S*), and you can see why using a magickal script could shatter a Witch's concentration.

On the other hand, using a script such as Theban might make you feel more magickal. This is especially true if you manage to memorize it! If its use becomes second nature and you reserve it for just magickal activities, it will probably amplify the energy you create. If using Theban is just a frustrating exercise in looking things up, it won't be much use.

We all agree, though, that magickal alphabets are especially effective if you are trying to keep something secret. If you are doing spellwork involving a roommate, writing that roommate's name down in Theban (or some other magickal script) will keep them from knowing you are focusing on them if they go through your stuff. Using a magickal alphabet in a Book of Shadows will keep people from learning whatever you want to keep hidden there. The use of a magickal alphabet might also scare someone from going through your stuff. People who are frightened of magick and Witchcraft are probably not going to look through anything with a bunch of unidentifiable symbols on it.

Similar to using a magickal alphabet is writing in our standard alphabet but backward! Writing something backward (or *drawkcab gnihtemos gnitirW*) can keep prying eyes away from your magickal work and might simply make you feel more magickal. There's also a more practical use for writing backward: it can serve to deflect or reverse magick directed at you.

If there are nasty Witches in your neck of the woods, the kind who curse and hex for no reason, writing *!em morf yawa dna uoy ot kcab lleps ruoy ecnuob I* ("I bounce your spell back to you and away from me!") can help redirect their energy back to them. This is a powerful little magickal trick and often one people overlook. While we think this makes perfect sense, if you disagree, then it probably won't work for you, so use it only if it resonates with you.

Writing things down in reverse doesn't generally produce the break in concentration that we might experience when writing things in a magickal script. Simply write down what you want to do in regular letters and then use that to guide you in writing it in reverse. It takes a bit of focus, but not nearly as much as shuffling through correspondence tables.

Sigils

Similar to magickal alphabets but a bit more abstract are sigils. Sigils are symbols that are linked to a specific magickal idea or goal. For example, if you were trying to lose weight, you might create a sigil dedicated to weight loss. Included in that sigil would be shapes and signs that you feel are connected to your goal and that resonate with you. You'd then place that sigil in a place (or places) where you would see it frequently. In the case of our scenario here, the refrigerator feels like an ideal place to place such a sigil. Instead of opening the refrigerator door, you'd be hit with the power of your sigil, reminding you of your weight loss goal and strengthening your resolve.

The modern use of sigil magick is quite different from the original intent of a sigil. In the grimoires of the Middle Ages and early modern period, sigils were most often used and created to aid in the manifestation of angels and demons, and, most importantly, to control those entities. Sigils were thought to be the secret names of powerful entities, and it was believed that possession of those secret names conferred power over figures such as the archangels Raphael, Gabriel, and Michael.[12] There are still people who use sigils for this purpose, and one of the most influential grimoires ever, the *Key of Solomon*, contains dozens of sigils dedicated to just this task.

There are no hard-and-fast rules when creating your own sigils. You can use well-known symbols (such as a heart for love) or abstract ones, or simply design your own. What's most important is that what you put down on paper resonates

---

12. Rosemary Ellen Guiley, *The Encyclopedia of Witches & Witchcraft* (New York: Facts On File, 1999), 310.

with you. It's easier than ever to draw a sigil on a computer, but for maximum effectiveness it should be drawn by hand. By drawing a sigil, you are infusing it with your power and energy, and every time you see it, either with your physical eyes or in your mind's eye, you are interacting with its power.

Create Your Own Sigil

For this exercise, Jason created a sigil to inspire him to get out of the house and exercise more (see illustration). It's an example of how simple it is to create a sigil and how easy it is to use symbols to represent ideas and actions. There are entire books dedicated to sigil magick, and we can't get too in-depth here. Think of this as a primer, and if you find yourself intrigued by sigil magick, take a look at the bibliography to further your studies.

To start, Jason drew a straight line pointing upward. To him this represents moving forward with his life. It also suggests physical activity. The phrase "onward and upward" also came to mind, as his goal was to move forward with his fitness goals.

The second thing Jason drew was a five-pointed star at the bottom of the line. A star can represent energy, but more important to him here was the pentagram's long association with Witchcraft. Invoking and banishing pentagrams have a long history in magick, and a pentagram conjures those two different energies based on the pattern on which they are drawn. Jason wanted to capture the energy of manifestation in his sigil, hence the pentagram.

Movement is really important if one is going to exercise, and the wavy lines added here are representative of that idea. They also remind Jason a bit of a flowing breeze, something he associates with running. The wavy lines are also symbolic of arms pumping, which is something that happens when you run.

Borrowing an idea from author Laura Tempest Zakroff, who suggests in her book *Sigil Witchery* that pyramids have a fierce energy, Jason next drew three pyramids.[13] Running in particular makes Jason feel strong, so it made sense to add these to his sigil. The triangles might also be representative of scaling a mountain, which relates to his goal here in both a literal and a metaphorical sense. (Being more active is a metaphorical mountain to climb, and while being more active, he might actually walk up a mountain, or at least a hill.)

---

13. Laura Tempest Zakroff, *Sigil Witchery: A Witch's Guide to Crafting Magick Symbols* (Woodbury, MN: Llewellyn, 2018), 50. Interested in sigils? This is *the* book!

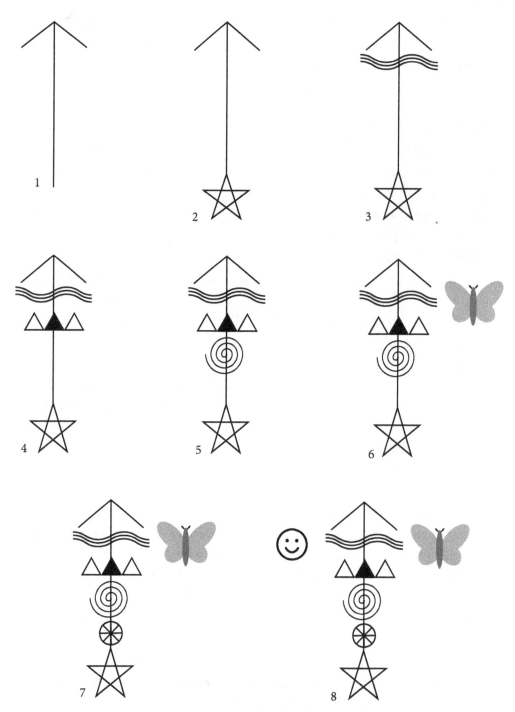

Exercise Sigil

Next Jason drew a spiral, which again is representative of movement, but he had an ulterior motive here: the spiral reminds him of his neighborhood. Jason and Ari live in a densely packed suburban area where the streets often feel like they spiral around one another. Every time Jason sees that spiral, he thinks of the jogging paths recorded on his phone.

One of the reasons for more exercise is to feel better and perhaps lose a little weight. Jason doesn't expect to be reborn like a butterfly emerging from a cocoon, but he does expect to see or feel some physical differences. The butterfly here is symbolic of those changes.

It's easy sometimes to limit our magickal work to one season, but the Wheel of the Year here represents the continual nature of the exercise project. Adding this to the sigil says that there will be exercise in the spring, summer, autumn, and winter. The Wheel of the Year suggests the seasons in motion, and exercise is motion.

The last symbol, a smiley face, might seem a bit silly, but Jason is happier when he's exercising regularly. Deep down he knows he's not taking care of himself in an optimal way when he sits at his writing desk all day. The smiley face represents who he wishes to be and is a reminder that movement will make him happier.

As a full-time writer, Jason placed this sigil on his writing desk. Now every time he looks at it, he is inspired to get outside for at least a little bit. While drawing his sigil, he was cognizant of what each symbol meant to him and infused those energies into his drawing. Sigils are a great way to keep your spellwork moving and to maintain focus on your magickal goals.

The Sigil Wheel

An alternative way to create sigils is by using a sigil wheel, which consists of a circle with twenty-six spaces, generally divided into three concentric rows of five, eight, and thirteen spaces. Unlike the sigil just discussed, the sigil wheel creates a unique sigil without any symbols. If you are worried about your artistic skills not being up to par to create a traditional sigil, using a sigil wheel is a great alternative.

With a sigil wheel, the Witch draws a series of lines linking together all the letters that form their magickal intention. For instance, if you were looking for a new place to live, your intention might be "new home." From there you'd go to your sigil wheel and draw a line from the first letter of your intention to the second letter, so from N to E. Then you'd draw a line from E to W, from W to H, and so on until you get to the last letter of your intention. The resulting line drawing is your sigil, which you can then use just like a traditional sigil.

Before working on this book, I (Jason) had never encountered this type of sigil magick until Amanda introduced me to it. Over the course of trying it out, I found it extremely empowering. I verbalized my intention, visualized my desire, and then connected the ~~dots~~ letters. It was simple, but I could feel the energy pouring forth from both me and the marker I was using.

To work with a sigil wheel, you'll have to either create your own wheel or (easily) find one online. We think it's best to create your own wheel, not only because that creation will add extra power to your magick but also because how you arrange the letters in the wheel has magickal significance.

Most sigil wheels found online begin with *A* at the top of the image in the outer row and then spiral around, with *N* at the beginning of the second row and *V* at the beginning of the inner row. This inward spiral suggests a stopping point or an end point, which works well with magick focused on stopping a habit or person.

By way of contrast, if your wheel begins with *A* in the inner row, then the letters are spiraling outward, which suggests gain and growth. This is the type of energy to use when looking to find a new lover or job. A third option is to randomly place the letters in the sigil, which is perfect if you are attempting to perform magick to cloak your actions or to confuse an adversary. The befuddling nature of the randomly arranged letters will extend to the sigil you create.

The optimal way to use a sigil wheel is with a piece of tracing paper. Set your paper on top of your wheel and then create your sigil. Ideally you want to separate the sigil from the wheel so that you can use the sigil as a point of focus without the distracting letters in the wheel getting in the way. The focus should be squarely on the sigil, not on the sigil wheel. No tracing paper? That's not a big deal. Most of the paper we use in our printers today is transparent enough to accomplish the same goal.

When you create your sigil, your lines will go through boxes of letters that are not connected to your spell. That's fine and can't be helped. You do want to make sure, though, that every letter of your intention is clearly touched by the line you are drawing to create your sigil.

You can add additional layers to your sigil wheel by using a magickal alphabet such as Theban. However, if you find yourself looking up the equivalent Theban letter for every Latin alphabet letter of your intent, you will most likely be focused on correspondences rather than your magickal intent.

Examples of Sigil Magick with the Sigil Wheel

The first sigil we created here was to promote growth in the garden in the back of Jason and Ari's house. Because we were focused on fostering growing things, we started with the letter *A* in the inner row of the wheel, with the rest of the letters spiraling outward from there. The word we used here was simply *garden*, because we didn't feel like it needed much embellishment.

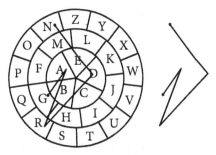

Garden Sigil

When we were done creating the sigil, Jason took the sigil tracing and drew the sigil on some flat rocks with a fine point marker. He then placed the actual sigil in the garden and ended up with the biggest pumpkin he's ever grown.

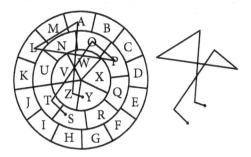

Stop Lazy Sigil

A big problem many of us face is an occasional bout of laziness. Sometimes we need to be lazy to recharge a bit, but other times we feel lazy because we are stuck in a rut or some other unwanted circumstances. Our second sigil for this book was "stop lazy," a very loud and emphatic cry for us to get to work. We think it's best to avoid negative words in spellwork, but in this case we really needed a jump start and "stop lazy" felt like the kick in the pants we all needed. For this sigil we utilized a sigil wheel starting with the letter *A* in the outer row and from there spiraling inward. When we were done with our sigil, we placed it near our workstations and altars to inspire us to get this book done (mostly) on time.

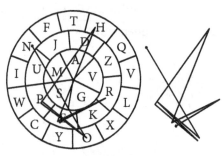

Nothing Sigil

The third sigil here is our befuddling sigil, one that utilizes letters that we placed in the wheel randomly. Have you ever had people over at your house and found them going through a drawer or medicine cabinet? This sigil is designed to keep people from going through your stuff. The word we chose for it was *nothing*, which is the idea you'd want to project to people who are too curious for their own good! Unlike with other sigils, you want to place this sigil *inside* the place you want to keep prying eyes out of. If you are using this sigil in a drawer, the ideal spot is on the inside of the drawer's face (or front), so that the sigil is facing outward toward the person opening the drawer. This means you will no longer be able to see the sigil inside the drawer, but its energy will radiate outward, confusing any snoopers in your home.

Chapter Four
Spells by Visualization and Script

Spellwork does not require a large number of tools or other accoutrements. Many spells can be cast with simple creative visualization, and others require nothing more than a pencil (or pen) and a piece of paper. Magick is often made needlessly complicated. The spells involving creative visualization and the written word included here are simple and effective. Many of these spells are among the most used items in our magickal bag of tricks.

Creative Visualization Spells

Spells involving creative visualization are usually cast because there is no other option. They are the type of spells you cast because you find yourself in very unexpected circumstances and need some magickal energy. All these spells require is a clear picture of what you are trying to accomplish, and because of that, we've deliberately kept them very simple. Because you might have to wield these spells at odd times, we suggest practicing them a few times before you actually need them. The more you practice and cast the spells below, the stronger the magick will be over time. Magick is like anything else: practice makes perfect!

Shields Up! A Quick Protection Spell

Whenever you feel threatened, it's best to put up a personal shield of energy. This energy won't necessarily stop people from saying cruel things, but it will make you more resilient and less affected by their barbs and bullshit. Shielding yourself also produces energy that says "leave me alone," and will often result in people moving on to their next target or simply ignoring you.

Start by visualizing yourself safe, confident, and secure. Once you've created that image, imagine energy collecting near your heart. This energy should well up within your body and then move toward your heart. We generally visualize that energy as blue-white in color, but picture it in whatever way works best for you. As you visualize the energy collecting near your heart, actively attempt to feel the energy pooling there. It should feel warm and comforting.

Take a deep breath and then actively push that energy outward from your body. Imagine it as a suit of armor, covering your body. (Other visualizations include a simple shield or a disco ball of energy surrounding you.) Imagine this armor deflecting any negative comments directed at you and serving as a warning for others to keep away. Once the energy has encircled your body, quietly say "so mote it be" to signify the spell's successful casting.[14]

Because energy doesn't stay still, you may have to repeat this process several times over the course of a few hours. When you feel the spell breaking up or you are no longer getting the results you want, place more of the protective energy around yourself.

Creative Visualization Pep Talk

We all have to deal with unpleasant tasks from time to time, but magick can help get us through them. If you are faced with an unwanted task, take a deep breath and visualize yourself accomplishing that task quickly and easily. For example, many of us are forced to give speeches or presentations at work, which can cause a lot of anxiety. In the days leading up to your speech, visualize yourself confident and successful.

As you are visualizing yourself accomplishing your task, begin chanting a mantra either out loud or in your head. In this case you might chant, "I'm going to nail this speech, I'm going to be strong." Before beginning the actual task, spend a minute or two repeating your mantra. As you speak, the energy of the visualization will be released, giving you the power to accomplish your goal. If you feel yourself faltering during your task, repeat your mantra in your head to release additional magickal energy.

Morning Mirror Mantra

We are bombarded daily with the message that no matter what we do, we aren't good enough. Advertising images often insult both our physical appearance and our intelligence. This morning mirror mantra is a great way to overcome those negative energies and begin your day (or night) in an empowering way.

---

14. "So mote it be" is a common phrase said at the end of spellwork. It is equivalent to using the word "amen" at the end of a prayer.

Stand in front of a mirror and take a good look at yourself. None of us are perfect, but most of us are at least pretty good! We all have desirable qualities and skills. As you look in the mirror, visualize all those good things and take a moment to feel positive about yourself.

Mirrors are magickal tools that are often used to reflect the energies projected at them. Since this spell is designed to be said in front of a mirror, the mirror will send our positive energy directly back to us!

Your mantra here can be anything you want it to be. We like to emphasize how strong we are and capable of overcoming life's obstacles. We also want our bodies to be healthy, so the mantra also sends some energy back to us that reinforces health and vitality.

Look into your mirror and begin saying your mantra. This is our mantra:

> *My bones are strong, my blood is strong, my breath is strong, my mind is clear and sharp.*

As you say those words, picture yourself strong and healthy and feel the full energy of your intention coming back to you, preparing you for the day. When you are done, let out a hearty "so mote it be," indicating that the spell is over.

Pen and Paper Spells

Pens and pencils are not usually listed as official Witch tools, but maybe they should be. Words and drawings have more energy than most people think! If you are new to Witchcraft, pen and paper spells are easy starting points. Pen and paper spells can easily be kept hidden as well, which is perfect if you are trying to hide your practice of Witchcraft from a roommate, lover, or parent.

A Circle for Protection and Deflection

On an ordinary piece of paper, draw a large circle. Then place the paper on a pentacle if you have one (and it's fine if you don't have one—you can just set the piece of paper on your working surface).[15] Now begin thinking of the people you want to keep safe. Envision them clearly in your mind's eye and then begin writing their names in the center of your circle. As you write down their names, say:

---

15. Not sure what a pentacle is or what it's used for? You can find out more about the pentacle in the glossary of this book.

To keep you all safe from harm,
I create for us this charm!

Repeat the rhyme while you write down all the names.

On the outside of the circle, write what you want your magick to do. While we were creating this spell, we chose to write the following phrases: "deflect all ill intent," "protect us all," and "keep us safe from harm." Follow this up by imagining negative energy being directed at your circle and then bouncing off of it. When you are done, your drawing should look like a sun or a flower. The circle you've created here should help keep negativity away from those within it by bouncing that energy back to those who sent it.

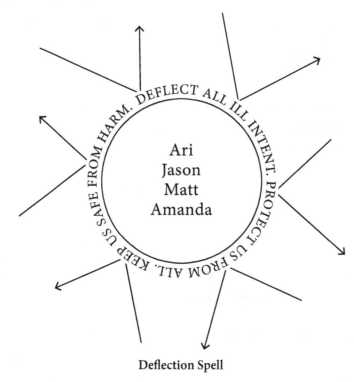

Deflection Spell

If you don't like the visualization of a circle, an alternative here is to draw a shield and place the names of those you are trying to protect behind that shield. Follow this up by drawing the negative energy bouncing off the shield and away.

When your illustration is complete, place it in an out-of-the-way place where it can't be seen. We suggest placing it in a frequently used room behind a picture. For maximum results, repeat this spell yearly to renew the magickal energy.

Money Pyramid Spell

No matter how one feels about money, it's hard to get by in society without it. This spell is designed to keep money flowing into your life so there's always plenty of cash on hand to pay your bills.

Draw a large pyramid on a piece of paper. Be sure to draw your pyramid right-side up, with the pyramid's point at the top of the paper. In the center of your pyramid, write down what it is you are trying to manifest (such as "money not to worry"). Asking to win the lottery here is not very practical. Instead, visualize yourself successful, with all the money you need and then some. Visualize your refrigerator full of food and your rent or mortgage paid easily, with cash to spare.

Now write down the qualities needed to reach that goal. Ideas include competency, wealth, and abundance. (When we did this spell together, we wrote "hard work," "success," and "determination.") For best results, write your name (or the person you are doing the spell for) in the center of the pyramid to better direct your magick.

At each of the three points of your pyramid in turn, say the following chant while drawing three small dollar signs:

> *Money come, money grow,*
> *Money stack, money flow.*

Imagine that money coming into your life and flowing around you. This spell is not about a one-time payout; it's about manifesting a continual flow of cash. Continue the money flow chant and draw a large dollar sign at the top of your pyramid. From that dollar sign, draw a wavy line down toward the left side of the pyramid. Stop at the left-hand point of the base and draw another large dollar sign. Now draw another wavy line to the right. At the right-hand pyramid point, draw one more large dollar sign and then a wavy line moving up the pyramid. Envision the energy of financial security moving around you, flowing and ever present.

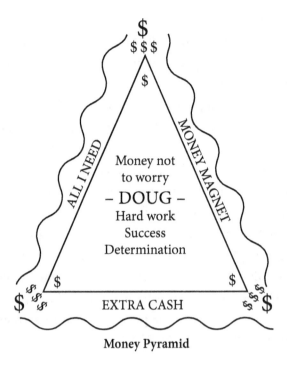

Money Pyramid

Between the pyramid and the wavy lines, write affirmative phrases stating what you want. We wrote "all I need," "money magnet," and "extra cash," all things we were trying to manifest. To signify the energy around the pyramid moving inside to fulfill your needs, draw three more dollar signs, this time inside the pyramid at each of the three points.

For maximum results, place your pyramid in a location associated with money, such as in a wallet or purse, in your checkbook (if you still use checks), or perhaps taped to your computer or under the case of your phone. Repeat the spell yearly.

Drawing for Love

Love spells have been popular for thousands of years, but they are also among the easiest spells to mess up! This spell will help you find exactly the kind of romantic partner you are looking for.

Start by drawing a large heart on a piece of paper. As you draw the heart, visualize love coming your way and on your terms. Follow this by writing down what you are looking for in a partner. Some suggested words and phrases include "stability," "passion," "eyes that will see only me," "a hand always there to hold me," "shared hobbies," etc. Once your list is complete, draw a version of yourself in the center of the heart. This doesn't have to be elaborate. A stick figure will work.

After you've drawn the image of yourself, begin writing the qualities you are looking for in a partner on and around your picture. As you write those things down, say them all aloud. Here are some examples:

I seek a stable partner free of drama.

I seek a partner who will be passionate about our relationship physically and emotionally.

I seek a partner who only has eyes for me.

I seek a partner whose hand will always be there for me.

I seek a partner with whom I can share my interests and hobbies.

The more lines you write down and say, the more precise your magick will be and the more likely it is that you will find exactly what you are seeking.

After you are done writing things down, say:

Not only do I seek love, but I deserve love! So mote it be!

After you are done with your spell, fold it up and carry it in your wallet or purse to attract the type of love you are seeking.

Envelope Spells

Envelope spells are great examples of sympathetic magick. You can use an empty envelope to send people luck, love, and energy. When you are using an envelope for magickal purposes, address the outside of the envelope as you normally would. Write down the recipient's name and their address as specifically as you can (though we aren't sure that magick cares about zip codes!). If you have something belonging to the recipient of the spellwork, add that to the envelope for an extra link to them. This can be something the person has owned, their signature, a bit of their hair, or even just a picture.

To send someone energy, fill the envelope with things you associate with energy while thinking of the person you are doing the spell for. When we think of energy, we think of things related to exercise and certain foods and drinks that make us more alert. Putting some coffee grounds in the envelope is appropriate, but you could also use pictures of energy drinks. If you want to use things related to exercise, something as simple as a pair of sneaker shoelaces would work. If an item represents energy and power to you, stick it in the envelope!

If you are trying to send someone some luck, fill the envelope with things associated with luck. Ideas include four-leaf clovers, drawings or pictures of horseshoes, a lucky rabbit's foot, and a certain cereal with the words *charms* and *lucky* in its name. The possibilities are endless! If it represents luck, put it in the envelope. You can repeat this process with just about anything you desire to send to someone else.

When you are done stuffing the envelope, place it on your pentacle and say:

> *This envelope is filled with what I wish to send.*
> *Bestow all these blessings upon my friend!*
> *So mote it be!*

As you say the final words of the spell, visualize the energies you've filled your envelope with entering your pentacle and going directly to your friend. Visualize your pentacle as an open and glowing portal, with the energy of your spell moving through it to your intended goal. Let the envelope lie on the pentacle for at least an hour, then either place the envelope in a secure place or dispose of it in whatever way you feel is appropriate (burning, trash, compost, etc.).

A Letter to the Dead

Death is an unwelcome part of life but also an inescapable one. There are times when we can be with those we love as they pass away and share with them how we feel. But death can also be sudden and unexpected, and when that is the case, there are often many things left unsaid. As Witches, we believe that the soul survives death and that we can share our emotions and feelings with those who have passed.

If you find yourself needing to share something with someone who has passed away, begin by addressing an envelope to them. Include their name and wherever you think they may be in the afterlife. Many Witches who believe in reincarnation refer to the land between lives as "the Summerlands," which is a fine way to address your envelope. Depending on your beliefs, other options could include Cerridwen's Cauldron, heaven, the Elysian Fields, etc. However you choose to address your envelope, be sure the delivery address resonates with both your beliefs and the beliefs of the person who has passed.

Before writing to the person who has passed about how you feel, take a moment to set up a picture of them in your writing space. If it doesn't hurt too much, you can go a bit further by playing some of the departed's favorite music, burning their favorite incense, or surrounding yourself in their favorite scent and perhaps filling a glass with their favorite beverage.

Once your writing area is set up, begin writing to your lost loved one. Visualize them in your mind's eye, and as you write, imagine yourself having a conversation with them. Feel the emotions inside of you, and actively visualize those emotions falling out of you and onto your paper. If you cry while writing, let those tears fall upon your paper. Be as honest as you can with both the departed and yourself.

When your letter is finished, place it in your envelope and seal it. The best way to help your letter and emotions cross the veil between the living and the dead is by burning the letter and envelope. We suggest doing this outside and always in a safe manner. Bonfires are great, but many of us can't light those in our backyards, so we suggest using a charcoal grill or even something as small as a large metal can (like a coffee can). As the letter burns, the smoke will carry your words and feelings to the person you have lost.

When you are done burning the letter, be sure to completely extinguish your fire and dispose of the remains properly. Be sure all of your words have been lost to the fire, as you don't want an unwanted pair of eyes to come across them.

Paid in Full

Keeping up on the bills can be a never-ending job. This spell is a little magickal trick to get ahead of the bills and ensure that you've always got enough money to cover your expenses. It can be tailored to pay a specific bill or used in a more general way for "all the bills."

Start by visualizing yourself paying off your monthly debts quickly and easily, with plenty of money left over. If you have your bills set to autopay, visualize your bank making the payments you owe "paid in full." With this visualization firmly in your mind's eye, begin writing "paid in full" on a piece of paper over and over while saying the phrase "paid in full" as you write. Write down and say "paid in full" as many times as you can. We suggest doing this at least forty times.

When you are done, triumphantly state, "All my bills will be paid in full!" Follow this up by taping your piece of paper to wherever you pay your bills (such as a computer) or placing it in your checkbook, purse, or wallet.

If you want to use this trick for a specific item, repeat this process but add the name of whatever it is you wish to pay off to the phrase "paid in full." An example of this is "car paid in full." Write down the phrase "car paid in full" as many times as necessary to match the terms of your loan. If it's a five-year loan, you'll want to write "car paid in full" sixty times, once for every month the bill is due. (If you use this spell for a house with a thirty-year mortgage, you'll be writing "house paid in full" 360 times, once for every month the bill is due.) When you are done writing, finish by saying, "This car will be paid in full!"

Place your piece of paper either in your car or near where you pay the car bill. If you use this spell for a house, place the spell under the doormat by the front door of your house or some other place that feels appropriate.

Chapter Five
Your Will, Personal Power, and the Earth and Sky

When people think of magick, they often visualize candles, wands, and jars of dried herbs. Especially in this day and age, there's a "look" to magickal practice, and we see it often in social media and on the covers of books. But all of that is mostly window dressing; you can do some pretty amazing magickal things without any tools or other magickal items. We all love our magickal stuff, but the most magickal tools at your disposal are yourself and the hum of the universe around you!

This chapter is a dramatic departure from most everything else in this book going forward. When we tap into magickal energy, we most often end up focusing it on objects such as poppets or stones. Here we are spending some time with the three biggest forces Witches generally use to raise energy: our personal will, our physical self, and the natural world.

Tapping into our personal will is one of the biggest sources of magickal power and a foundation of magickal practice. In addition, we as human beings are capable of generating a great deal of energy from the things we do, whether that's dancing, clapping, or singing. And then there's the natural world around us, which is just bubbling with energy if we know how to gather it up.

It's possible to do magick with just these three energy conduits, but most often they are used in conjunction with other practices. While working with a candle, you'll eventually find yourself transferring energy from your will, your physical self, and the world around you into your candle, often without being conscious of it. So this chapter is about the energy we raise and then add to other forms of magickal practice. Mastering the techniques to raise energy in this chapter will make your magickal work that much more effective.

Your Magickal Will and Intuition

The most powerful magickal tool you will ever yield is your magickal will. We spent some time exploring the concept of will back in the introduction, but some of it bears repeating here. *Will* in a magickal sense has a variety of definitions and interpretations, but most people agree that it's essentially the core of your being. Your will is the ultimate accumulation of all your experiences in life. It represents your truest essence and knows what it is that you most desire, which will often differ from what your conscious mind thinks you want.

Your will is also a magickal furnace capable of emitting voluminous amounts of energy. Think back to an intensely emotional moment in your life. Imagine, for instance, the first time you truly had your heart broken. For most of us, that's an experience involving lots of tears, desperate sadness, and complete hopelessness. When the pain is especially strong, the grief and heartache feel as if they are hanging in the air around us. That energy is the direct result of our will; when we feel an intense emotion, our will is being engaged, and we produce an energy appropriate to that emotion.

The energy produced by will can also be felt by other people. Have you ever been deliriously happy? Have you ever noticed that those you come into contact with during those moments often end up feeling happy too? It's all because of that inner furnace, your will, producing energy and then emitting that energy out into the world where it's then felt by others.

When the words we say in ritual are completely honest and come from our deepest recesses, we are tapping into our will. When we truly desire an outcome and use magick to help obtain it, our will is actively engaged and adding energy to the spellwork we do. And when our emotions are pouring out of us, our spellwork is often even more powerful because of the energy being produced by our will.

Your will is also a magickal guide in a sense. It represents what you truly want. If you are doing a spell to help a person you don't like buy a new car, the spell will be less effective than usual because your will won't be engaged. You don't really want the person you are helping to get a new car, so there's a part of your magickal self that has checked out of the spell. This applies to yourself, too. Maybe you don't really want a relationship right now despite doing a love spell on Valentine's Day. Your will knows and will react accordingly.

Along with your will, there's a second force that's important in magickal work: your intuition. In this book we repeat the phrase "do what makes sense to you" multiple times in various ways. Someone can tell you that spearmint leaves are good for increasing wealth, but if that doesn't make sense to you, then those leaves aren't going to do you any good. We all react to things differently, and this is especially true with magick.

This book has dozens of different spells in it, and many of them are very specific: say these words, use that stone, etc. But none of that matters if there's a voice in your head suggesting that you do something another way. Trust that voice! Use books like this as a starting point, not an ending one.

A few people in our coven joke that there's nothing more powerful than watching Ari, Matt, and Amanda put together a spell. A covener will ask for magickal assistance for a certain problem, and all three will jump up and start assembling a variety of magickal items to be used to fix that problem. Ari often describes her intuitive magickal process as an unseen hand guiding her around our ritual room, instructing her to pick up certain oils, stones, and candles. Like our will, our intuition is an unconscious process that takes place outside of normal thinking.

When you work magick, trust that unseen hand and let it guide you where it will. Listen to your intuition and have confidence in it. Magick isn't quite like breathing, but it comes naturally to a lot of us, and often does so without much thought. Unlike your will, your magickal intuition isn't a battery full of energy waiting to be released, but is the part of you that will best utilize the magick you have in the most effective way possible.

Muscle and Movement

If magick is energy infused with intent, then every step we take has the potential to be magickal. Even something as simple as walking can be turned into a means to cast a spell. When our muscles tighten, we are using energy, and when our muscles relax, we are then releasing that energy. Most of the time when we are walking we are probably not consciously thinking of turning our footfalls into a spell, but theoretically it could be done.

One of the easiest ways to feel energy is by tensing your arm muscles. Hold your arms in front of you, bent at the elbows, with your hands parallel to each other at the level of your heart. Ball your hands up into fists and tense the muscles in your arms. Tense the muscles in your upper arms and pull upward, bringing your fists even with your shoulders. After you tense your muscles, relax them. Repeat this action nine to ten times. Eventually you should start to feel a little pool of energy gather between your fists in front of you.

At this point that pool of energy is just that: energy. But if you fill it with intent and then send it out on its merry way through the universe, you will have just cast a spell. You can fill that energy with intent in a number of ways. Without saying a word, you could simply form an idea in your mind, visualize it, then mentally push that picture into your pool of energy.

If you don't want to just project an image into your energy, you could verbalize your intention while flexing your muscles. If you were waiting on a package from the post office that was overdue, you could say something as simple as "package, come to me" over and over again. That would be enough to infuse your energy with intent and create magick. To release the spell and send it out into the world, you would stop flexing your muscles, open up your hands, and then fling the energy you've created out into the universe to do your bidding.

Writing about magick this way makes it feel so easy to do! If all a person has to do is flex their muscles for a few minutes and say some words, then why doesn't everyone do it and get whatever they want? The problem with our little "flexing the muscles" example spell is that we haven't really raised that much energy. It's a small spell, and the smaller your spell, the smaller your chance of success.

Magick takes time and energy, and the more time and energy you put into it, the greater your results will be. Our little muscle spell is a jab, not a knockout punch. If you wanted this particular type of spell to be truly effective, you'd have to tense your muscles for an extended period of time.

However, if you get a bunch of Witches doing the same thing together, your chance for success will increase dramatically. In this instance, a circle of Witches could stand around flexing their arm muscles, but movement—especially dancing—is a far more common (and fun!) way to raise energy. Movement also allows Witches to add other magickal tricks to their energy raising, such as chanting, which is especially effective.

Sound and Chanting

Chanting adds a lot of power to spellwork for several different reasons. The first is that sound is created from moving parts of our body. Chanting may not be as visceral as dancing to a dozen thundering drums, but muscles are still contracting and releasing, producing energy we can use for magick.

When the words we chant or say in ritual are honest and represent our truest desires and ideals, we are activating the energy within our will. This is why chants will often bring about an emotional response while they are being articulated.

While doing a chant to raise energy with the goal of healing a sick friend, you might find tears in your eyes as you cry out. That's your will accompanying the words of the chant.

Chants are also useful because they provide focus during a magickal working. It's impossible to forget the purpose of a spell if you are continually chanting the end goal during a magickal working. Chants are also a bit hypnotic. One of the biggest obstacles in magick is turning off our generally overactive brains. If your focus during a spell is on a late work assignment you need to finish, your magick will be less effective. Getting lost in a chant turns off that part of your mind and lets you focus exclusively on magick.

For these reasons, chants are a part of all sorts of magickal operations. Chanting while lighting a candle or working with a stone will add to the spellwork you are performing. The more layers you can add to your magick, the stronger it will be, and chanting is an easy layer to add.

Many spell books include complicated chants, and there are Witches who love those types of chants. A sixteen-line chant that rhymes completely, with the same number of syllables per line, is impressive, but in the moment it can be difficult to memorize. We think the most effective chants are ones that are nearly effortless. Worrying about getting the words right to an extremely long chant can take away from a spell's focus.

When trying to keep things simple, a good rule of thumb is to include no more than two or four lines per chant. Rhyming your two lines will make it easier to memorize, but there's no point in getting caught up in finding an exact rhyme to the word *orange*. What's most important is always the intent: a chant should sum up the idea of whatever you are trying to accomplish.

Chants that are just a couple of words long are more than adequate. Simply chanting the same word over and over is also effective. The expression "keep it simple, stupid" (KISS) applies to magick in general but especially to chants and the spoken word.

Similar to chanting is toning, which in some ways is even easier because it doesn't require coming up with any words. When we tone, we simply emit energy from our body mixed with intent by making a vowel sound. Toning produces a large amount of energy. Again, we are utilizing muscles in our diaphragm, but we are also engaging our will. Not having to worry about being in rhythm with others or remembering a series of words allows us to focus entirely on our magickal intent when we tone.

Toning and chanting are very similar, but the kinds of energy they create are different. As a coven, we use toning when dealing with heavy issues, such as sending healing energy to a gravely ill friend. There's an intensity of focus that comes with toning, making it especially effective for spells focusing on just one person.

Chanting, while it can also be serious, has a festive nature to it. Chants in group settings forge bonds between Witches and have an infectious energy. Holding hands and skipping around the circle are things you do while chanting. Toning is often something you do while standing still, with the energies of your will radiating outward for all to feel.

Chanting and toning are the most common forms of magickal sounds, but there are other things that can be utilized as well. Accompanying a chant or dance with a drum or other percussive instrument will add extra energy to your rite. No drums? Hand claps, foot stomps, or finger snaps are effective, too, and produce even more energy! If it makes noise and doesn't annoy everyone around you, it's fair game.

Do you lack a sense of rhythm? (Jason completely lacks rhythm, so you aren't alone here.) Add some recorded music to your ritual while you move, dance, or chant. While many Witches frown upon recorded music in ritual and magick, we think it can be effective if used properly.

Music activates our emotions, and when our emotions are engaged, our magick is stronger. Music can also simply make us feel more like Witches. If your inner Witch feels stronger when listening to goth music, do it! If your inner Witch feels stronger listening to country music, that's fine too.

Body and Blood: Personal Bits in Magick

In addition to our personal energy, we all have something else that we can use in spellwork: bits of ourselves. Many Witches actively run away from blood and other bodily fluids, hair, and nail trimmings, but these things have the potential to be powerful allies in magick. If one of the first tricks of magick is knowing exactly what you want, then nothing "knows" a person better than bits of their own body.

People have been using blood in various magickal workings for thousands of years. Blood is a part of our life force; without it we are dead. Consciously cutting oneself is not a part of mundane life and is a transgressive act. Harming oneself, no matter the reason, is generally looked upon with scorn and concern.

Before continuing, we think it's worth mentioning that if you are going to use blood for magickal purposes, it should be done safely and hygienically. The easiest way to do this is by purchasing a sterile lancet, some antiseptic, and a bandage. To draw blood, the easiest method is to squeeze the tip of a finger and, as the blood collects there, prick it quickly with the lancet. Squeezing the finger a second time should result in a drop or two of blood coming out of the tip. Once you've collected the blood, wipe down the area of the finger with an antiseptic and then bandage it. Care should always be taken when handling bloody items, and they should be disposed of as quickly as possible. It goes without saying that swapping blood with other Witches should not be done.

When we think of blood, we usually associate it with its primary function: carrying nutrients throughout the body. However, blood is much more than that. Blood and other bodily materials contain all our genetic information, basically all the information that makes us *us*. Nothing identifies us more than our DNA. If you are trying to link a piece of magick directly to yourself, there's no better way to do so than with something intensely personal, like a part of yourself.

When making an oath or a promise to yourself or others, blood is a powerful bonding force. Writing a vow on a piece of paper and then "signing" it with a bloody thumbprint is magickal. The blood from the thumbprint will link you nearly forever to that vow. If you throw away such a written vow, it will still exist and remain connected to you. The only way to release a vow sealed with blood is by burning the paper on which you've written and sealed your vow.

Because blood is such a powerful identifying force, there are Witches who use it to actively mark their tools. Pricking yourself with the point of a new athame is an easy way to share your energy with your new tool. A small drop of blood applied to a wand links the individual Witch directly to their wand and will probably make it that much harder for any other Witch to wield that wand. Are we suggesting that you smear blood on every tool on your altar? No, but if you are especially close to a particular tool, marking it with blood and sharing some of yourself with it has value.

Blood contains more than just our DNA; blood is rich in metals such as copper and iron. Like those metals, blood is powerful. It can be an accessory in any spell you cast to gain control over a situation. Blood also contains white blood cells, which fight against bacteria and viruses, and because of this, blood is a powerful ally in healing spells. If you've been given the blood (or hair or fingernails) of a sick friend, you can use that blood as a focal point in a healing spell to help that person.

Sexual fluids contain our DNA, but their use can also be linked to their primary purpose. Sex is a way for people to connect physically and often emotionally. Sexual fluids are useful when creating spells to grow closer to another person (with that person's consent, of course). We aren't suggesting that your handfasting ceremony consist of a public mixing of sexual fluids, but if you were trying to improve a bond with a committed partner, those fluids could come in handy.

After blood, urine is probably the most easily accessible bodily fluid, but urine is quite different magickally from blood. Urine is waste; it consists of substances the body does not need, and it's hardly ever wanted. (We give blood to others to preserve lives. No one collects urine for similar reasons.) Therefore, urine is useful when you are doing magick to rid yourself of unwanted habits or tendencies and as a repellent to keep people away. Urine is also used by many animals to mark their territory. While we don't suggest urinating around the perimeter of your property, if your neighbors were especially bad, this could be a powerful piece of magick.

Saliva is another useful bodily fluid. Like blood, it can be used as a personal marker of either yourself or another individual. The act of spitting generally reflects disgust with something, and that can easily be applied to spellwork. Visualizing an unwanted trait or tendency and then spitting is a magickal act. Energy and intent are poured into the saliva, and the act of spitting discards that unwanted energy.

Blood and bits of the body are probably most associated with spells directed at specific people. If you are trying to bind someone to keep them from harming others, using their name as a focus for your spellwork is satisfactory, but your spell will be even more powerful if you can use some of their hair or a fingernail. The link to a person when using some of their bodily fluids or extraneous pieces is profound and has been used by magicians and Witches for thousands of years. However, it's not a requirement, and a Witch should never go out of their way to collect hair from a comb or brush. Using someone else's personal bits for magick is generally done only when every other option has been exhausted.

Earth Energy

After ourselves, the second greatest depository of magickal energy is our planet and the universe it's a part of. Earth energy is also incredibly easy to tap into, and we often use its power without even really being conscious of it. Earth energy is the power that shifts continents and drives the rains and the winds. Further afield we can feel the energy of the moon affecting both ourselves and the tides of the oceans. Much more distant is the movement of the planets in our solar system, and how those movements correlate to our lives on Earth, as recorded in astrology.

The power of the earth can be felt in specific objects such as stones or herbs, but it also constantly moves around us. It's easiest to notice the earth's energy when a breeze is blowing or we're standing in a particularly majestic part of nature, but it's always there no matter how still or urban an area is. When we tap into the earth's energy, we can add it to our own and use it in our own spellwork. With practice, it's possible to do this subconsciously, too.

If you've never felt the raw energy of our world before, it's easy enough to access. If possible, go outside and sit under a tree, with your back pressed straight against the trunk. (No tree? That's okay. You can do this against a wall or even in an empty field. Just remember to keep your back as straight as possible.) Close your eyes and focus on your mind, with its kaleidoscope of ideas and colors. From your mind, send your awareness down your spine. Visualize your spinal cord and imagine it like a lightning rod, capable of conducting power and energy.

Now comes the tricky part. As your awareness reaches the end of your spinal cord, push it out even further beyond your body. Feel the earth you are sitting upon and go down even further. Feel the roots of trees and the coolness of the soil as you descend. Be on the lookout for a feeling like a constant pulse; that's the heartbeat of the earth. When you feel that pulse, you are ready to tap into the energies of the earth. Draw that power up from the earth, as if your spinal cord were a lightning rod conducting energy.

You should now feel the energy of the earth moving upward through your body. That energy might fill you with strength or even make you feel a little giddy. This exercise is a good one to practice if you are tired or are having problems concentrating, but it can also be used to charge your magick. As the energy of the earth begins to flow through you, you can direct it to an end point where it will leave the body. The easiest end point is generally your hands, but if you are more comfortable with another part of your body, that's fine too.

As with our exercise earlier to activate energy from the body by contracting and relaxing our arm muscles, the energy you've drawn up from the earth will gather between your hands (or at whatever terminal point you've chosen). Once that energy is filled with intent, it becomes magick that you can then send out into the world to transform your life. Or you can take that energy and add it to the magick you are currently doing, such as putting it inside a candle or stone.

The downside to this exercise is that it's not very conducive to practicing magick. Most of us aren't going to go sit under a tree and meditate while performing a spell to find a new place to live. Luckily, once you've mastered drawing energy from the earth, it gets easier and easier to do.

Common in public Witch circles is the meditation "your feet are the roots of a tree." This is similar to the method of tapping into earth energy just described in this book, though the "earth are the roots of a tree" meditation is often performed both sitting down and standing up. The idea is basically the same though: you push your awareness down through your body and eventually through your feet and into the earth. The imagined "roots" that emerge from your feet are then used to bring the earth's energy upward and into the body.

When this technique is practiced enough, you may find yourself doing it all the time without thinking. With every footfall, your inner self will reach down into the earth, pulling energy up toward you. This is especially true when working magick where we are consciously (and unconsciously) searching for energy to add to our spellwork.

Another way to tap into the earth's natural energies is through breathwork. The energy that sustains life and transforms our planet isn't just in the ground; it also floats in the air and can be accessed there. If you've never absorbed the earth's energy through your breath, it's a pretty easy process.

Start by sitting or standing comfortably and inhaling deeply. As you breathe in, imagine the air moving into your lungs as a blue-white light, filling up your being. Hold the air there for a moment and feel the energy in that air move through your body. At this point you can choose to keep that extra energy you've breathed in or exhale and release it.

Breathing in natural energy is especially effective when performing spellwork. When we work on a spell, we are actively engaged in manifesting an outcome. Our desire is placed firmly in our mind, and everything we do while working the spell is infused with that desired result. When we are conscious of our breath, the air and energy in our lungs is filled with our intent. As we exhale, that charged energy is released into the space around us, where it can then be used in our spellwork.

All of this might sound rather complicated, but when we become aware of what our world truly offers us, tapping into that energy becomes second nature. While preparing a candle for a spell, you'll eventually find yourself instinctively pulling energy up from the earth and bringing it into your lungs. That energy is then added to your own, making your magick stronger!

The Magick of the Sun and Moon

While a discussion of astrology is beyond the scope of this book, working with the powers of the sun and moon is not. Many Witches time their magickal workings to harness the energies of these two entities, and for good reason. The magick of these two celestial bodies is both easy to understand and easy to utilize. Using their energies in magick only requires a bit of patience and the awareness to observe the sky above you.

Over the course of about twenty-eight days, the moon moves from darkness (the new moon) to light, slowly waxing until it shines full in the sky. Then it wanes as it returns to its new phase, its light gradually decreasing until it's dark once more. Not surprisingly, the most important of the moon's eight phases are the new and full moons.

To utilize the energy of the moon in spellcraft, your spellwork should match the energy of the moon in the sky. If the moon is growing larger (waxing), you want to focus on magick having to do with growth or gain. The most advantageous time for magick dealing with banishing or diminishing is when the moon is waning and its light is decreasing in the sky.

The two most powerful nights of the lunar cycle for magick are the new moon and the full moon. If you are doing a spell to bring money or love into your life, and that spell will take only one night to perform, for best results you should enact it under the light of a full moon. If you are casting a spell to get over the loss of a lover or to banish a bad habit, the ideal time for that spell would be under the new (dark) moon.

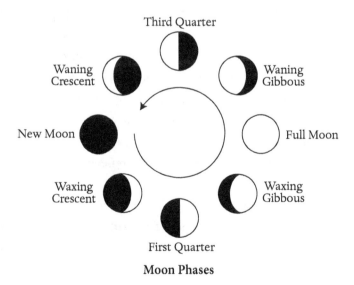

Third Quarter

Waning Crescent

Waning Gibbous

New Moon

Full Moon

Waxing Crescent

Waxing Gibbous

First Quarter

Moon Phases

Many spells, though, are designed to be enacted over a series of days and not just minutes or hours. Candle spells involving pillar or jar candles can sometimes take days or even weeks! To harness the power of the moon on such occasions, you might consider starting a banishing spell at the full moon and then putting the finishing touches on it two weeks later at the new moon. New and full moons find the moon at the height of both its banishing and gainful powers, but these two phases are also transition points and mark the beginning of the moon's waxing and waning periods.

To charge an item with the moon's energy, set it in a place of personal power, such as on an altar or a dresser, where the moon's rays can reach it. Do this on a new moon night, so your item can slowly be charged with the moon's energy over the course of the next two weeks. It should reach maximum charge on the night of the full moon.

Moon energy is often labeled as feminine, but we find gendering energies to be an antiquated way of describing such powers. What makes moon energy truly special is how it slowly washes over our magickal work. The moon's energy works much like the tides, gradually extending and then receding, eventually covering everything in its way before being drawn outward again. The moon's energy is subtle but all-pervasive, creating change one small step at a time until what lies before us is truly transformed.

The sun's daily energy, in contrast, is quick. It reminds us of a quick slap, momentarily stinging but often lacking any serious consequences. The energy from the sun's daily journey through the sky will find your magickal target quite quickly, leave a mark, and then retreat. While the moon's energy slowly engulfs a magickal operation, the energy of the sun rushes in and rushes out in equal measure.

This is not to suggest that the sun's everyday power is weak; it just works differently. Sometimes we need a very quick resolution that won't have a lot of long-lasting repercussions, and other times we need long and lasting change. If you need a one-time infusion of cash in a hurry, the daily rays of the sun provide an effective way to do so. But if you need a continual and renewing source of funds, moon magick is your best bet.

The sun's daily energy works in a way similar to that of the moon. For magick involving increase or gain, work your spells from sunrise to noon. Noon to sunset is the time for working magick to get rid of or banish something. That "ridding" energy will then be at its peak at sunset.

Utilizing the energy of the sun can also be useful when you don't have time to wait for the moon to change from waxing to waning, or vice versa. Perhaps you need to work a spell *now* and have no time to wait. The sun's energy is urgent and quick; it comes directly to us as the sun shines down upon us from the sky. By way of contrast, the moon reflects the sun's light, meaning there is an extra step in there before we see or feel moonlight.

Much as moon energy is sometimes labeled as feminine, there are many in Witchcraft circles who equate the sun with masculinity and male deities. In many Witchcraft circles, the rebirth of the sun on Yule (the Winter Solstice or sometimes Midwinter) is heralded as the rebirth of the male solar deity. And while there certainly are lots of male sun gods out there in the world, there are also female sun deities and male lunar deities. Boxes like "male" and "female" may seem quick and easy, but we find them lazy, simplistic, and generally unrepresentative of the world around us.

While the moon moves through a complete cycle over the course of about twenty-eight days, the sun takes a whole 365 days and some change to do the same. This means there are two types of sun energy that can be utilized in magick. The first is the energy of the sun's daily rays and its cycle from sunrise to sunset. The second is the sun's annual long game, the energy it provides over the course of the Wheel of the Year.

If you are working on a very slow-moving spell, something that you will be repeating for weeks or even months on end, you can line up this type of magick with the sun's annual journey through the sky. Magick for banishing will be most effective when done during the period from the Summer Solstice (sometimes called Litha or Midsummer) to the Winter Solstice, as the hours of sunlight we receive gradually decrease. Magick for gain or increase will be most powerful when done during the period beginning at the Winter Solstice, reaching its apex on the Summer Solstice, the day when we receive the most hours of sunlight.

Working with the sun's cycle throughout the course of a year or a few months is big, slow magick. It's for when you need to make a drastic change in your life, such as a new beginning or forever closing the door on a relationship or career. When we use the sun's daily energy, we cast a spell and then move on to something else soon after. When we use the sun's bigger, cyclical energy, we generally do so slowly over time.

There are some exceptions to how we might use the sun's annual cycle for magick. A banishing ritual done on the Winter Solstice (or the night before) will have a lot of extra energy due to where we are on the Wheel of the Year. Rituals for gain are especially powerful when done at noon on the Summer Solstice. Magick and rituals for balance are also popular on the Autumn and Vernal Equinoxes, and this is powerful magick to tap into, especially if you can wait that long for such a celestial occasion.

Often when we are doing magick, there's no time to wait. If things are out of whack in November, it's going to be hard to wait until the first day of spring to perform a spell for balance. Even waiting two weeks to utilize the magick of the moon can be too long sometimes. While using the moon and sun for magick will add a little extra *oomph* to your magickal workings, your spells will still work if they aren't in sync with the moon's current phase.

We also see the full moon as a three-day occurrence and not just something that happens one night a month. The moon looks plenty big both the day before and the day after it's technically "full." The time for magick is when we are ready and in a position to do it. If the new moon occurs on a night when you have to work or attend your child's piano recital, it's okay if you wait until the following night to do your spell. Witchcraft is not about rigid rules and fixed deadlines. Witchcraft is about making magick work for you, and sometimes you can fudge things a bit to keep that magick on your own schedule.

Chapter Six
Spells by Moon and Will

Our personal power can be utilized in a variety of different ways magickally. Perhaps the easiest ways to utilize our personal energy involve the cone of power and the Witches' Mill. Both of these magickal techniques require little more than a handful of Witches and a bit of space.

Using our own personal bits and fluids is also an easy way to create magick. Because those substances have so much of ourselves within them, spells that utilize them can be done quickly and easily, often without anyone being any the wiser that we are working magick.

The magick of the sun and moon is most often an accompaniment to magick. We plan our magickal operations around solar and lunar cycles, for instance. However, the moon is a powerful ally in magick, and this chapter includes a formula for magickal moon water from our friend Madame Pamita.

The Cone of Power

The cone of power is an advanced magickal technique that, to be most effective, requires several Witches. Unlike the vast majority of spells in this book, the cone of power must also be done in sacred space, within a well-cast magick circle. Building a cone of power is not particularly complicated, but without multiple Witches and a vessel to contain magickal energy, it lacks magickal punch.

So what exactly is a cone of power? The simplest answer is that the cone of power is an accumulation of energy produced by individuals that is infused with intent. The energy used to build the cone of power can be created in a multitude of ways, but the most common methods include dancing or other movement and chanting or clapping. Both movement and sound create and release energy. Chanting has the additional benefit of verbalizing intent while building the cone of power.

As more and more energy is added to the cone of power, that energy will begin to move upward in a clockwise direction. If you could see the energy, it would look like a cone or upside-down tornado (hence the name "cone of power"). As the energy builds, intent is added to that energy, creating magickal energy. At the climax of the rite, when the energy is at its peak, the magickal force created through the cone of power is released through the top of the circle (which is, in actuality, much like a sphere) and out into the universe to do the bidding of the Witches who created it.

In group work, the cone of power is an easy magickal activity because it requires virtually no training or expertise. If someone can move, clap, or make noise, they can contribute to the cone of power. The only other requirement is that intent be added to those actions. In addition, building the cone of power can be exhilarating! It is energy that one can both easily feel and take a hand in creating.

The cone of power can be used for just about any magickal desire. It could be focused on healing a sick coven member or finding someone a new place to live. In our coven we've used it to help promote fertility in a coven member wanting to conceive a child. If you can easily identify the intent, you can attach the cone of power to it. In appendix IV, we list the cone of power in a number of spell categories because it is so versatile!

Building the Cone of Power

You can build a cone of power in just five easy steps! All that's required is a little space and a couple of Witches.

Determine Your Intent

It's not necessary to have an end goal in mind when creating a cone of power, but if you are hoping to utilize the cone for magickal purposes, you'll need to decide where you want to direct the energy you'll raise. The energy created by a cone of power can be used in both a general and a specific way. You might want to raise energy to stop racism or transphobia. Those are worthwhile goals, and magick can most certainly be used to tackle such large problems.

The cone of power can also be used to focus on specific goals and items. A cone of power can be built to help find a home or lover, to heal a sick friend, to help someone gain employment, and so on. If you can articulate your end goal, the cone of power can be used to achieve that goal! When working with other Witches, it's important that everyone involved understands the purpose of the magick you are creating together. You don't want contradictory magickal goals colliding with one another while building the cone of power.

Decide How to Raise Energy and Who Will Direct That Energy

There is no one way to raise energy when building the cone of power. You can chant, walk, dance, tone, clap, or yell, along with whatever else you can think of, and you can also do many of these things together! If it comes from you and it produces energy, it's in play to build the cone of power. Ideally you want to pick a method of energy raising that accommodates everyone you are working with and takes into consideration all the limitations imposed by the space you are using. (Our coven's ritual room is tiny, so we can't dance around the altar if attendance is high!)

It's important that everyone feels included in whatever way you choose to build the cone of power. In our coven we have people with mobility issues who love the energy produced by dancing and chanting but can't move around the circle particularly well. They participate by clapping along with the dancers. You don't need everyone to do exactly the same thing.

If you use a chant while creating your cone of power, agree on the words in advance and keep them as simple as possible. Ideally, any chant you use will verbalize the intent of your energy raising.

You'll also want to appoint one person to lead the building of the cone of power. That person will be responsible for releasing the energy raised and telling everyone when the rite is about to end. The person appointed to do this has the most challenging job involved in creating the cone of power! More on this below.

Cast the Circle

A well-cast circle is a must for building the cone of power. We create circles by projecting concentrated energy from within ourselves, often with the assistance of an athame, sword, or wand. The energy of a circle is designed to hold on to the magick we raise until we are ready to release it. Casting a circle takes practice, and some people are better at it than others.

If you choose not to cast a circle when building the cone of power, you might still get some results, but they will be less than what you could have achieved otherwise. Without a circle, all the energy you are raising will simply drift away. You want your magickal energy to go out into the universe in a big blast, like a volcano erupting!

Raise the Energy

This is the best part of the process. Raise the energy in whatever manner you previously decided on. As you raise the energy, keep your end goal in mind so that the energy being created can be infused with your magickal intent. If you are using movement to raise the energy, remember that the cone of power is not a marathon. You don't want to run your fellow Witches ragged!

Release the Energy

Ideally you want to release the energy created in a cone of power at the apex of the ritual. At the point where everyone involved is at the height of their energy raising and the air in the circle starts to feel thick and heavy, you'll want to send your raised energy out into the universe. Whoever you appoint to lead the cone building will be in charge of signaling the end of the rite. In our coven that person is usually Ari, who will typically start a countdown telling us that the end is near. She does this by yelling numbers when appropriate or holding up her hand and counting down using her fingers.

When Ari begins that countdown, we generally step up our energy work, chanting louder and with more focus, for instance. The idea is to reach the height of what we can project outward when Ari gets to one. When we've reached the end, Ari is then responsible for directing all our energy upward and out of the circle. This means she must be in tune with the energy of the circle so that she can create a hole in the top of it, and she must be in tune with the energy we've created as a group in order to push that power out into the world. (The person in charge is also responsible for repairing the hole at the top of the circle, though in our experience the circle will typically repair itself.)

How do you know that your energy has been released? The atmosphere in the circle will start to change immediately. The air around you will cool off and things will feel much less "soupy." We've noticed that the temperature in our ritual room usually drops about ten to twenty degrees!

The Witches' Mill

Similar to the cone of power is the Witches' Mill. Practitioners who create the mill are often said to be *treading* it, an apt word for reasons we'll get to later. The Witches' Mill is a practice that comes to us from Traditional Witchcraft, one of the earliest alternatives to Wiccan-Witchcraft. The mill as we know it today was first written about by English Witch Robert Cochrane (1931–66), who also called it the "grinding of fate."

When raising the cone of power, movement is generally done *deosil*, or clockwise. But in the Witches' Mill, the movement is just the opposite: the participants move *widdershins*, or counterclockwise. Witches who enact the Witches' Mill are actively working against the natural clockwise flow of energy.[16] This creates a grinding effect between the two different waves of energy, hence the name *mill*.

The energy raised by the Witches' Mill is very different from that raised by the cone of power. It's a befuddling kind of energy, better used to confuse or curse one's enemy. It's also an energy best used to get rid of something, whether that be a lover or a bad habit. Unlike the cone of power, the Witches' Mill is described as "cold." Instead of the temperature going up in ritual space, a group of Witches treading the mill will most often see their magickal space grow colder. Because movement in opposition to the general flow of the circle is more difficult, Witches are thought to "tread" in magickal space when working the mill.

When treading the mill, the focal point of the rite is most often the *stang*, the tool most associated with Cochrane's Craft. A stang is a forked staff or pitchfork that can be used to symbolize an altar or wield energy. The most common chant used with the Witches' Mill is the otherworldly *Io Io Evohe* (pronounced "Yo Yo Evo-hey"), repeated over and over. This is my favorite way to tread the mill, but Cochrane thought the most powerful way to "grind fate" was to do so in silence.

In addition to using the Witches' Mill for spellwork, it's often used to produce a trancelike state. In this state it's generally easier to have encounters with deities and other higher powers, most notably the Horned God. When we've used the mill in ritual, it's either been for a magickal purpose or to induce an altered state of consciousness. Trancework and spellwork are two very different disciplines, so when treading the mill, it's best to have a specific goal in mind before you begin.

When using the Witches' Mill for trancework, you'll want to arrange everyone you're working with into a circle and have them face the stang. From there they should all turn to their right and place their right arm on the right shoulder of the person in front of them. The left arm should then be extended toward the stang as the circle begins to move widdershins. (We've found that a relatively fast walking

---

16. Traditional Witches often call their magickal space a *compass* instead of the more common *circle*, but the ideas behind both are similar. Jason writes more about the Witches' Compass in his book *Witch's Wheel of the Year*.

pace is the most effective.) It's important that everyone keeps their focus specifically on the stang as they move about the circle.

Knowing exactly when to end the Witches' Mill can be tricky. If you are using the mill for spellwork, its use is similar to that of the cone of power. When the energy in the mill reaches its peak, you'll want to end the grinding. When using the mill to facilitate trance, you'll want to end your chanting and walking when someone in the rite has had a vision of the Horned One or the energy in the mill begins to lag.

Using the Witches' Mill for trancework takes a bit of time, and three or four circuits around the stang are not likely to produce an altered state of consciousness. But eventually, as *Io Io Evohe* is chanted and everyone begins treading the mill, your group's patience will be rewarded and your ritual space will start to shift. Minds will wander and eyes will lose focus, and many Witches will find themselves losing touch with the mundane world. It's in those moments that mysteries are revealed and deities let themselves be known. The magick of the Witches' Mill lies in actually doing it and being open to whatever experiences you may have.

Put It on Ice!

This is one of the simplest spells one can do, and has appeared in hundreds of Witch books since the 1970s. If someone is bothering you or is a threat to themselves or others, write down their name or acquire a piece of their hair, a nail, or a fingerprint. Place whatever you choose to use in an ice cube tray and fill the tray with water. As you stick the tray deep into your freezer, say:

> *Away from me! No harm to yourself or others! I put you on ice.*
> *For your misdeeds, in the freezer you pay the price!*

Follow this up by forgetting about the offending person, because they are no longer a part of your life.

This spell can easily be modified as a self-help tool. Instead of writing down another person's name, write down your own, or better yet, use a piece of your hair or a clipped nail and place it in the ice tray. Next to whatever you put in the ice tray, place whatever it is you are trying to banish from your life. If you are trying to quit smoking, a dead cigarette butt would work well, or of course you could simply write down whatever trait you are trying to rid yourself of. As you place the tray in the freezer, say:

Away from me, quality that is unwanted!
This trait in me is now halted!

If you find yourself backsliding, redo the spell or make more ice cubes to take away your unwanted habits and qualities.

Spit Magick

Spitting in public is not particularly polite, but it's very potent magickally. In our practice we usually use it as a deterrent against others or to rid ourselves of something unwanted.

If you live in a large city, holding on to a parking place, even just one in front of your house, can be quite challenging. If someone is parked in your spot, you can get rid of their car with a well-placed loogie. As you walk past their car, spit onto their tires, followed (or proceeded) by the words "away" or "get out." Your spit will send your magickal intention straight to their car. Repeat every time you walk past the offending car until it's gone.

A similar spell can be done in regard to people. Find yourself with a houseguest you don't want to ever see return? After you escort them to the front door and they've gotten into their car, spit outside onto your porch or entryway. Follow that up with the words "never again" to verbalize your intention. You should never have to deal with that person again.

Shared Spellcraft: Make Some Magical Moon Water
by Madame Pamita

What's more magical than the moon? Is there anything more beautiful than a full moon on a clear night, the silver light glistening in the crisp, fresh air? Whenever the full moon shows her face, it's the perfect time to do some powerful moon magic.

When I was a little girl, long before the internet allowed us to find anything we wanted at the touch of a Google "I Feel Lucky" button, I was always searching for any information I could find on magic. In a book somewhere, I read that witches would spin around three times and bow to the moon on the night when it was full. So that little witch girl that I was would go out into the backyard, look up at the full moon, spin around three times, and then make what I thought was a graceful, dizzy curtsy.

I was born under the sign of Cancer, and Cancers are ruled by the moon, so it was only natural that I gravitate to what I call my "Moon Mama," but any sign can benefit from working with the moon. Full moons are the perfect time for doing spells to increase psychic abilities and powers of divination. It's the perfect night to dust off the old tarot deck or do a tea leaf reading for your friend, for example.

Full moons are also amazing for creating powerful intentions for love, prosperity, and blessings. But you don't have to limit that kind of magic to just that one night. If you want to carry the power of the full moon over to the rest of the month, you can capture the magic by making Full Moon Water, which is an extremely powerful water for blessing in any context.

Before you get started, check your favorite online moon phase calendar to see when the full moon is going to be at its peak. If it's early in the morning or during the day, this spell can be started on the night before so that you capture the magic of the waxing moon.

Fill a clear glass or white porcelain bowl with spring water on the night of the full moon. You don't have to go to a spring to get the water (although that *would* be amazing). Bottled spring water will work perfectly for you city spellworkers. As an alternative, you can gather rainwater or melted snow for this spell, which is another amazing way to add an extra level of magic to the working.

If you would like to supercharge your spell and really draw in some extra magnetic force, you can place some moonstones around your bowl of water to amplify the lunar energy.

At moonrise, place the bowl outside or, if you're going to do your spellwork inside, place it next to a window where the moon can shine down on it.

Close your eyes, hold your hands over the bowl as the moon begins to shine, and say a prayer or intention for the water; for example, "Open my psychic abilities and strengthen my intuition," "May my true love be drawn to me," or "Bring bright blessings into my life." Whatever you are asking for, ask for it with a clear, confident, and powerful intention.

Leave your water in the light of the moon for the entire night. The next day you can decant your water to a bottle. If you plan to use your water right away, then there is no need to do anything more. If you plan to use it over the next week, then store it in the fridge. Longer than that, add about a half ounce of clear alcohol, such as vodka, to each cup of water, and that will preserve it for the entire month.

Here are some ways to use your Magical Full Moon Water:

- You can sprinkle this holy moon water around your house to bless and protect it.
- If you've added a bit of clear alcohol to preserve the moon water, you can keep it in the fridge and drink it all month long.

- You can use it to make magic potions, such as teas.
- You can add it to your bathwater for a spiritual cleansing.
- You can use it to bless and consecrate your magical tools.
- You can place a cup of it as an offering on your ancestor altar.
- You can pour it over your body for a self-love ritual.
- You can plant a magical plant and water it with this amazing water (without the alcohol) to infuse it with your intention.

There are so many beautiful ways that you can use this holy moon water. Let your inspiration guide you and let the bright moon shower you with blessings.

Madame Pamita is a professional tarot reader/scholar, rootworker, teacher, author, and maker of magic, music, and mischief. She is the author of Madame Pamita's Magical Tarot *and the host of her popular YouTube channel, which includes the playlist "Hoodoo How To with Madame Pamita," as well as the* Magic and the Law of Attraction *podcast. She is the owner of Madame Pamita's Parlour of Wonders, an old-time spiritualist's shop in Los Angeles, where she offers tarot readings in her salon, teaches classes in tarot and magic, and creates spiritual-magical tools for transforming lives. Visit Madame Pamita online at www.parlourofwonders.com.*

Melt Away the Hex

After meeting a local Witch with a rather nasty reputation, Ari and Jason noticed that everything in their lives started turning upside down. They had been cursed, and the sooner that curse was dealt with, the sooner they could go on with their lives.

Since time was of the essence, they weren't in a position to wait for a new moon or a coven gathering. Things needed to be dealt with immediately! Luckily the sun has its own daily waning energy, and that energy is perfect for dealing with curses and hexes. To utilize the power of the sun to rid yourself of a curse, all you need is an ice cube and a waning sun.

Once the sun has passed its apex in the sky (known as solar noon), the spell can be enacted. Hold on to your ice cube as long as possible while saying the name of the person who hexed you (if known) and the words "go away." (If you don't know the name of the person who hexed you, simply say "hex, be gone!" or "hex, go away!") When the ice cube begins to hurt your hand, throw it as far away from you as possible. (This works best in a backyard or some other place where you won't be disturbed.) As the ice cube melts, the hex will melt along with it!

Chapter Seven
Candle Magick

Perhaps the most popular form of magick among Witches is candle magick. There's just something enchanting about a lit candle in a dark room, and that's long before any magick has been raised or any spell has been cast. Candle magick is popular not just because it's pretty to look at but also because it's both effective and simple. The only thing you need for candle magick is a white candle and a lighter or match.

During the course of working on this book, one of us remarked that "an altar is just a place until a candle is lit." Although that's an oversimplification, it's not untrue. The simple act of lighting a candle makes a room or space feel more magickal. Our ancestors used fire for heating, cooking, lighting, and probably dozens of other things, but we are mostly removed from it in the twenty-first century. Because it's less common than it used to be, seeing raw fire can be transformative, as its presence in our lives changes our perceptions when we are near it.

Fire is intensely powerful, and it's a power we often see the direct results of. As Californians, we've watched wildfires devastate our natural areas over the last ten years. While writing this book, the second and third largest wildfires in California history have burned all around us, and we've had friends lose homes because of it. Fire is a useful tool when we can control it, but it's also something that has deadly consequences when free of any constraints.

Many Witches like to assign correspondences to certain objects, especially correspondences related to the elements of earth, air, fire, and water. Items such as chalices are generally associated with water since they hold liquids, and not surprisingly, candles are thought of as a tool of fire. However, in many ways candles actually encompass all four elements, adding to their power in magickal work.

A candle is designed to hold a flame, representing the element of fire. That part is obvious, but less obvious is how the other three elements are a part of the candle. Candles are generally "poured" into being, meaning they start out as a liquid, and when lit, parts of the candle again turn into a liquid. Liquids, not surprisingly, are typically associated with water. Candles also release a little bit of steam while they burn.

Most candles today are made of paraffin wax, which is a by-product of refined petroleum, a resource extracted from the earth. The most common form of candle wick is cotton, which comes to us from the cotton plant. You probably see where we are going with this: the candle owes its existence to earthly things. Natural types of wax, such as beeswax, can also be connected to the element of earth since bees subsist on nectar, which comes from flowers that grow up out of the ground.

Candles also rely on the power of air to burn. No air means no oxygen, and no oxygen means no flame. In addition, many candles contain pockets or bubbles of air that are produced during their manufacture. As you can see, candles contain the power of all four elemental energies in at least some way.

One of the reasons for the popularity of candle magick within Witchcraft traditions is its accessibility. Candles can be purchased nearly everywhere, and a basic pillar or votive candle costs only a couple of dollars at most. A giant box of tealight candles will last the thrifty Witch for at least a year, without setting them back more than ten bucks. If a Witch is down to their last dollar and needs to spend that dollar on magickal supplies, the candle is a wise investment.

Candles are also ubiquitous. Nearly everyone burns them. A large pillar candle on the fireplace mantel isn't likely to attract that much attention, even if it's being used for spellwork. The current popularity of Witchcraft means that many mainstream stores are also stocking candles specifically created for magickal purposes (though the magickal effectiveness of a spell candle from a chain store is a bit dubious). This is great for those who don't have a Witch or metaphysical shop nearby. Hobby stores also stock dozens of candles in nearly every shape and color. Candle magick has never been easier to do than it is right now.

The magick within a candle spell is released gradually by the burning wick. Unlike building the cone of power and releasing a blast of energy, the magick within a candle slowly flickers out and away. That magick also moves away from the candle in every direction. It's not always the most precise form of magick, but it's often the most thorough, because the candle's energy is coming into contact with so many different facets of your life.

With candle magick, we let the candle do the heavy lifting instead of doing it ourselves. We transfer our intent and energy into the candle, and once that's within the candle, we allow the burning flame to disperse that power. Many spells require the individual Witch to maintain some sort of creative visualization while the spell is being cast, but with candle magick we are doing that while preparing the candle. By the time we light the candle, our part in the spell is mostly over with; it's the burning flame that's releasing the magick.

Candle magick is also especially easy to do because a candle is an excellent focal point. Even in a well-lit room, our eyes are generally drawn to a candle flame. Every time we look at a spell candle, we are focusing more of our intention and energy into our magickal work. With a candle, we don't have to visualize our energy going out into the universe because we can feel and see that energy. The light of a candle is a visual manifestation of our magickal energy, and the candle flame's heat is a tactile manifestation that we can feel.

Getting Started: Practicing Safe Candle Magick

Because of the destructive nature of fire, candle magick has the potential to cause serious harm and damage. It's easy to be dismissive of the power of one small flame, but that one little flame can have some pretty serious consequences. Magick is good for all sorts of things, but it can't prevent a fire due to an inattentive Witch.

Attend to Your Candles

This is one of the most important rules of candle magick. If you are burning a candle, you should be in the room where the candle is burning. You don't have to stare at the candle for four straight hours, but it should be in a place where you can easily see it.

Trim the Wick

This one can be tough to remember, but forgetting it could have deadly consequences. Ideally the wick of a candle shouldn't be much longer than a quarter of an inch. Giant candle flames look cool, but they can easily start a major fire. For most candles, a pair of scissors works to trim the wick, but if you are using a jar candle, you'll probably want to buy a wick trimmer. You'll want to trim the wick of any candle you burn after about four hours of burn time.

If your candle has been previously lit, you can quickly trim the wick before you light it by snapping off a piece of the wick. A charred wick breaks apart pretty easily, and snapping it as a form of trimming works well in a pinch. After trimming your wick, make sure to dispose of it properly. Don't leave it swimming in wax, as it's still capable of starting a fire.

Place Your Candle in a Safe Place

Be sure to set your candle at least three inches away from anything that's flammable and keep it away from drafty areas. Setting your candle in a window might look cool, but a strong breeze might knock the candle over, causing a fire or splattering hot wax everywhere. Be sure the candle is in a place where it can't be disturbed by children or animals.

Use a Candleholder and Find a Heat-Resistant Surface

If you aren't using a jar candle, you'll want to make sure your candle is securely placed in a candleholder. Tealight candles come in their own little containers, but those containers get incredibly hot. Tealight candles should be placed on a heat-resistant surface to avoid fire danger.

Avoid Moving a Candle While It's Burning

Be careful when picking up or moving a burning candle. Not only is moving a live flame a fire danger, but there's also a chance you could burn yourself as the hot wax drips. If you have to pick up a burning candle, make sure the candle is firmly in a holder. We don't recommend ever trying to pick up a burning tealight or jar candle, but if you have to do it, make sure to do so within the first minute or two of the candle being lit.

Extinguish Your Candles before They Fully Burn Down

A candle is most dangerous at the end of its life, so extinguish your candles before they fully burn down. When there's only about half an inch of pillar or jar candle left, extinguish it. A tealight candle should be extinguished once the wick begins to easily move around inside the candle.

Be Extra Careful Outdoors

If you are going to burn candles outdoors, use jar candles or other types of container candles that keep your candle flame contained and won't easily tip over. A lit candle has the capacity to produce sparks and embers, which can be picked up by a strong breeze and start a fire. Avoid an unprotected flame outdoors as much as is possible.

Check Your Candle before Burning It

Make sure that any packaging has been removed from your candle before lighting it and the candle is free of dust. If you are using a candle especially prepared for magick, make sure you know what's in the candle wax. Many candle makers like to melt things like herbs, flower petals, and plastic junk into the wax of their "magickal candles," which, while poetic, can be a very real fire hazard. If there's anything plastic in your candle, we suggest not burning it at all. If your candle is laced with herbs or other natural materials, be especially wary while it's lit.

Preparing and Dressing a Candle for Magickal Use

Candle magick is not complicated, but it requires a little bit more work than simply buying a candle and then lighting it. For best results, any candle that you buy for magickal purposes should be prepared and dressed before you light it. Dressing and preparing a candle can involve several different steps, and the more steps you use, the more effective your magick will be. However, there will be instances when you may not have the time or resources for all three steps.

The most important preparatory step when it comes to candle magick is charging your candle. Luckily, charging a candle is not difficult nor time-consuming; it just requires going back to that most important first step in magick: creative visualization. Charging a candle involves infusing the candle you are going to burn with the specific and focused energy of the spell you wish to cast.

Before starting your candle spell, visualize what it is you are trying to accomplish. If you are working on a spell to keep your relatives from arguing over a holiday dinner, visualize that dinner in your mind. Picture everyone in attendance happy and getting along with one another. As you picture that image of a happy supper in your mind, push that energy into your candle.

To push the energy into your candle, hold the candle in your dominant hand. Grasp the candle tightly and visualize a peaceful dinner in your mind's eye. Once you've established that particular picture, you should feel energy moving down your body: from your head, to your neck, to your shoulder, through your arm, and then finally to your hand and into your candle. The longer you hold the visualization and push the energy into the candle, the stronger your spell will be. This does not mean you need to spend thirty minutes pushing energy into your candle, but thirty seconds isn't going to cut it either. If you want your magick to be strong, you should dedicate some time to it! A properly charged candle should feel warm in your hand and should radiate energy. If those two things don't happen, you should spend a little more time putting energy into your candle.

If you want to add a little extra energy to your candle, you can verbalize your intention as you transfer that energy into the candle. This could be a simple chant such as "peace and harmony, peace and harmony" or some toning. What's most important isn't the words or the lack thereof; it's the intent behind the sounds you are making.

When you are done pushing the energy of your intention into the candle, the candle should feel warm to the touch. Some of that is from the warmth of your hand, but some of it is the energy you've transferred into the candle. If you are preparing your candle a day or two ahead of working your spell, your candle will likely remain warm until you start working your magick.

If you find creative visualization to be challenging, an alternative to pushing your energy into the candle is to write down the results you are looking for on an index card or a small piece of paper. As you write down what you are trying to achieve, you can also verbalize those intentions out loud. For our hypothetical holiday dinner spell, you might write things such as "civility," "cooperation," "mutually agreed-upon topics," "kindness," "shared values," "hospitality," "selflessness," "harmony," etc. Remember to avoid the negatives, which in this case might be something like "no politics." By writing all of this information down, you are putting your intentions into the index card, which will then transfer to the candle, building up your energy. If you choose to write everything down, set your card aside when you are done.

The second step in candle magick is "dressing," or anointing, the candle. The most commonly used substances to anoint candles are essential oils. Before using an essential oil on your candle, check to see that the oil you are using is natural. You don't want to burn something with a bunch of weird chemicals in it! (We'll talk more about essential oils in chapter 13.) When using an essential oil to dress your candle, you should choose one whose energy complements the goal of your spellwork. For this hypothetical spell, we are going to use peppermint oil because it promotes cooperation.

You could simply dribble some peppermint oil on your candle and then smear it around, but most Witches make every act they do deliberate. When performing a spell for gain, you generally want to apply the oil to your candle by starting at the candle's bottom and then moving upward toward the wick. If you are trying to banish or get rid of something, you will usually start at the top of your candle and apply the oil downward toward the candle's base. As you apply the oil to your candle, visualize the end goal of your spell, which in our hypothetical example is to increase goodwill and ensure some peace.

Is it absolutely essential to dress your candle? Of course not. But the more time you spend with your candle, the more energy you'll put into it and the stronger your magick will be. If you don't have a complementary essential oil to use with your candle, something as basic as olive oil will work, too. In a pinch, some of us have been known to anoint candles with water. A good essential oil will amplify the effects of your candle magick, but so will the actions involved in dressing the candle. A dressed candle does not have to be used immediately, either (which is especially useful if you are using water), since the energy put into the candle will last until the candle is lit.

Depending on the type of candle you use, you may be in a position to write directly onto your candle. It's difficult to write anything too elaborate on a pillar candle, and even simple phrases and words take a long time to etch into candle wax, but on the upside, the more time you spend preparing your candle, the more energy you are putting into it. The easiest way to write on a candle is with a pin or needle or the tip of a sharp athame or white-handled knife.[17] Some Witches prefer to use scripts like Theban when writing on a candle, but we are far more likely to use the Latin alphabet. Another option here is to use symbols. For a money spell, for instance, you could use a dollar sign, or a heart for a love spell.

If you are using a candle that can't be etched into, there are alternatives. If there's a paper wrapper on the outside of your seven-day candle, you could write on that paper, or you could use a marker to draw directly onto the glass housing of a jar candle. You could do some writing on the outside of a tealight candle, and even scratch the metal surface a little bit to form symbols. Where there's a Witch, there's a way! Writing on your candle is not necessary, but again, the more you work with your candle, the stronger your magick will be.

If you wrote down what you wanted your spell to achieve when you began preparing your candle for use, place your index card or piece of paper under your candle/candleholder. If possible, place the card in a place where you can continue to read much of what you wrote. The more you look at those words, the more it will reinforce your magickal work. As the candle burns, it will draw up the energy you used to write your intention down and disperse that energy out into the universe.

---

17. Jason wrote an entire book about athames and other sharp objects called *The Witch's Athame*, published by Llewellyn in 2016. We are sorry for this gratuitous plug.

If you frequent Witch shops either in person or online, you'll come across candles labeled "success" and all kinds of other things. If the place you are shopping at is reputable, these candles will come "pre-infused" with magickal energy, and most likely will be pre-anointed with oil. Because there's already energy in these candles, they are great to use in spellwork; however, unless the candle is created specifically for you, that energy is probably not very targeted. To increase the likelihood of your magick being effective, spend a little time putting some of *your own energy* into such candles. The manager of your local Witch shop might be one of the most capable Witches ever born, but your candle will still benefit from a bit of personal attention.

Color Correspondences

Color can be used in a variety of ways in magickal practice. The first use is psychological: colors make us feel a particular way. For many people, light blue is a calming presence and bright red is energizing. We also associate certain ideas and concepts with color. The most common of these is perhaps the association of the color green with money.

Simply lighting a green candle won't bring you more money, but when you light a green candle during a money spell, you are creating a channel that will release more of your personal energy out into the universe. Every interaction you have with that green candle will trigger thoughts about how you are seeking more money, adding additional energy and power to your spellwork. If you do not associate the color green with money, then using a green candle during a money spell would be pointless. The color of the candle you use should be based on your own intuition and feelings, not on a list of correspondences from a book like this one. In other words, the correspondences we list in this book are the ones that work for us, but if they don't work for you, change them to something that resonates with you.

Color magick is not limited to candles. The following list of color correspondences (and your own thoughts on the matter) can be used in various other types of spellwork. For example, you might want to use red ink when writing the words of a love spell or use a black sachet when doing magick to banish an idea or a thought. We use color magick in as many situations as possible.

Common Color Correspondences

These color correspondences come from our own experiences over the last twenty-plus years of practicing Witchcraft and working magick. Interpretations of color can and will differ among Witches. Feel free to make your own list of color correspondences based on your own experiences.

Black: Dispelling negativity, getting rid of things, mourning; black also absorbs energy and all visible light

Blue: Healing, banishing sadness or melancholy, cooling, calming, harmony, relaxing, restful sleep, water

Brown: Grounding, balance, the natural world, earth, rational decisions

Green: Money, prosperity, success, achievement, material things, good health, growth, luck, earth

Gold: Wealth, sun, energy, power, gaining influence

Orange: Creativity, energy, communication, overcoming jealousy

Pink: Friendship, platonic love, self-worth, self-acceptance, beauty, youth

Purple: Royalty, power, divination, ambition, wisdom

Red: Love, passion, anger, revenge, initiation, fire

Silver: Moon, money, psychic powers, prophecy, divination

White: Purifying, cleansing, clarity, truth, calm (White can be substituted for any other color.)

Yellow: Clarity, activating intuition, provoking dreams, supports intellectual pursuits, inspiration, air

Types of Candles

Candles come in a variety of styles, and the type you buy will play at least a small role in your magickal work. Any type of candle you buy for magickal work will most likely serve you well, but certain styles are best suited for certain types of work. When choosing a candle, consider how "big" your spell will be and how quickly you want it to manifest.

Pillar Candles

Pillar candles are typically wide free-standing candles. Other than a heat-resistant surface to burn on, they don't require much in the way of candleholders or other accoutrements. Pillar candles are most often used for decoration and can take days or even months to burn. If your spell is designed to be cast over the course of a few months, a pillar candle is ideal. If you want to keep a candle in your living room to emit a certain type of energy, pillar candles are a great choice. Because they are decorative, pillars are generally dripless, so if you collect candle wax to add to your magickal workings, pillar candles are the wrong choice.

Taper Candles

Taper candles are long, thin candles. Some of them taper from base to top, growing narrower the closer you get to the wick. Many "taper" candles don't taper at all and are the same width the entire length of the candle. Tapers always require a candleholder!

Depending on the size of your taper candle, it might burn down to a nub in just a couple of hours, or it might take a few days of on-and-off lighting. Tapers are generally solid colors, are easy to write on and anoint, and will drip wax. (Even the "dripless" varieties will produce some runoff.) Tapers are probably the candles that most people think of when they imagine candle magick.

When using taper candles, it's always best to be actively aware of them. We've met a few High Priestesses who have caught their hair on fire on a taper when leaning over the altar. Also, you want to make sure the taper candle is snug in its holder. A less than secure fit can result in your taper falling over.

Chime (or Mini Taper) Candles

Chime candles are short, thin candles with a round base. In Witch shops they are often sold for fifty cents or less. For many Witches, these types of candle are their first introduction to candle magick. Chime candles burn down to nothing in just a couple of hours and don't produce much leftover wax. They are ideal when you need to do a quick spell or are doing spellwork with a group.

Votive Candles

Votive candles are short, plump candles that are usually no more than two or three inches high. They are often scented and can usually be found at discount stores. Votive candles are great for personal work, and if they are made with essential oils, those oils will add to your spellwork. Votives generally melt into a small puddle before dying. Votive candles stand well on their own but should always be placed on a heat-resistant surface if you don't have a candleholder available.

Tealight Candles

Tealights are one of the cheapest and easiest types of candles to use in magick. They burn for a short time, generally under four hours, and come in a small metal (or plastic) container, which means you don't need a candleholder to use them. Tealight candles are available in a variety of colors, but be aware that colored tealights often contain synthetic scents.

One downside to tealight candles is that they produce a lot of extra refuse that's hard to recycle. They also have a tendency to flair up near the end of their usefulness, so at about the time you've forgotten that your candle is burning, it's going to be at its most dangerous. Despite these problems, tealights are a great choice thanks to their low cost and ease of use.

Jar Candles

These are candles that come in jars. Often these are decorative or aromatic candles and cost more than most of the alternatives. One of the advantages of a jar candle is that it can easily be used outside without the risk of it being extinguished by a slight breeze. Jar candles also don't require a candleholder since the jar serves that purpose.

Seven-Day Candles

A seven-day candle is a specific type of jar candle. If you've ever seen a glass candle with a picture of Jesus or the Virgin Mary on it at your local grocery store, you've seen a seven-day candle. Seven-day candles get their name from their burning time, as they are traditionally burned over seven days. Many Witch shops that sell custom candles for spells often sell them as seven-day candles. Seven-day candles come in solid colors as well as varieties dedicated to particular religious figures and even pop-culture figures. There's a David Bowie candle in our coven's temple room.

Seven-day candles are often burned to petition Christian saints for assistance with a vexing problem. This practice has also spread to folk saints such as Santa Muerte. (In California, her seven-day candles can be found at our local grocery store.) There are many Witches who work with both Catholic and folk saints.

Seven-day candles are relatively inexpensive and can often be purchased for just a couple of dollars. Their popularity in Catholic circles means they are also readily available. They will last for years if you use them in honor of deity or to signify the elements. Seven-day candles generally require a wick trimmer and either extremely long matches or a long-reach lighter. Like other types of jar candles, seven-day candles are useful for outdoor rites.

While seven-day candles are common, there are other types of day candles available as well. Three-day, five-day, and six-day candles will get your magick done a little faster than the seven-day variety, and fourteen-day candles are an option when you want your spell to take a bit longer. Many church supply stores sell candle inserts that can be placed in colored glass jars, allowing you to reuse the jar again and again. (The candle inserts themselves are generally housed in plastic.)

Knob Candles

These are candles with a variety of round knobs that look like someone stacked a bunch of small, squat candles on top of one another. Knob candles are designed to be used over a period of days, with the magickal practitioner burning one knob daily to enact the spell. Knob candles come in a variety of colors and are increasingly popular.

Types of Candle Wax

In addition to the style of candle you choose, you might want to think about the type of wax used to make it. Most candles are made of paraffin wax, which is made from petroleum. Paraffin wax candles are cheap, don't produce too much runoff, and are the most common type of material used for candles. Paraffin wax can be a bit sooty when it burns and is far from "natural." If you are doing a spell to fight pollution, we would not recommend paraffin.

Beeswax candles burn much faster than paraffin and cost more, too, but they release a pleasant smell, are completely natural, and aren't particularly messy. Beeswax, because it's natural, is more powerful than paraffin, but its price makes it unaffordable for some Witches. Beeswax has another benefit: these candles are great for people bothered by candle soot. If the smoke from a paraffin wax candle is irritating, try beeswax.

Another more expensive but more natural option is a candle made of soy wax. Soy wax is biodegradable and doesn't produce any unwanted soot while burning. Due to their price, soy wax candles aren't available in as many varieties as paraffin and beeswax candles, but they are a good choice for Witches who prioritize sustainability.

Casting Your Candle Spell

So far in this chapter we've picked out our candle type and color and dressed and prepared our candle, but what comes after that? Most of us want to feel like we are casting a spell, not shopping for living room accessories or alternative light sources. But every step of the journey is a part of casting the spell, from a mundane trip to the store to buy a box of candles to scratching words or symbols on a candle and anointing it with oil. Every moment we spend with our candle is part of the spell, even if it doesn't feel magickal.

After your candle has been properly prepared, there's no great secret to releasing its energy. You simply light the wick, keep an eye on your burning candle, and then wait for the results you are seeking. For many Witches, though, there's something ultimately unsatisfying about that—they want something that feels like a *spell*. And while an extra amount of buildup is not necessary for the release of your magick, it certainly won't hurt anything, and will add even more energy to what you are trying to accomplish.

For us, the best place to burn a candle is on one's personal altar. An altar is in tune with your own personal energies and will add an extra bit of *oomph* to your spellwork. If an altar is out of the question, a place that holds meaning to you will work just as well and be equally powerful. In the house where Jason and Ari live, they do much of their candle magick on the mantel above their fireplace. It's not technically an altar, but as a focal point of their magickal household, it acts much like one.

It's perfectly acceptable to flick a lighter and light your candle without much fuss, but the more thought you put into lighting your candle, the more power-ful your spell will be. There are many Witches who like to light their candles with matches for this reason. Lighting a match isn't an especially drawn-out process, but it takes more time and deliberation than using a lighter. You pull a match from the matchbox, hold the match between your thumb and forefinger, strike it, and watch as an intense flame appears as if by magick. Holding raw fire in one's hands is pow-erful! Then there's the lighting of the candle itself and the blowing out of the match when done.

An alternative here is to use a taper candle and light it with the flame of another candle. If you are doing ritual in sacred space, you might light candles for the ele-ments of earth, air, fire, and water as well as certain deities you are close to. Lighting your magickal candle from the flame of one of those candles is a provocative act. You are transferring the energy of your elemental or deity candle to your spellwork. This might come in especially handy if you honor the goddess of Aphrodite and use a candle lit in her honor to light the candle you are using for a love spell.

Words can add extra gravity to your spell, and articulating your goals out loud will always add power to your work. The words said in such instances can be simple and sparse or poetic and numerous. What's most important is that you feel comfortable saying them.

Many Witches like to articulate their spells as rhyming couplets or poems. Rhymes are generally easy to memorize, but they also feel magickal. Saying a rhyming verse such as the following at the moment you light your candle can only add to the power of your spellwork:

> *Fire burn bright, fire refine my sight.*
> *My oppressor revealed this night!*

However, if thinking of a rhyme is too taxing or distracts you from visualizing your end goal, it's not worth the trouble.

If you begin your spell in sacred space, it's unlikely that your candle will have fully burned down before you feel the need to close your circle. In such instances, you might want to acknowledge that the candle is out of sacred space but will continue to do its work in your mundane space by saying something like this:

> *This circle is open but my spell will not rest.*
> *What I seek this night shall manifest!*

Sometimes a candle spell will take days to complete. In such instances, it's not necessary to re-create sacred space or repeat previously said words. A quick acknowledgment that the spell is continuing is usually all that's needed. As you relight the candle each day, say:

> *My spell has begun once more.*
> *I shall obtain what I long for!*

We also like to say a few words when we have to extinguish our candle for whatever reason. If the candle is being extinguished before the spell is complete, it's often appropriate to say words suggesting that things are "to be continued":

> *My work here is not yet done.*
> *My final results, not yet won!*

When extinguishing a candle (remember, letting a candle burn out completely on its own can be a fire hazard), a few words can serve to finalize the spell in your mind. Those words can harken back to the original intent of your spell (such as "I cast this spell for peace and harmony") or can be more general, like this:

My magick now spun, my spell has now been cast.
With light and love, long may my magick last!
So mote it be!

There's nothing wrong with blowing out a candle, but there are many Witches who find the practice disrespectful. If extinguishing your candle for the last time with a candle snuffer or even your fingers feels most magickal to you, do it! There's no right or wrong way to extinguish a candle.

Chapter Eight
Spells by Candlelight

One of the best things about candle magick is its simplicity. To perform a spell with a candle, you shouldn't need much more than a lighter, a candle, and a bit of space. However, some of the earliest Witchcraft books on the subject often suggested the use of multiple candles per spell, plus a few accompanying items. In this chapter we've tried to keep the spells as simple as possible, though in a few cases we do suggest using a few extra items.

However, if you don't have those extra items, whether it's a particular kind of oil or a certain stone, don't sweat it. These spells can be done without the extras. For the purposes of this book, we just wanted the spells to be as powerful and complete as possible. Sometimes it's simply not possible to use extra stuff, and that's fine—the magick will still work!

Ari's Find My Community Spell

Ari found the Craft while in Catholic high school, and her first few years as a Witch were spent in her parents' townhouse in the room she shared with her younger sister. During that period of time, she'd wake up in the middle of the night and perform this spell to find the Witch community she longed for. Not surprisingly, she met Jason on her second day at Michigan State University at the age of eighteen, and they've been together ever since.

For this spell you will need:

- 5 colored candles (white, yellow, red, blue, and green) or 5 white candles (We recommend small tapers.)

Start by envisioning the type of community you are searching for. Is it a coven of Witches or something less formal? In your mind, picture that group and you being an active and accepted part of it. After you have envisioned what you are looking for, start the spell.

Begin by lighting the white candle and placing it in the center of your working area. As you light the white candle, say:

> *A community of Witches is what I seek tonight.*
> *May I be drawn to their power and light!*

The next four candles are all representative of the qualities you wish for in a community. If the ideas expressed in these next eight lines aren't in sync with your desires, change them to something more appropriate.

Pick up the yellow candle and, while lighting it, say:

> *People with which to share, give, and grow,*
> *United together, our magick will flow!*

Place the yellow candle in the east, about six or seven inches from the white candle.

Pick up the red candle and light it while saying:

> *A group of people who will let me be me,*
> *Where devoted Witches we are free to be!*

Place the red candle in the south, again about six or seven inches from the white candle.

Now pick up the blue candle and, while lighting it, say:

> *A place of magick, acceptance, and love,*
> *Within and without, as below, so above!*

The red candle is now set in the south, again six or seven inches away from the white candle.

And finally pick up the green candle and say while lighting it:

> *A place to settle, a people to call my own,*
> *For I shall no more be a Witch alone!*

Place the green candle in the north, about six or seven inches away from the white candle, and as the five candles burn, say this incantation:

> *I light these candles to find my community,*
> *A place of shared love and unity.*

I shall find my chosen family,
A place to weave Witchcraft's tapestry!

If you are in a situation similar to Ari's, where you have to secretly work your magick in the middle of the night, it's likely that you'll have to repeat this spell at least a couple of times before your candles burn down completely. Each time you relight your candles, move them closer together, bringing you ever closer to the community you are looking for.

Jason's Invisibility Spell

Many years ago Jason worked in a grocery store where he was being sexually harassed by a customer. After struggling with the situation for a couple of months, Jason remembered, "Oh yeah, I'm a Witch!" and quickly went about crafting a spell that would make him invisible to the offending party. Several weeks later, Jason was standing right next to this person and was completely ignored by them. Success!

For this spell you will need:

- 2 candles (Votive candles are recommended. Use whatever colors work best for you.)
- A pin, athame, or white-handled knife (for carving your candles)

Start by carving the name of each party involved on the two candles. In Jason's case, he carved his name on the candle that represented him, and "bad person" on the candle representing his problem customer. While carving the candles, visualize the offending party looking through you as if you were invisible.

Now place the candles close to each other. As you light the candle representing the person to whom you want to be invisible, say:

You will no longer be able to see me.
From now on you shall just let me be.
Out of your sight and out of your mind,
From me you will ever more be blind!

Now light the candle that represents you while saying:

I will now disappear from your sight,
As if shrouded in the darkest night.
I will be free from your unwanted attention.
For myself I cast this spell of deception!

It's recommended that you cast this spell over several days, slowly moving the candles farther apart from each other. Halfway through every session of your candle burning, blow out the candle representing the bad actor. As you do this, say:

I extinguish your line of sight.
This spell will make all right!

In this spell you want your candle to burn twice as long as the bad person's candle. So if you blow out their candle after thirty minutes, let your candle burn an additional thirty minutes. When you are done with your spellwork for the day, extinguish your candle and say:

I shall be invisible to your eyes.
With magick I cast my disguise.

Repeat your work on this spell until the candle representing you burns almost completely away. Remember to move the candles farther and farther apart each time you work on the spell and to let the candle representing you burn twice as long. As the wax melts away from your candle, you will melt away from the eyesight of the person bothering you!

Shared Spellcraft: A Simple Spell for Solstice (or Any Time You Need to Remember Your Brightness) *by Irisanya Moon*

This spell utilizes the power of the reborn sun on the Winter Solstice to awaken the magick inside of you.

For this spell you will need:

- All the candles in your home that are unfinished
- All the candles in your home that still hold magick
- Matches/lighter
- Bowls of water to place the candles in for safety, or a place where you can leave candles to burn all the way down (such as a bathtub, an enclosed shower, etc.)

Each year a beloved of mine gives candles as solstice presents, carefully wrapped in paper, and a card of blessings in the wintertime. Over a decade I have received candles from other loved ones, and there are spells that sit on my altars:

- Candles from initiations and classes
- Candles from secret spells
- Candles from out-loud spells

I have plenty of light, if only I remember.

So I take the candles out. I take out the spells that need tending or haven't quite wrapped up. I place all the candles in their various stages of illumination.

I reaffirm the circle around my house or I cast another circle to hold the energy in a more contained way, often when I have a lot of unfinished work for some reason.

Then I light all the candles in the dark of the house. I light them one by one and ask them to grow.

I keep a vigil (as much as possible) to witness the burning. I make prayers and offerings and feel the warmth of magick fresh and magick ongoing.

The light grows over the hours. Some candles will drown in wax. Some candles will need extra tending and wick trimming. But I light them all. And I leave the artificial lights off until the candles are out.

Then I open the circle or clear the space. I thank. I remember.

No matter where you are or what you feel in these days, whether you are filled with joy in the shadow or sing loudly for the returning light, let all the candles in the house of your heart burn brightly.

Let the spell of your being fill the places that forget. Let the spell of your growing turn from promise to reality. Let the light grow inside and outside.

And even as the candles complete their work and fold back into dark, may you remember the burning.

The spark. The flame. The fuel of your intention—spoken and not. Light all the candles of your heart. And remember, no one can hold back your dawn.

Irisanya Moon is a Reclaiming Witch and initiate, Moon Books author, priestess of Aphrodite, and international teacher. She is interested in shifting stories and cultivating resilience through magick and wonder.

Open Your Roads: Remove Blockages and Be Open to New Opportunities

No matter how focused or determined we are, we will eventually run into obstacles blocking our way forward. When those sorts of roadblocks appear, they may keep us from realizing all the opportunities that lie before us. This spell is designed to remove those blockages and put us in the proper frame of mind to realize when new possibilities are right in front of us.

For this spell you will need:

- 1 candle (We recommend a yellow taper.)
- A pin, athame, or white-handled knife (for carving your candle)
- Oil for anointing (Our suggestions include Road Opener oil, sunflower seed oil, or virgin olive oil.)

Start by carving words and phrases related to your goal into your candle. We suggest words and phrases such as success, opportunity, open eyes, clarity, clear vision, openness, lucidity, possibilities, and potential. Carve your words starting near the candle's bottom and then moving upward. Be careful about where you begin the first letter of each word, as you don't want to run out of space before you get to the final *y* or *s*. As you carve each word or phrase, envision new opportunities ahead of you.

After the words are carved, dress your candle with oil. Sunflower seed oil and virgin olive oil are easy enough to obtain and might already be in your kitchen. Road Opener oil is specially formulated for the purpose of this spell and is in the magickal cupboard of many Witches. (For more on oils, see chapter 13.) As you dress your candle, start at the bottom and move upward, repeating the phrases you carved into your candle as you anoint.

After your candle is properly prepared, light it while saying the following words:

Nothing in my way, my path is now clear and free.
I see the opportunities in front of me!

Let your candle burn for one hour, then repeat each day until your candle is spent, repeating the "clear and free" verse every time you light it. As you light the candle, picture yourself a little bit closer to your goals.

Candle and Pins Spell for Sending Blessings

This spell can be used for a variety of ailments, but we originally used it to help a friend of ours who needed healing. If you choose not to use it for healing, it can also be used to help a friend who is down on their luck or someone facing a major life change, such as a divorce, a breakup, or a new job. The spell is designed to be used for a specific person, so the stronger the link you have to that person, the stronger the spell will be. We originally did this spell as a coven, but it can easily be adapted for solitary practice.

For this spell you will need:

- A small mirror (If you don't have a mirror, a piece of aluminum foil wrapped around a coaster will work.)
- Something representing the person for whom the spell is being cast (such as their picture, an item they own or have touched, a few strands of their hair, or their name written on a piece of a paper)
- 1 light blue or white taper candle
- Citrine or bloodstone
- Pins

Place the mirror on your working space and take a moment to verbalize your intention for the spell. If you are doing this spell to help someone heal, say something like this:

> *Tonight we cast this spell for Janet*
> *To invoke the blessings of the universe*
> *And to help with her healing.*
> *So mote it be!*

Follow this up by placing the picture (or other item) of the person you are doing the spell for on your mirror. The reflective nature of the mirror helps focus your energy toward the target of the spell. Place the candle on top of the picture or written name of the person you are working magick for. If you are using an item the candle can't be set on top of, simply place the candle next to the item on your mirror. Finally, place the citrine or bloodstone on the mirror. (Citrine and bloodstone are great for healing, and their inclusion here will add a little extra energy to your spell. See chapter 11 for more about stones and crystals.)

Once the spell is set up, have everyone present take a pin and hold it in their dominant hand. Remind everyone of the gravity of the situation at hand and ask them to form a strong mental picture of your friend strongly in their minds. Once everyone is properly focused, have them stick their pins into the candle while saying a blessing or giving words of encouragement to the person you are doing the spell for. Here are some things you could say here:

I give blessings to Janet so she can fight the infection in her body.

Blessings be to Janet, that she can financially get through this time.

I send love and energy to Janet. I want her to know she is not alone.

Once everyone has inserted their pin (or pins—everyone can go more than once) into the candle, light the candle. You don't have to say anything as you light the candle, but verbalizing your intention never hurts. It can be something simple, like this:

May Janet receive our blessings this night. So mote it be!

As each pin drops out of the candle as it burns, the wish inserted into the candle goes out into the universe. If you are in a hurry, encourage people to stick their pins near the top of the candle. If you are doing this spell as part of your normal coven work, after you light the candle, you can set it aside to do its work. When using a large taper candle, you may have to light and extinguish the candle several times.

Amanda's Tealight Love Candle Spell

This spell requires a little work, but the more work you put into preparing your candle, the stronger your spell will be! This spell utilizes the idea of "like attracts like" and includes several elements associated with love in the preparation of the candle. In addition to love, this spell can easily be used to ignite passion if your current relationship is feeling a bit stagnant.

For this spell you will need:

- The wax of 1 white tealight candle, chopped into small pieces (Keep the empty container and the wick; you will use them later.)
- A small glass measuring cup
- A small pot of water, heated to simmering
- 5 drops of liquid red food coloring
- 1 small garnet chip (optional)
- A few drops of rose essential oil
- A toothpick
- Dried rose petals ground into powder (You won't need more than a couple of petals at most.)
- Biodegradable glitter for sprinkling on top of the candle (optional)

Place your chopped-up tealight candle wax in the small glass measuring cup. When your pot of water has become hot (about 180 degrees Fahrenheit), carefully place your measuring cup full of wax in the simmering water, essentially creating a double boiler. (The measuring cup does not have to float on top of the water. Simply set it in the water.) Once the wax has all melted, add the red food coloring. Stir thoroughly until the candle wax is a rich red color.

Place your garnet chip (if using) in the empty tealight container, then pour the melted wax over it, keeping the wick in the center of your candle. When the wax begins to cool around the edges, add the essential oil and blend with a toothpick. Be careful not to add the essential oil to the candle wax too soon or the heat of the wax will dissipate the oil, causing you to lose the oil's scent. Once the wax reaches a semisoft state, sprinkle the ground rose petals and glitter onto the top, gently pressing them into the wax to secure them.

Once your candle is cool, it's ready to be used. Before lighting your candle, verbalize your spell's intention:

> *I am worthy of love and of being loved.*
> *I cast this spell so that I might receive the love*
> *That has been missing from my life.*

The spell is done when the candle has burned down. For extra impact, perform this spell on a Friday, the day of the week that is sacred to the goddess Frigga.

Spell to Drive Away Enemies

No matter how nice you are, it's likely that you'll pick up at least one enemy over the course of your lifetime. Luckily, because we are Witches, we can rid such people from our lives.

For this spell you will need:

- 1 candle to represent your enemy
- Tools to inscribe the candle (pin, athame, scissors, etc.)
- Be Gone oil

Start by carving the name of the person who needs to go away three times into your candle. Over their name, carve the words "be gone" or something similar that states your intention.

Grip the candle at the base with one hand and hold it out and away from you. Get a little bit of oil on your other hand and anoint the candle by grasping the candle near the base and moving your grip upward toward the wick. When you reach the candle's wick, take your hand off the candle and start over at the base. The motion you are using to anoint the candle is symbolic of pushing the unwanted person out of your life. Once you've dressed your candle, light it while saying:

> *(Name of individual), you will be gone from my life!*
> *Be gone! Be gone! Be gone! So mote it be!*

You can let your candle burn down all at once or burn it for thirty minutes a day until the candle is gone. When finished, dispose of the candle in the garbage, where this person belongs!

Bewitch Yourself

We all have moments when we doubt ourselves or feel as if we are somehow inadequate and don't deserve the things we want in life. This is a spell to help overcome those feelings. In effect, it's a spell to bewitch yourself!

For this spell you will need:

- A candle to represent you (We recommend picking your favorite color.)
- Anointing oil (optional)
- A pin, athame, or white-handled knife (for carving your candle—optional)
- A small mirror or other reflective surface

Charge and prepare your candle with oil if desired. If you want to use an oil, we suggest one that manifests self-confidence and self love. You can also carve the spell's mantra into your candle: "I am worthy of what I seek and deserve." Start by setting your reflective surface on your working space. If you don't have a mirrored surface to set your candle on, that's okay, but this spell will benefit mightily from that. A reflective surface will bounce the energy coming out of the candle back up toward you! Place your candle on top of the mirror and pause for a moment before lighting it.

During this pause you should be able to see at least a small part of yourself reflected in the mirror. Sometimes it can be difficult to look at our reflection, especially when we are hurting, but don't ignore yourself this time. Look at yourself for a moment and know that you are worthy of what you want in life, such as love, success, security, friends, and family. If you can look at yourself in the mirror without hate or malice, you are worthy of all these things and more.

Light your candle and state your intention:

I am worthy of what I seek and deserve.

After you light your candle, look at the candlelight and the reflection coming up from the mirror. Let your eyes lose focus, and concentrate on what you see in that moment. Visualize yourself happy and whole, feeling free to embrace the things you care about. As you look into the light, repeat your mantra. When you extinguish your candle, you should feel refreshed and confident in yourself. Repeat this spell anytime self-doubt creeps into your life.

Breaking Up with a Person Spell

Sometimes breaking up with someone is intensely difficult, no matter how right the decision might be. This spell is designed to aid in a breakup and to keep you whole in the process.

For this spell you will need:

- 1 candle to represent the person you want to be rid of
- 1 candle to represent yourself
- Be Gone oil, Get Away oil, or another essential oil related to your intent (optional)
- A healing oil of your choice or an oil representative of strength (optional)
- A pin, athame, or white-handled knife (for carving your candles)
- A pair of scissors

If you are anointing your candles with oil, first anoint the candle representing the person you want to be rid of with Be Gone oil, Get Away oil, or another essential oil related to your intent. As you anoint the candle, start at the top of the candle and apply the oil with a counterclockwise (widdershins) motion. Anoint the candle representing yourself with a healing oil of your choice or an oil representative of strength. Apply the oil from the bottom up, in a clockwise direction.

After the oil has been applied, carve your name and the name of the person you are breaking up with on your respective candles. For an extra bit of energy in the spell, include each person's birthday on their candle. Start by placing the candle representing you in the middle of your working space. Place the candle representing the person you are trying to get rid of six to eight inches away from the candle representing you. Open up your pair of scissors and position the blades so they are facing the candle representing the person you are getting rid of. As you do this, say:

I cut the ties with which we were bound.
We will be as we once were, safe and sound.

Light the candle representing the person you are breaking up with while saying:

Your road shall no longer have me in it.
From you I have now forever quit!

Now light the candle representing you and say:

I shall emerge from this healed and whole.
Strong are my mind, heart, and soul!

Let the candles burn for a while and then snuff them out. Repeat every day until the candles burn down, each time moving the candle representing the person you are breaking up with farther from the candle representing you. As you move the candle farther away, restate the intention of your spell. When the candle representing the person you are breaking up with has burned down entirely, your spell is complete.

Personalize Your Seven-Day Candle

Seven-day candles are powerful tools in spellcraft. Thanks to their popularity, they are also inexpensive and available in a variety of places. Many Witch and magickal shops sell seven-day candles specially prepared for a variety of workings. This spell allows you to customize your own seven-day candle focused on your specific needs and desires.

For this spell you will need:

- A seven-day candle in the color of your choosing
- An image to add to the outside of your candle or a marker to draw on the outside of it (optional)
- Adhesive such as Mod Podge or a glue stick (optional)
- 2–3 essential oils associated with your end goal (to add to the candle)
- A long skewer or piece of wire
- Finely ground herbs related to your candle's purpose (to sprinkle onto the candle)

Start by determining the focus of your candle. Is it money, health, opportunities, love, or something else? Once you have identified the purpose of your candle, round up two or three essential oils in line with your end goal. (See chapter 13.)

Next, decide how you will decorate the outside of your candle. Is there a picture you'd like to place around the jar? The picture could be something related to your end goal or perhaps an image of a deity or higher power you work with. Many of the Christian saints commonly found on seven-day candles can be worked with too, so you wouldn't have to add your own image to the candle. When you've created your image, glue it to the outside of your candle using an adhesive such as Mod Podge or a glue stick.

Alternatively, you could simply draw on the outside of the candle with a marker. This has the added benefit of allowing you to push more of your personal energy into the candle. What you "draw" doesn't have to be a figure or symbol, either; words that are representative of your end goal are fine here too. No matter what you choose to do, be sure to let the marker or glue dry on your candle before moving on to the next step.

Specialty seven-day candles often have essential oils infused into their wax, but if yours is free of oil, you can easily add some with a long skewer or solid piece of wire. Along the outside edge of the candle's wax, away from the wick, push your skewer or wire as deep into the candle as possible, creating a hole at least four or five inches deep in the wax. Make three or four different holes in the wax to fill with oil. Once the holes have been made, drip some essential oil onto your candle and swirl it around so the oil goes down into the holes. You only need a couple of drops; too much oil and you risk drowning the wick. It may take a bit of time for all the oil to absorb into the candle, so be patient and keep swirling the oil as much as needed. To make this as easy as possible, leave your candle in a warm spot for an hour or two before you make your holes to soften the wax. A sunny spot in your house or a place near a warm oven or heating vent will provide more than enough warmth to make the wax more supple.

Once the oil has been absorbed into the candle, sprinkle your finely ground herbs around the outer rim of the candle wax. Don't be overly generous with the powdered herbs; you want to avoid turning your candle into a fire hazard. Once the herbs have been sprinkled, pick up your candle and infuse it with some more of your own energy related to the task it was created for. And voilà! You have your own seven-day candle to aid you in your magickal workings!

Matt's Knob Candles for Luck

There are times in life when we need a little bit of extra luck for whatever reason. This is a spell for those situations. It is based on the old Irish poem "May the Road Rise Up to Meet You," which is a surprisingly strong piece of magick. It includes invocations to the four elements, a blessing for chosen family, and a petition to deity. This spell requires seven days to cast, as you will burn one knob of the candle each day over the course of that period.

For this spell you will need:

- 1 seven-knob candle (We recommend yellow.)
- Oil for anointing (We recommend Road Opener oil or another oil you associate with positive energies.)
- A pin, athame, or white-handled knife (for carving your candle)

Start by charging and anointing your candle. Anoint one knob of the candle at a time, treating each knob as a separate candle. Anoint for growth, with an upward, clockwise motion.

The phrases in this traditional Irish poem aren't particularly long, but they'll seem long as you carve them into your candle. It isn't necessary to carve an entire verse into each knob, but you will want to scratch either some symbols representative of the ideas or at least some of the major words of each line.

Start at the top of the candle and carve these words (or the equivalent) into the first knob:

May the road rise up to meet me.

This particular line is about easy journeying; instead of presenting obstacles, the road ahead intentionally makes your path easy to navigate. Envision yourself easily obtaining the things you want in life as you carve and chant the words of the candle's first knob.

On the candle's second knob, carve these words (or the equivalent):

May the wind be always at my back.

As you carve these words, imagine a powerful force gently moving you forward to accomplish your goals. As a Witch, many of us often feel pushed ahead in positive ways by unseen energies. Keep that picture in your mind as you carve and chant the words of the candle's second knob.

On the third knob of the candle, add these words (or the equivalent):

May the sun shine warm upon my face.

Imagine for a moment a warm and bright morning, where you feel safe and healthy. Keep that energy in your mind as you carve and chant the words of the candle's third knob.

Traditionally, the poem's fourth line is "[May] the rains fall soft upon your fields until we meet again," but we've amended them here, splitting that line into two parts. For the first part of the line, the fourth knob of your candle, carve these words (or the equivalent):

May the rains fall soft upon my domain.

Rains are necessary and usually are a blessing, provided they don't spill uncontrollably from the sky. Imagine the rain as the blessings in life, the sweet moments we all cherish, even if they aren't always big and boisterous affairs. Picture those blessings falling into your life again and again while you walk the Wheel of the Year. Here your domain is your life, because as a Witch you are the ruler of your own destiny. Chant these words as you carve them into the fourth knob of your candle.

For many of us, Witchcraft has given us a chosen family, one that remains strong even when we are separated from one another. On the fifth knob of your candle, carve these words (or the equivalent):

May I always meet again those I love.

As you carve these words into the fifth knob of your candle, chant them and picture the people who are most dear to you in life. Visualize them being a part of your experiences, and if they are far away, see yourself reuniting with them in your mind's eye.

Belief in deity is not necessary to be a Witch, but for many of us it's an important part of our practice. If you are an atheist Witch, feel free to replace the word *gods* with *the earth* in the next line. What's important is to visualize whatever higher power is most important to you. As you visualize that power looking out for you, carve these words (or the equivalent) on the sixth knob of your candle:

May the gods hold me in the palm of their hands.

If you are close to specific deities, you can include them in this part of the spell. If you are particularly close to your ancestors, you could call on them too. What's most important is being comfortable with the higher power you are carving and chanting about.

The original Irish poem ends here, but after invoking the road (earth), the sun (fire), rain (water), wind (air), deity, and family, it feels like we should invoke ourselves as well. As Witches who wield magick, we are active controllers and creators of our own lives. On the seventh knob of your candle, carve these words (or the equivalent):

> *And may I always have a hand in creating my own luck!*

Often overlooked is the fact that we really do help create our own luck, and we do so by wielding magick. At this stage of the spell, visualize good things happening to you, and you being happy and secure. Hold these thoughts as you chant these words and carve them into the seventh knob of your candle.

Over the next seven days, burn one knob every day. As you prepare to burn each knob, say that day's line aloud several times, reminding yourself of the intention. Make sure each knob burns down completely each day. On the seventh day, end your spell by letting out a resounding "so mote it be!" as the candle nearly finishes burning.

Shared Spellcraft: Truth Spell
by Jessica Ripley

I developed this truth spell during a time of great need when I thought someone who was my adversary was hiding something that would be extremely detrimental to me. Since it was already a situation in which I was at a severe disadvantage, I channeled this spell through my ancestors. It worked for me in an unexpected way.

Instead of bringing to light a deception, the spell opened this person's eyes to the way they were treating me and the way their treatment of me was getting in the way of their desired outcome. It made a very volatile situation bearable until I was able to leave.

Be aware that when you complete this spell, it can work in a variety of ways. It might bring about a confession from someone who has wronged you, or illuminate a truth you might have missed. Be specific and thoughtful in your petition. In my original spell, I used three oils (Master Key oil, Van Van oil, and dragon's blood oil) created by a trusted rootworker named Fredericka Turner at Conjuria. You can substitute High John the Conqueror oil for these three oils.

For this spell you will need:

- Petition paper
- A writing utensil
- 1 blue chime candle (and holder)
- Master Key oil, Van Van oil, and dragon's blood oil (or substitute High John the Conqueror oil for these three oils)
- Ground cinnamon
- Ground coffee

Cleanse yourself, your space, and your tools. If desired, leave your ancestors a libation and call on their protection during the casting of your spell.

Create a crosshatch petition by writing the person's name (or the situation) nine times on your paper, then turning the paper 90 degrees and writing your name over theirs nine times.

Without lifting your pen from the paper, write your desire ("the truth about X comes out," or whatever it is you want to come to light) in a circle around the names.

Dress the candle with the oils and lightly sprinkle the ground cinnamon and coffee on the outside of the candle.

Place the candle in a holder on top of the petition paper. Focus on your intention and light the candle. Speak your intention out loud.

Let the candle burn down and out. Once your candle has burned out, collect the petition and any wax remains and dispose of them in whatever way you see fit. As you dispose of your candle's remains, speak your intention so the truth will be revealed to you.

Jessica Ripley is a Hekatean witch and writer from Minnesota.

Chapter Nine
Herb and Plant Magick

Up to this point, all the magick in this book has come from us. *We* create the energy we use for magick when we draw a picture or say our intention aloud. Even a candle is just a focus for the personal energy we raise during magickal work; the candle itself doesn't contain any magickal energy when we begin working with it. This is the chapter where everything starts to change, because the magick of plants and herbs is quite different from the magick we create mostly on our own.

As once living things, the herbs and plants we use in magick don't have to be charged because they are already full of energy. Whether cinnamon is in stick form or ground into a fine powder, it is radiating energy—energy we can use in our spell-work. Cinnamon has strong associations with power, success, and protection, and when we use cinnamon in our spellcraft, those powers will come through.

If we carry cinnamon with us, the energies it emits will affect us. Carrying a stick of cinnamon in your pocket will probably make you feel more confident (that's how you get to power and success) and will keep people away from you (that's the protection part). Carrying around an herb may not feel like magick, but it's most definitely a type of spell, because herbs and plants influence their surroundings, including ourselves and the people we interact with.

How we use plants and herbs in magick will vary. Simply carrying an herb on your person is the simplest way to use one in magick. However, herbs and plants are perfect accompaniments to other types of spellwork. Sprinkling rose petals on your altar while working a candle spell will add more energy to your spellwork. Red rose petals have long been associated with love and lust, and when we use them in a spell, we are adding their energies of love and lust to the magick we are creating.

Rosemary not only smells wonderful but has also been used to cleanse and protect for thousands of years. Putting out a couple of sprigs of rosemary when having the relatives over will help protect your home from negative energies and hopefully stop a political argument long before one erupts. The simple act of putting out the rosemary is a spell, and it's the kind of magick that can be done without anyone even realizing it.

If there's a downside to the magickal energy of herbs and plants, it's that the energies involved are not particularly strong. Think of an ounce of catnip versus a hundred-plus pounds of human, and it's not surprising that we have the capability to emit more energy. Carrying a certain herb in your pocket will probably have a small effect on you and those around you, but it's not capable of protecting you from every possible problem or conflict that might arise in your life. Will it help? Yes, we absolutely believe it will. But its power is limited. Magick doesn't fix everything or rule out every possibility. For this reason, herbs and plants are often used as an "extra" in conjunction with other forms of magick.

Because people have been working with certain plants for millennia, we know how people typically react to them. But there are very few absolutes in life. As you use herbs and plants in your magick, be aware of how *you* react to them and how they influence your work. You never know—you might be one of those people who react in an unexpected way to a particular plant.

In addition to the natural energies that herbs and plants possess, they affect us in other ways as well. Smell is an often overlooked sense, but odors and scents carry powerful energies with them. For example, our coven uses a particular incense blend created by Ari, and when we smell that incense, we are instantly put in ritual mode. Just smelling that incense makes us think of magick and Witch rituals. We tend to burn our coven's incense only when we are doing ritual together, but sometimes we burn it individually because we need to conjure up the feelings and emotions it brings out in us. Sometimes we simply associate certain smells with specific ideas, and when we use those associations to change our consciousness, we are doing magick.

Herbs and plants also contain properties and substances that affect us on a very real level when we ingest them or rub them on our skin. Herbal Witchcraft is not just using herbs in traditional spellwork; it's also using natural plants for health and healing. Willow bark contains salicin, a compound similar to aspirin. It wasn't a doctor who figured that out, but individuals we'd probably associate today with Witchcraft. Herbs and plants can affect us on a physical level and not just a magickal one.

We are not going to spend a lot of time in this book discussing the ingestion of herbs and plants for healing. Using your Witch cupboard as a personal apothecary is outside the scope of this book (and we are not doctors). However, looking into the effects on the body that result from eating certain herbs and plants is definitely worth your time, and there are thousands of books that contain such information.

The magick of herbs and plants works on three very different levels. There's the physical level, where what we ingest or absorb changes our body chemistry or results in healing. There's also the olfactory level, where scents have the power to change our consciousness in ways both positive and negative. And then there's the level that we will be exploring in this chapter: the magickal level, where the natural energy emitted by herbs and plants has the potential to affect both us and those around us.

Awakening the Power of Herbs and Plants

While there is latent energy in herbs and plants, you can make those energies more effective with a few simple steps. We call this process "awakening." By awakening your herbs, you are acknowledging them as co-creators of the magick you are working to manifest. Is this a process that has to be done? No, but we feel it will make your magick stronger and build a better relationship between you and the herbs you use.

It's easy enough to open up a book and read that sassafras can be used to attract money and good health, but there are lots of herbs that do those things. What makes sassafras special and different from other plants? Awakening your herbs before using them will often answer these types of questions.

To awaken an herb, you want to tap into its energy to truly feel how it affects you and possibly others it will come into contact with. Start by holding the herb in your hands and noting any sensations you feel. Do you feel a shift in your consciousness while it's in your hands? Is the herb releasing any energy that you can tangibly feel?

While holding the herb that you are awakening, take a moment to truly look at it. By *look* we mean not just a passing glance but a deep dive into your herb's physical characteristics. What colors are present? Is the herb's form pleasing? While it's easy to assume that all dried herbs look the same, that's not true at all. They all have differences, even if they are crushed or ground up. Look at the herbs in your hands both up close and from a distance. You'll be surprised by what you see.

Cup the herb in your hands, bring it up to your nose, and inhale deeply. Notice all the smells your herb emits. Inhaling the herb's scent is a way to bring its energies directly into your body, and it's possible that the inhalation will conjure up emotions, feelings, and sensations within you. Take note of these.

If you rub the herb between your thumb and fingers, you'll release additional oil from it. This oil will make the herb's scent more intense. Breathe again. Do you notice anything new now that the oils have been released? Depending on the herb, the rubbing of the herb might result in certain sounds. These are also worth noting. If you know with 100 percent certainty that your herb is edible, place a small piece of it on your tongue and again notice what feelings this awakens within you.

Breathing in the scent of your herb is more than an exercise in olfactory sensations; it's an acknowledgment to the herb that you value its energy and life force. The petals of a lavender are not alive in the sense that you or I are, but they emit energy, and when that energy is welcomed and acknowledged, it will be more powerful. By engaging with the herb using most of your senses, you are building up an understanding of the herb that goes far beyond what's in books.

After you've engaged with the herb as much as possible, speak to it. Thank the herb for being with you and lending its energies to your magickal work. Yes, we know that herbs don't have ears and can't respond in a traditional way, but the energy of the herb will respond to you. It will sense your positive intentions toward it and respond in kind. The awakening of the herb makes its energies compatible with yours. Instead of being separate pieces of a puzzle, you and the herb are now connected on a magickal level.

There are many Witchcraft books on the market today that talk about "plant spirits." This doesn't mean that every time you mow your yard you are creating dandelion ghosts, but all plants radiate a type of energy. When we tap into that energy and take the time to truly understand it, we are honoring the spirit of the plant.

Because the spirit of every plant species is different, there will be certain herbs and plants that we are more drawn to than others, making those particular herbs and plants stronger magickal partners. This is why some Witches call certain plants "familiars." Those Witches are acknowledging a special bond they have with a particular plant or herb.

You don't have to awaken your herbs every time you use them in your magickal practice, but acknowledging them before you use them is a good habit to get into. When measuring out herbs to use in a spell, Amanda "knocks" on them to reawaken the energy they contain. If the herbs are in a glass jar, this might entail knocking on the glass and saying something along the lines of, "I acknowledge and call upon the energy of vervain once more to use in my spellwork." If you are very familiar with an herb, your entreaty can be more informal, like "Wake up! It's time for magick again." However you touch your herb (or its container) and no matter what you say to it, knocking is both a physical and an energetic cue to the herb you'll be using that you will be tapping into its energies again.

Awakening an herb might seem like a lot of work for something that already emits its own energy, but the more you work with a magickal tool, whether it's an athame or a bit of goldenrod, the stronger that tool will become and the more effectively you'll be able to wield it in your magick.

Using Herbs and Plants in Your Spellwork

Before we get into lists of the magickal properties of herbs and other natural items, it's worth taking a moment to discuss just how to use them in your magickal workings. Long lists of magickal properties are great and everything, but they don't really convey any sense of how to use a particular item. We've all used herbs in our spellwork over the years, but before writing this book, we had never really thought about it in a way that might benefit other practitioners.

It's certainly possible to pick up a bay leaf, stick it in your pocket, and then allow that leaf's energy to influence your life. However, in such circumstances your bay leaf is not going to last a particularly long time. Within a day or two it will most likely disintegrate into tiny pieces, and, perhaps most importantly, without much focus on the leaf, it probably won't be particularly effective magickally.

It's also easy enough to simply place a few herbs on your altar while working on a spell. The energy of those herbs will get caught up in the other energies being raised and utilized, and then when the spell is cast they'll be directed where they need to go. The more magickal power we can surround ourselves with, the better our chance of success magickally, and simply putting a few herbs on our altar doesn't require a lot of work. It's a simple addition to magickal work.

Herbs and plants are often more beneficial to magickal work when they are in other forms or when they are used in tandem with other magickal techniques. Herbs are frequent additions to charm bags (see chapter 15), container spells (see chapter 17), and poppets (also chapter 17). In such work, the herbs are added to a focused spell that generally contains a variety of other ingredients. Also, placing herbs in a container, whether it's a glass jar or a cloth bag, will keep your herbs from making a mess in your purse or pocket. This is how we most often utilize herbs in our spellwork, because these ways of doing magick provide focus and contain a variety of energies.

Finely ground and powdered herbs can also be added to candle wax if you make your own candles. This is an especially powerful way to utilize herbs, as the energy placed in your candle works in tandem with the energy of your herbs. When the candle is burned, those powers are released together to work your will. If you don't want to make your own candles, you can also sprinkle powdered herbs onto large candles (especially jar candles). Just keep the powder away from the candle's flame as much as possible.

Powdered herbs are another way to utilize the power of our plant allies. Most herbs can be easily ground with a mortar and pestle, which has the bonus effect of charging the herbs you are grinding with your own natural energy. While grinding the herbs, focus on your intent, infusing the herbs with your magickal goal. This works especially well if you grind your herbs before every new spell that utilizes them.

Roots used in magick (such as High John the Conqueror root—see chapter 17) can be especially hard to grind into a fine powder, particularly by hand using a mortar and pestle. A trick we've learned over the years is to place your herbs in a small sealable plastic bag and then pound them with a hammer. It sounds rather inelegant, but using a hammer will also transfer your intent and energy into the herbs. Witches do what works, not just what's always esthetically pleasing. Food processors and coffee grinders are other options, but you risk breaking the food processer, and you won't be infusing the herb with as much of your intent, either.

A fine powder can be used as more than just a supplement to candle wax, as it has a lot of power all on its own. You can sprinkle that powder in your shoes (or someone else's shoes!) or across doorways and windowsills to attract (or keep away) various energies. If this is something you choose to do, you can make your powdered herbs last even longer by mixing them with cornstarch.

Cornstarch is a magickally neutral substance and won't counteract the energies of the herb you are utilizing. It also offers a few other benefits. Sprinkled on the ground, cornstarch isn't especially noticeable, meaning no one will know that you've surrounded your doorway with a particular herb. Cornstarch is also sticky, and if you want your herbal powder to stay in the same place for a while, cornstarch will help.

Powdered herbs often show up in incense, and non-powdered herbs can be burned too. Burning releases the energy of the plant material directly out into the universe to do your bidding. The downside to burning many herbs is that they often don't smell good while burning! If you do choose to burn herbs, we suggest doing so only outside in a contained fire or by burning a small amount on a charcoal disc designed for indoor burning. A few herbs burned before going out for the evening can be beneficial. (Burning safflower on a charcoal disc at the start of the night is an old Conjure trick used by male magick workers to attract other men.)

Herbs thrown in an outdoor bonfire can also be effective, but make sure you're throwing something with some weight onto that fire. You don't want wispy burning pieces of leaves floating through your neighborhood or backyard. We can tell you from experience that the right herb infused with magickal energy raised through movement and chanting and then thrown into a fire is a powerful way to work magick in a group.

Herbs can be used in both the bath and the shower for cleansing and to bring things into your life. The idea of a soothing, warm bath infused with the right mix of herbs sounds like a great way to get rid of unwanted energies, and this works for many people, but there are some caveats worth pointing out when using herbs in this manner. Unless you change your bathwater with some frequency, that unwanted energy will just stay in the water. When bathing to get rid of something, showers are more effective, because both the dirty water and the unwanted energy will move quickly down the drain.

Taking a bath with some of your favorite herbs to absorb their energies is a great use of herbs in the bathtub. The longer you stay in the water with your herbs, the more of their energy you'll soak up. In this type of instance, you want to take your time and let their energies seep into you.

And finally, of course, there are certain herbs that you can ingest as food and drink. In our coven we do a Yule ritual where we place magickally infused herbs in a Crock-Pot full of warm (apple) cider. Cinnamon, vanilla, orange slices, nutmeg, sugar, and allspice work to bring adventure, prosperity, sunshine, and sweetness (among other things) into our lives. We then bring those energies into our lives by drinking the cider.[18]

The process is the same whether you cook with an herb or use it to brew a cup of tea. To fully activate the power of an herb in edible (or sippable) form, take a moment to acknowledge what you are trying to gain from the herb and verbalize your intention. Be sure that what you are using in your food and drink in edible! Spices from your kitchen are great, but herbs from your local Witch store might not be suitable for eating and drinking.

We are only scratching the surface here with how to use herbs in magickal practice. If you can imagine it, you can do it! As long as the process you are using makes

---

18. This ritual is detailed in chapter 10 of Jason's *Witch's Wheel of the Year: Rituals for Circles, Solitaries & Covens*, published by Llewellyn in 2019.

sense to you, it's fair game to use in magick. The energies of our plant allies are there to use in whatever ways work best for us individually.

Matt's Favorite Common Herbs for Witches

There are herb books that list thousands of different plants and their various magickal qualities. While working on this book, we decided that the majority of herbs and plants we'd write about would be ones that are easy to obtain and not particularly expensive. Many of the herbs in this section are already on your spice rack.

We also wanted to avoid listing the same plants over and over. Many common plants not listed here show up in other parts of the book, particularly in chapter 13 on oils and incense. The properties of a flower like jasmine are the same whether it is in its natural state or an oil, so we didn't think that writing about jasmine twice would do anything but pad the word count of this already lengthy book. Like all the lists in this book, the information here comes from personal practice and the books that have influenced that practice over the years.

Basil

Basil is beneficial for a variety of purposes, such as attracting love and money, bringing success in business, and promoting peace of mind. Basil is also good for purification rituals, driving away evil, and bringing about happiness. Sprinkling some basil around your ritual circle will not only help bring beneficial energies into your magickal space but also protect against malevolent spirits and entities.

Bay Leaf

Bay leaf can be used to cleanse the spirit and break curses. It's also a great herb to use when making a wish or focusing on spellcraft about wish fulfillment. On a windy day, write a wish on a dried bay leaf and then let it get swept up in the breeze, taking your wish wherever it needs to go to come true.

Bayberry

Bayberry is famous for its magickal abilities in relation to money and wealth. It brings success and good luck in all financial situations. Jason grew up with bayberry around over the December holidays and swears by its ability to attract happiness and fortune at Yuletide. Sprinkle some dried bayberry bark around your holiday tree for an abundant Yule, or burn a bayberry candle to lend its energies to your Yuletide celebrations.

Catnip

Catnip is not just for cats! It is potent in romance and glamour spells and can bring love and joy into your life. Sprinkle some catnip between your mattress and box spring to take advantage of catnip's potent and playful sexual energy!

Chamomile

Chamomile is a gentle herb that can be used to promote and ensure pleasant dreams. Away from the bed, it also attracts good luck and peaceful feelings. Some Witches use it for purification as well. We probably use chamomile most often as a tea, drinking it before going to bed.

Cloves

Cloves are a general-purpose herb and can be used in spells for success, prosperity, and protection. They can also energize your love life. Cloves are often used in uncrossing spells to remove negative energies. In the autumn, boil a small handful of cloves in clean water and then wash your front porch (or the entryway to your dwelling) with the clove-infused water to keep out unwanted energies and attract wealth.

Damiana

Damiana is known primarily as an aphrodisiac and can be used to stimulate passion. It's also a powerful ally in spells focused on matters of the heart. Damiana is sometimes used to induce psychic visions. Because of damiana's associations with sex and love, keep a small bowl of it on your dresser or nightstand to promote feelings of desire and romance.

Garlic

Perhaps most famous for keeping away vampires, garlic can also be used to protect against other forces both mundane and supernatural. Garlic is routinely hung on walls and on doors to keep away vengeful spirits and other entities. Don't want to hang it on your door? A clove on your altar will work, too. Garlic is often given as an offering to the goddess Hecate and left at a crossroads for her.

Ginger Root

Ginger helps keep energies moving. Because of this, it's good to include in spells enacted over the course of days, weeks, or months. In such spells, sprinkling a little dried ginger root on your candle, in your jar, or in your charm bag will keep the magickal energies you've built up moving and bringing about transformation in your life. Due to its spicy nature, ginger can also be used to remove psychic blockages and to heat up your love life.

Hibiscus

Hibiscus flowers are great for love in all its forms. Need to sweeten your own disposition in order to receive and give love? Keep some hibiscus on your person or ingest some in the form of a tea. Hibiscus promotes more innocent forms of love as well as lusty encounters.

Hyssop

Hyssop was used in ancient Jewish rites to purify the Temple in Jerusalem and for general protection. All of us are most likely to use it in purification spells, especially ones done in the bathtub or shower. If you are feeling spiritually stagnant and completely unable to connect with your magick or the other things in your life that you hold sacred, a cleansing bath with hyssop will go a long way toward fixing those issues.

Lavender

Lavender is one of the most popular flowers in Witchcraft and can be used for a variety of purposes. A common ingredient in soap, lavender cleanses and protects. Using lavender soap is an easy way to start your day in a magickal way! Lavender can also be used to promote peace and relaxation and to open your psychic senses. The color lavender has long been associated with the queer community, and lavender is especially powerful in LGBTQ+ love spells.

Mandrake Root

Mandrake root is extremely magickal but also difficult to grow and poisonous to ingest. Whole mandrake root often resembles a human being, which makes it a popular root to use when casting a spell on a person, including yourself. Mandrake root has myriad uses and is a common ingredient in love, protection, and money spells. Because of its rather unnerving appearance, mandrake often shows up in pop-culture books and movies about Witchcraft.

Mugwort

Another classic Witch herb, mugwort is most famous as an aid in divination. Mugwort can help relax the mind, which makes a person more open to messages and energies from higher powers. It can also be used to induce psychic visions. Having mugwort around, either as a dried herb, incense, or oil, will make it easier to interpret readings using tea leaves, tarot cards, or runes.

Rose

A classic ingredient in many love spells, roses are a magickal powerhouse. The various colors of roses allow them to be used in a wide variety of love and relationship spells: red roses attract passion and desire, pink roses stimulate deep emotional love, and white roses promote friendship. But roses are for more than just love. The stem of a rose, with its hard-to-miss thorns, can be used in protection magick and to drive away enemies. A magick circle outlined with dried rose petals promotes the ideal of perfect love and perfect trust while keeping away any energies that would hamper such a condition.

Rosemary

The rich, deep scent of rosemary wards off evil and keeps jealousy out of the home. It can be used to keep a partner faithful. A sprig of rosemary placed over the threshold of your home will keep out unwanted energies. Rosemary can also be used to promote memory. When a friend moves away, share a sprig of rosemary with them so you'll both remember to stay in touch.

Rue

Matt thinks so highly of rue that he calls it the "Queen of the Witches" due to its magickal potency! Rue has a long history in magick and has traditionally been used to drive away evil spirits and protect against the evil eye. Sprinkle dried rue or rue-infused water on your altar to cleanse and consecrate it. You can also do the same with your tools. When you are having argumentative friends or family members over, some rue placed in public spaces will help curtail their most negative impulses.

Vervain

If you have the space or resources for only one herb, vervain would be a most excellent choice. An all-around magickal herb, vervain can be used in spells for protection, money, un-hexing, divination, luck, and love. Need a replacement herb in an elaborate spell? Vervain complements just about anything.

Tree Magick

Most of us wouldn't feel too bad about clipping a few leaves from a basil plant. In most parts of the United States, an herb like basil is an annual, meaning its life cycle is completed in one growing year. A perennial is a plant that lives for several growing seasons, but even then, much of the plant is designed to die each year so that its seeds may be shared. Trees are an altogether different form of life. The oldest tree in the world is thought to be over five thousand years old.[19]

Because of the special nature of trees, we thought it was worth giving them their own section in this book. There are many ways to use the magick of trees in your spellwork without giving it a second thought. The easiest method is to only use things that have fallen off a tree. This means that leaves, pine cones, acorns, seeds, fruits, and branches are all fair game. These are magickal gifts given freely by our tree friends and are meant to be utilized. But what happens if you need something growing on a tree?

A tree is a living thing, and while it might not have the same type of soul that you or I do, there's a very real power residing in its limbs and trunk. It's always best to respect that spirit and let it know that it's appreciated. If you find yourself needing a branch from a tree for a wand or some fresh leaves for a spell, be sure to leave some sort of offering for the tree. The most traditional offerings are coins, but what's a tree going to do with a quarter? Instead, how about giving that tree a healthy drink of water or perhaps picking up any trash that might be near it? Your magick will be all the stronger for having the blessings of the tree you are utilizing.

There are many ways to utilize the energy and magick of trees. Every part of a tree will include that tree variety's specific energy, which makes leaves the easiest way to utilize tree energy. When dried, tree leaves can be ground up and used like any other herb. If you happen to come across some tree bark, you can do the same with that.

Any Witch tool made from the wood of a particular tree will carry that tree's specific energy. The yew tree is toxic to humans, linking yew to death and the world beyond this one. Because of this, an athame, wand, or stang made of yew can help facilitate journeys to the world of the dead during ritual. One of the best things

19. Bryan Nelson, "The World's Ten Oldest Living Trees," Treehugger, updated October 19, 2020, https://www.treehugger.com/the-worlds-oldest-living-trees-4869356.

about wood is that it's easily worked with, and fashioning Witch tools from wood allows you to choose what sort of extra energies you want contained within your tools.

One of the easiest ways to release the energy of a tree is through burning. Cherries and the cherry tree are associated with luck, love, and truthfulness. When you throw a log of cherry wood into the fireplace, you are releasing those energies into your home. This is an easy way to do a bit of subtle magick if you have guests over and want them to be more in tune with certain emotions or states of being.

The following is a list of attributes and magickal uses for some common types of trees. There are several varieties of some trees, such as oak and pine, which means that the energies will vary from species to species. These guidelines are based on our own experiences, but spend some time with any branch, leaf, or piece of bark that you use to gauge how it affects you personally.

Ash

In Norse traditions, the world tree Yggdrasil is commonly thought to be an ash, making ash an excellent wood for facilitating travel between the worlds. The ash tree is especially versatile and has been used in magick for prosperity, health, and protection.

Birch

Traditionally birch is used for protection and cleansing. The energy of birch is so protective that it's often been used to cast out evil spirits. Due to the paperlike bark of a birch tree, spells can be written on birch bark.

Cedar

Using the smoke that comes from a bundle of dried cedar is an especially powerful way to cleanse your home or ritual space. In addition to cleansing, the smoke also offers protective energies and is good for attracting wealth. Burning cedar is also said to increase a Witch's psychic power, making it great to burn when engaging in divination.

Cottonwood (Poplar)

Cottonwood, poplar, and aspen trees are all members of the same genus (*Populus*) and have similar attributes. Their wood is very soft, making it easy to work with when creating tools; however, those tools may not be particularly durable.

Most often used in money spells, the "cotton" that falls from a cottonwood tree is a versatile magickal tool. The cotton contains seeds, which provide energies associated with growth, possibilities, and new beginnings. The cotton is also designed to be carried by the wind, which makes it a useful tool when you want to get rid of something.

Elder

Elder is an extremely protective wood and is a powerful defense against unwanted spirits and mundane intruders. The sap of an elder tree is red, making it a ready substitute for blood in any spell that calls for it. Elderberries are said to aid in sleep, and because of this tree's protective nature, its energies are also useful in healing spells.

Maple

With maple trees, the first thing that comes to mind is their sap. The sap is a sweetening force and can be used when you are looking to sweeten someone's attitude or disposition. Because of their sweetness, maple trees are sometimes thought to bring love. The sap of a maple tree is sometimes called "liquid gold" due to its value, which makes the tree useful in money spells.

Oak

Oak trees are often associated with Druids, which makes their energies especially useful when working with Celtic deities. Acorns are symbols of fertility and abundance and are sacred to the Horned God honored in many Witchcraft traditions. As especially strong and hardy trees, oaks are also excellent to use in protection spells and when creating new foundations. Oaks are used exclusively in the production of wine and whisky barrels, so every time a person drinks from a spirit finished in an oak barrel, they are taking in some of an oak tree's energy. We will admit to being partial to oak trees, as the name of our coven is the Oak Court.

Pine

Pine is an extremely useful tree in magick. The pine cone is a fertility symbol *par excellence* and can be used in any magickal operation designed for gain. Pine cones are great for money and vitality spells, and piñons (pine nuts) are thought to have healing energies. The smoke from a bundle of pine needles can add protective energy to the home. It's also believed that the energy from pine needles can reverse curses and cause the energy of negative spells to bounce back to the sender. Spreading pine needles around the perimeter of your house is an effective form of protective magick.

Rowan

Rowan berries are frequently used in healing spells and can also aid in spells focused on success. The fernlike leaves of a rowan tree are ideal for dispersing liquids, which adds the rowan tree's own cleansing power to mixtures of salted water. The wood of a rowan tree is protective and can be used to keep supernatural intruders out of the home. Rowan's protective powers can also be used as a shield against bad weather. Rowan is thought to repel lightning strikes.

Thorn

Thorn trees are prized for their healing ability and association with virility. Given their "thorny" nature, thorn trees are also effective when used in banishing, hexing, and cursing spells.

Willow

Given the sweeping, romantic look of willow trees, it's not surprising that this tree is often associated with love. It also has divinatory properties, most often used to predict whom one will marry or partner up with. In the summer, willow trees are great places to hide from the sun, which is why they are used in protective magick. The belief that knocking on wood brings good luck was originally specifically about the willow tree.

Edible Magick from the Pantry

It's fine to read books about magickal herbs and stock your apothecary accordingly, but if you've got a semi-full pantry and/or refrigerator, you probably already have nearly everything you need to wield herbal and plant magick. We believe that magick should be easy to do and work for any budget, and magick from the pantry is one of the easiest ways to make magick accessible to everyone.

This section is one of our favorites in this book! It's full of magickal ideas and foods that can probably already be found in your kitchen.

Apple

"An apple a day keeps the doctor away" isn't exactly true, but apples are great for healing magick. Place a few apple slices on your altar when sending healing energy to a friend or loved one. Apples are thought by many to be the "forbidden fruit" in the Garden of Eden, so for this reason apples are useful when doing magick focused on learning a new skill. In Norse mythology, apples were the fruit of the gods, making them appropriate for deity offerings.

Slicing an apple at midnight on Samhain and eating the slices in front of a mirror was said to reveal a future lover or spouse. Modern Halloween games such as bobbing for apples originated as a divination technique for finding a partner. Apple cider has been used to bless English apple orchards for several hundred years. Try pouring some apple cider onto your garden every year around December or January to prepare it for the coming year.

Banana

Because of their phallic nature, bananas are great for spells focused on sexuality. If you are looking to attract a male lover, use a banana to represent your ideal lover! Due to its phallic associations, bananas can be added to magick focused on fertility or growth.

Being harassed by a male? Write their name on a banana and then stick that banana full of pins and needles while calling for the harassment to stop. When the banana has turned black and soft, the spell has been cast.

Canola Oil

Canola is the commercial name for rapeseed oil (you can see why they changed the name) and is one of the most common types of oil in modern pantries. It is heavily processed to remove erucic acid, which is poisonous to humans. Because of this, canola oil comes with ingenuity and cleverness bred into it. The high smoke point of canola means that it's an especially hearty oil, perfect for spells focused on strength. Use canola oil to anoint a candle or other magickal focal point.

Chocolate

Chocolate has long been considered an aphrodisiac, making it perfect for spells focused on lust and love. Cacao beans (from which we get chocolate) were used as currency by the ancient Maya, and chocolate's current status as a luxury food makes it ideal for money spells. Simply ingesting a few cacao beans is a way to bring more money into your life.

Because of how easily chocolate melts, it's also useful in magick focused on decrease or getting rid of something. Write the name of something you want to remove from your life on a bar of chocolate, then place your chocolate bar outside on a sunny day and watch the unwanted thing in your life melt away!

Coffee and Coffee Beans

Most of us use the caffeine in coffee on a daily basis. It's our "eye-opener," which makes it great for use in divination and getting a peek into the future. When adding cream to your coffee in the morning, ask, "Today what shall I see?" and see if any images show up as the cream splashes into the warm coffee. Simply drinking coffee before attempting to use a psychic power or a deck of tarot cards can add to your power (but only in moderation—don't drink a pot of coffee before beginning a divination).

Coffee is a quick pick-me-up, so if you are in a hurry for a particular spell to work, place a couple of coffee beans around your spellwork or use brewed coffee in it. For example, you could anoint your candles with coffee or place a few drops of it on a piece of paper or a stone.

Coffee grounds generally go in the garbage or compost pile, making them an excellent tool for getting rid of things. Using your finger, draw symbols of unwanted traits you want out of your life into your coffee grounds before disposing of them. This is a magickal way of "taking out the trash."

Flour

We don't usually think of flour as an herb or plant, but it's a milled grain, so it definitely counts. Cereal crops are the building blocks of modern civilization and the foundation of modern agriculture. Because of this, flour is a civilizing influence and encourages cooperation and teamwork. It's also super easy (though a bit messy) to sprinkle around any spell calling for such qualities. As the main ingredient in bread, flour is also symbolic of abundance and plenty. For this reason, it can be added to spells focused on money or increase.

Due to just how light it is, flour also dissipates easily. On a windy day, take a healthy pinch of flour and sprinkle it in the palm of your hand while saying aloud something you wish to be rid of. Hold the flour in your palm and, once outside, repeat whatever it is you wish to be rid of. Then open your hand and blow. The winds will take away whatever you put into the flour.

Hot Peppers

Is your love life not as hot as you want it to be? Work some magick with a hot pepper to spice it up! If all you need is a little nudge, use a jalapeno, but if you need a bigger boost, grab a habanero. Dried peppers are also effective for keeping people away from things. For a little extra protection around your house, dry some hot peppers, grind them up, and sprinkle the powder around the outside of your house, paying special attention to the windows and doorways.

Because peppers can physically hurt people (Have you ever had the oil from a pepper reach your eye? Ouch!), they are also useful in aggressive types of magick, such as hexing and cursing. The seeds contain the majority of the heat in a pepper and can easily be added to spellwork focused on protection. No hot peppers in your house? Don't worry, regular black pepper will work, too!

Olives and Olive Oil

Olive oil has been used for thousands of years to power lamps. Because of olive oil's association with light and illumination, it's a useful oil to use when working magick focused on learning or acquiring a new skill. When we think of olives, we often think of ancient Greece, making the olive a great conduit for getting to know the goddesses and gods of Olympus better.

There's also something very civilizing about the olive. Use olives and olive oil when doing magick to restore order in your life. Olives are associated with abundance, so use them when doing spellwork focused on growing things in your life. Olive oil is a great base oil, which we will talk about more in chapter 13.

Onions

In popular culture, onions are most associated with crying. It really is true that slicing an onion will cause a few tears to well up. Because of the onion's association with crying, it's a powerful tool to use in magickal operations where you want to bind or banish a person or an idea. Having some serious trouble with a neighbor? Write down your neighbor's address on a slip of paper and dice up an onion to put over it. Your neighbor will be so overcome with grief that they'll probably leave you alone for a while. (When we do this spell, as we pile on the onions, we also add a caveat such as "may no harm come to this person.")

Because onions make us cry, they are also useful if you are trying to expel some emotional pain. Crying is healthy and is a way to release sadness. Onions are powerful allies when we need to purge unwanted emotions.

Oranges

When looking at a perfectly round orange, many of us see the sun reflected back at us. If you need to bring a little light and happiness into your life, oranges (or their juice) will do the trick! Most of us know that oranges are rich in vitamin C, and they've been used to treat colds for centuries. This makes them an excellent partner in healing magick.

Oranges are an extremely versatile fruit. When trying to bring a little happiness into your life, dry some orange peels, place them in a sachet, and carry it in your pocket or purse. When you feel doom and gloom coming upon you, take the sachet out and smell the orange peel. You'll instantly feel better and more energized.

Pomegranates

Because of their use in the tale of Persephone's abduction by Hades in Greek mythology, we think of pomegranate seeds as the food of the dead. If you are trying to get in touch with your ancestors or beloved dead, eat a few pomegranate seeds before beginning your ritual. At Samhain, we have everyone in our coven eat pomegranate seeds before crossing the veil between the worlds. These seeds are also a welcome addition to the plate of a deceased loved one when holding a dumb supper.

Pomegranate seeds are a food of autumn and winter. They are welcome additions to every sabbat from the Autumn Equinox to Imbolc. They connect us to the dark half of the year and its promise of rest and rejuvenation.

Sesame Seeds

The phrase "open sesame" derives from sesame seeds, making them the perfect accompaniment to magick focused on new opportunities, growth, and fresh beginnings. Sprinkle sesame seeds on your altar when performing magick focused on increase or gain.

If you have a specific new opportunity in mind, scatter a couple of sesame seeds in a place that is symbolic of that opportunity. If it's a new job, scatter them at the place where you'd like to work. While you scatter them, say "open sesame!" and use the magick of the sesame seed to help you achieve your goals.

Sugar

It doesn't matter if the sugar in your pantry is made from sugarcane or beets—it's still sweet! Because of this, sugar is effective in spells where you are trying to sweeten the disposition of someone, whether it be your boss or your partner. Because sugar is a bit addicting, it's also useful in magick where you are trying to attract something. Looking for a new house? Pour a little sugar on your altar when you're doing your spellwork.

Sugar is also useful if you're looking to tap into youthful energies. As kids, most of us were probably obsessed with cookies and candy. Sugar contains the energy of childhood, and will cause the youthful feelings of wonder and excitement to rise to the surface within us. This can be especially useful when trying to look at the world with fresh eyes and less cynicism.

Wine and Grapes

Grapes have been used for thousands of years in fertility, wealth, and abundance magick. They are also associated with nobility and taking it easy. (When we see grapes, it's hard not to conjure up images of people lying on a couch and being fed grapes!) Grapes are playful and childish and can be useful when you want your rituals or magickal activities to revolve around fun and positive feelings.

Grapes in the form of wine are the most common libation to deity and are always an appropriate offering. Because of wine's connection to Dionysus, it's a gateway to both ecstasy and madness. Wine is also a symbol of civilization, since it takes a coordinated effort by many people to produce wine from grapes. Wine can also be used as an anointing liquid when performing initiations or handfastings.

Issues with Herbs

Most Witches use dried herbs. There are several practical reasons for this, the biggest one being that dried herbs simply last longer than fresh ones. Most herbs sold for magickal purposes come dried, and as long as those herbs are stored properly, they should last for years. While there's something romantic about the notion of collecting fresh herbs glistening with morning dew on the morning of the Summer Solstice, that's not practical for most Witches.

However, even if dried herbs are the most abundant ones in magickal cupboards, fresh herbs are perfectly acceptable too. Jason finds that herbs and plants gathered from his garden are especially powerful in his magickal work, most likely because some of his own energy has been infused into them. There's also an emotional attachment between a gardener and their plants that adds to the energy those plants contain. Gathering fresh herbs also allows a Witch to thank a plant directly for their sacrifice in many cases, and perhaps present the plant with an offering if the entire plant doesn't have to be harvested.

There are times when gathering fresh herbs to use in magickal work might lend energy to a working or spell. If you were doing a love spell involving lilies and chose to gather those lilies on the day of a full moon, a Friday (the day of the week that is sacred to Venus), or a sabbat such as Beltane or Ostara, the circumstances in which those lilies were gathered would add to their magickal effectiveness. Again, the problem is that most of us probably don't have the free time to gather lilies if they aren't growing in our own backyard.

Whether you choose to use fresh or dried herbs and plants comes down to personal preference and availability. It's usually easy to find fresh flowers for magickal work in the spring or summer, but harder to find fresh basil in December. When a spell calls for dried herbs and you choose to use fresh ones, you will need more of the fresh herb than the dried one. The rule of thumb is about one tablespoon of fresh herbs for every teaspoon of a dried one. Dried herbs are generally more concentrated, and with the water removed from them, a teaspoon is a lot of plant matter.

We thoroughly believe that magick should be available to everyone, regardless of how much money is in their wallet. Because of this, we always recommend using and buying what you can afford. While there are a lot of Witchcraft books today that advocate avoiding GMOs (genetically modified organisms) and non-organic herbs and foodstuffs, we are not among them. However, if those issues are very important to you, you should let your conscience be your guide.

The energy of the place where an herb is raised can have an effect on its effectiveness. If you are purchasing herbs from a farm that treats its employees poorly and uses destructive agricultural practices, that negative energy might seep into the herbs you are using. As with everything having to do with magick, trust your intuition and make the choices that will best aid you in your practice of the Craft.

One of the most contentious issues in the Witchcraft world today is the use of white sage in the form of smudge or a smudge stick. Smudging with white sage is not a traditional part of most Witchcraft practices. The first modern public Witches in England, for example, did not use white sage and would have been perplexed by the use of the word *smudge*. As parts of the New Age movement began to creep into

Modern Witchcraft in the 1970s and '80s, smudging with white sage became an increasingly common practice in the Witchcraft community.

When it comes to the use of white sage, there are two issues that are worth exploring. The first involves its harvest. While white sage is not yet an endangered plant, the plant's current popularity makes the possibility of it being added to the endangered plant species list in the near future very real. In addition, most of the white sage being harvested today does not come from commercial growers. Instead, most of it is "wild harvested," meaning it comes from wild areas, and most often illegally.[20] The illegal gathering of sage by poachers also plays havoc with the sage's surroundings, since most people doing the harvesting don't seem to have much concern for the well-being of our planet.

The second area of concern with sage involves cultural appropriation. Using white sage to cleanse an area of negative energy was originally a technique used by many Native American (First Nations) groups. Most instructions on how to use sage for cleansing strip the white sage of its cultural origins and the context in which it was used. The use of white sage in smudging was also popularized by "plastic shamans," individuals who claimed to practice Native American spiritualities but were generally white imposters.

Why is all of this problematic? Remember all that talk about plant spirits and plant energy at the beginning of this chapter? Using white sage with no appreciation for its history or origins is simply disrespectful. When we disrespect something, whether it be a plant or a person, it stands to reason that it won't be as effective as we want it to be in our magickal work.

So what's a Witch to do? If you choose to use white sage in your work, there are some ways you can do so more ethically. The first is to find out where the white sage you are using has been harvested. There are many Native American groups that sell white sage that they personally grow, so if you can buy from those groups, please do so. Not only will you be helping the people growing the white sage, but you will be more likely to get a product that was raised and harvested in an ecologically sustainable way.

People around the world have been using herbs and dried plant matter to clear negative energy for thousands of years. While white sage is native to Southern California, common sage (generally used in cooking) comes from the Mediterranean and was used by the ancient Romans for both cleansing and culinary purposes. Using

---

20. Kimon de Greef, "The White Sage Black Market," Vice, August 24, 2020, https://www.vice.com /en_us/article/m7jkma/the-white-sage-black-market-v27n3.

common sage instead of white sage is a viable alternative. In our own practice, we like to use both dried pine and cedar to purify our magickal spaces.

For those who still wish to use white sage, just be careful how you implement it. Study its history and use in Native traditions and avoid ceremonies and practices calling for white sage that were written by charlatans and people pretending to be Native Americans. Perhaps most importantly, be respectful of the plant and its long history in the sacred practices of the first people to call the Americas home.

If you choose not to work with sage, there are a variety of other herbs to choose from that are commonly burned for cleansing and creating sacred space. Juniper, lemongrass, lavender, thyme, bay leaves, and peppermint are just a few. These can be easily grown in your own garden or found at any local market or out in nature. All of these herbs have affiliations with purifying and cleansing energies as well as promoting happiness and other positive associations. They are also widely available and are not under scrutiny for potential cultural appropriation.

Chapter Ten
Spells by Plant, Tree, and Flower

When trying to access the magickal energies of a plant or herb, there are several quick and easy ways to do so. Carrying a plant will allow its energy to interact with both you and your surroundings. Certain herbs can be ingested. Is sprinkling basil on your dinner a magickal act? Of course it is, if you choose it to be. But like most magickal tools, the more we work with an herb and surround it with complementary pieces, the more effective it will be.

The following spells feature herbs and plants as the primary sources of magick. Because keeping a bunch of dried herbs in your pocket is not a viable long-term way to enact a spell, these spells often require a few extra items, such as a small sachet bag. We will be looking at sachet bags and knots in chapter 15, and the techniques we include there can easily be added to some of these spells and many others in this book.

Amanda's Herbal Charm Bag for Protection

This spell utilizes herbs associated with protection. To make the spell as easy as possible, I've chosen four common herbs, but you can add and subtract whatever herbs you think will work best.

The herbs I recommend for this spell are burdock, dill, rose buds, and mugwort. Burdock is a purifying herb and brings with it energies that promote positive thinking in yourself and others. Dill is a protective herb that is often used to repel negative energies and hexes. Rose buds bring love and luck but also protect the physical body. Mugwort is commonly used for protection by travelers, which makes this charm bag especially useful when traveling.

For this spell you will need:

- Four herbs (I recommend burdock, dill, rose buds, and mugwort.)
- Four small bowls, one for each individual herb

- A larger bowl for mixing the four herbs
- A small pouch or sachet to carry the herbs
- A spoon for transferring the herbs from bowl to pouch/sachet
- A trusted magickal tool such as an athame or wand (optional)
- An airtight glass jar (optional)

Begin by setting up your magickal space, then gather your four herbs and place them in their individual bowls. Set your larger empty bowl in the middle of the four herb bowls. Awaken the herbs for the working in your preferred way. Once you have awakened the herbs, hold each herb individually in your dominant hand and chant the following line to magically charge the herb:

> *Protect me well, protect me well.*
> *Work your magick with this spell.*

As you chant, you should feel your magickal energy entering the herb. Once that power has reached your herb, place the herb in the larger empty bowl in the center. Repeat this step until all four of the herbs have been moved to the larger bowl. As you continue to chant, mix the four herbs in your larger bowl and feel their powers of protection together. For this step you can use either a finger (preferably the index finger of your dominant hand), the spoon that you'll use later for scooping, or a trusted magickal tool such as an athame or wand.

When your herbs are thoroughly mixed together, both physically and energetically, gently spoon them into your pouch/sachet and then firmly seal it. You have now created a charm bag for protection that you can easily carry with you when entering unknown or uncomfortable situations!

If you have any remaining herbs, you can put them in an airtight glass jar and label them as your protection blend. Keep the jar in your apothecary for future spellwork.

Shower for Spiritual Cleansing

This herbal brew is great to remove any unwanted energies that could be weighing you down from a stressful day. There are a variety of herbs that can be used for this spell, but our version includes rosemary to remove jealousy and evil, hyssop for spiritual cleansing, and sage for protection.

For this spell you will need:

- A large pot of boiling water
- Herbs: rosemary, hyssop, and sage

- A strainer
- Your shower

Fill a large pot with clean water and set it on the stove to boil. Make sure the amount of water you put in the pot is not so much that you can't easily carry the pot from your kitchen to your bathroom. Once the water is boiling, add each herb to your pot, stating your intention while adding each one. For example, you might say the following words while adding your herbs:

> *Sage to my spell for its protection and power,*
> *My magickal self I cleanse and scour!*
>
> *Rosemary to remove what is not wanted,*
> *Others' evil shall now be blunted!*
>
> *Hyssop to renew both my body and my mind,*
> *The physical and magickal realigned!*

Once all your herbs have been added, allow the pot to boil for about fifteen minutes. Remove it from the heat and allow it to cool, then strain the herbs and discard them. Take your pot to the bathroom and set it next to your shower.

Start by taking a relaxing shower. Enjoy the warmth of the water, and as it falls upon you, visualize any negative energy on your body falling away. Let this shower be an indulgence—you're worth it! To add to the ambience, you can play some peaceful music or something that simply puts you in a good state of mind. Clean your body! Let the soap take away the physical things that are not wanted. Once you are nice and clean, turn off the shower and then set the pot with your herbal brew on the floor of the shower.

Using your hands, scoop the water up from your pot and pour it over your body, starting at the top of your body and moving downward as you do so. Rub every handful of water over your entire body, allowing the energy of the herbs to work their magick. As you rub, rub in a downward direction, this will take unwanted energies away from you. The herbal water should be rubbed on every part of your body, from head to toe.

Don't forget the bottoms of your feet! The energy you are removing is moving down your body and might reaccumulate at your feet. Because our feet frequently touch the ground, they tend to pick up negative energy more easily than other parts of the body do.

As you pour the herbal water over yourself, focus on what you are doing. Visualize and feel the enchanted water refreshing your body and taking away all that is not wanted. For extra added power, you can chant while washing yourself. This can be something simple, such as "renew the self," or something more elaborate.

When you have rinsed your entire body with your herbal water, step out of the shower and draw three *X*'s in the air. The *X*'s will keep any residual energy from returning and reattaching itself to you. Instead of drying yourself with a towel, allow yourself to air-dry while wearing a bathrobe or some comfy light clothing. Toweling off would remove the energy of the herbs you used, and you want their power to stay with you, forming a sacred fabric over your skin. If you feel tired after this spell or as if something is missing from yourself, anoint yourself with a magickal oil to replace the energies that were removed.

Home and Yard Protection Spell with Sunflower Seeds

Jason is an avid gardener, and one of his favorite things to grow is sunflowers. Unlike most domestic flowers, sunflowers can grow to truly mammoth proportions, with many varieties capable of reaching ten feet or more! Those sunflowers then stand tall in the wind, rain, snails, squirrels, and heat of summer, looming over almost everything around them.

Because of the protective power we associate with sunflowers, we use their seeds to guard our homes and yards. If you live in an apartment, this spell can easily be adapted: just sprinkle your sunflower seeds around your apartment complex! You aren't limited to just your immediate home, either; seeds can be sprinkled around street corners and in any place you wish to keep safe. This spell can be cast at any time of year, but the ideal time is late summer to early fall after your sunflowers have been harvested

For this spell Jason recommends using seeds you've grown yourself, but that's not entirely necessary. Besides, what if you don't have the space or time for a garden? If you don't have your own sunflowers to harvest, perhaps find a neighbor or friend who has some extra ones. Alternatively, you can buy entire sunflower heads on places like eBay, which is much less expensive than buying several packages of seeds, and even better, you can set some seeds aside to grow the following year. You'll want as many seeds as you can gather. For an average-size yard, Jason recommends one hundred seeds, or more if your yard is large.

For this spell you will need:

- Sunflower seeds: at least fifty—the more the better!
- A small bowl or dish for your seeds

Place your seeds in a small bowl or dish and then set them (ideally) on the pentacle of your working altar. (If you don't have a pentacle, simply setting your bowl of seeds on your altar will work just fine, too.) Once they are there, invoke the powers of the elements, the sun, the Goddess, the God, and all that lies in between. Charge your seeds by saying:

> *By the power of the noonday sun, sentinel of the skies,*
> *By the power of my garden's flowers, my magickal allies,*
> *By the power of the Goddess fair, mother to us all,*
> *By the power of the Horned One, deity of the fall,*
> *By the power of what lies between, all that I surmise,*
> *Safety, protection, hearth, and home, these I visualize!*
> *May my home be safe from intruder, weather, and harm.*
> *In that work these seeds shall be my charm!*
> *Powers of the universe, through my seeds come to me.*
> *The spell now cast, my will be done, and so mote it be!*

As you say your invocation, you should feel energy rushing into your seeds. While saying these words, be sure to visualize your home safe from threats during the coming winter months. Jason likes to picture a blue-white energy encircling his house, shielding his home from vandalism, threat, and natural disasters. Once your seeds are charged, walk around the perimeter of where you live and scatter the seeds at the boundaries. For extra protection I'll sometimes sprinkle additional seeds outside the doors and windows of my home. As you scatter your seeds, say:

> *By the power of these seeds,*
> *Evil shall let me be!*

When you are done, thank the powers you invoked and set some seeds aside to plant next year or use in future magickal workings.

Citrus for Justice

There will be times when we find ourselves wronged in life, either by another person or by a circumstance. This is a spell to bring justice in those situations.

For this spell you will need:

- 1 candle (and something to light it with)
- A small piece of paper or a small item that is symbolic of the unjust situation

- A pencil or pen
- A cleansing piece of citrus fruit (such as a lemon, an orange, or a grapefruit)
- A knife
- 9 pins

Start by lighting your candle and visualizing the wrong that was done to you. Imagine either the particular incident or the person who caused it to happen. As you light your candle, say:

May justice be served!

Write down the offense or the offensive person's name on your small piece of paper. As an alternative to writing down a particular injustice or a name, you could use something symbolic of the situation. If there's a person who has wronged you, you could use a picture of them, a strand of their hair, a small piece of their clothing, or something they have touched. Whatever you use should be small enough to fit inside your citrus fruit.

Take your knife and cut a slit into your citrus fruit large enough for you to slip your piece of paper (or whatever else) securely inside of the fruit. What type of fruit should you use here? We suggest a lemon, because it's commonly associated with cleansing. But other citrus fruits such as oranges and grapefruits can also be found in some cleaning products, so if those resonate more with you, feel free to use one! We are using citrus in this spell not just because it's often associated with cleaning (a form of purification) but also because of its high acidity. We want that acid to eat away at the injustice!

Once you've slid your paper (or other item) inside the citrus fruit, take one of your pins and hold it in your candle flame for a moment. Imagine the fires of justice burning away what has wronged you. Then stick the pin somewhere in your citrus fruit while saying the first line of the incantation below, and imagine truth entering the situation you find yourself in. Repeat this process with the other eight pins, imagining the ideas suggested in the words of this spell when you stick the pins in your fruit. (Note: the last two lines are for the final, ninth pin.)

May the fires of verity burn,	(Pin 1)
May justice be received,	(Pin 2)
The truth to be revealed,	(Pin 3)
Compensation for the aggrieved.	(Pin 4)
With nowhere to run or hide,	(Pin 5)

And nowhere to escape or flee,	(Pin 6)
All shall see the truth before them,	(Pin 7)
The truth shall now be set free.	(Pin 8)
Justice will now come to me,	(Pin 9)
This I say so mote it be!	

When you are done, place your fruit in a secure place. By the time it dries up, justice will have come to you. When justice if finally done, remove the pins from your fruit and dispose of the fruit and pins properly. The pins can most likely be reused after they are cleansed, and the fruit should go in the compost or trash bin.

Shared Spellcraft: How to Turn Your Tea into a Magic Potion
by Madame Pamita

Everyone knows that tea leaf reading is a magical act of divination, but did you know that drinking tea can be a great way to do magic? Yes, teas really are the magic potions we read about in fairy tales! Tea leaves and certain herbs have been recognized for their magical and medicinal qualities throughout the ages and can be made into teas or tisanes (herbal infusions) to bring in improved conditions. The difference between your regular cuppa and a tea spell is in the intention. Putting thought, words, and will into your tea can make it a magical potion that will transform your life!

Here is how to make a truly magical potion out of your tea.

1. Put some fresh spring water in a kettle or saucepan and place on the stove to heat.

2. While waiting for the water to boil, concentrate on the intention of your spell as you put your herbs in a teapot or infuser.

3. Pour boiling water into the teapot or a teacup with the infuser. As you do so, ask the herbs to do their work and say the words of your intention with loving conviction. For example, with a mint infusion you might say something like, "Mint, clear away my blocks to prosperity and protect my money."

4. Hold your hands in the steam over the teapot or cup and focus your intention on your spell.

5. Let the herbs steep for a magical number of minutes: 1, 3, 5, 7, 9, 13, or 21 minutes. (For green teas, the recommended steeping time is 1–2

minutes; for black teas, 3 minutes; for herbal tisanes, you can choose any number of minutes.)

6. Pour the tea or tisane into a cup or pull the infuser out of your cup.

7. If you need to let the infusion cool a little, speak your words of intention again over the infusion until the brew is cool enough to drink. You will have imbued your potion with all the words of intention, thoughts, and will to make it a truly magic potion.

8. Your potion is ready. Close your eyes and, sip by sip, drink it all in and feel the power of the magic permeating your body.

There are many magical herbs that can be made into teas and tisanes. While most people are familiar with mint and chamomile (both of which are powerfully magical herbs), there are so many more herbs that can be made into magical potions!

Just a warning: some herbs taste amazing and some of them not so much. You can always add a sweetener (and honey itself has its own magical qualities), but don't be afraid to drink something a little bitter. After all, a truly magical potion might require you to have courage! Some favorites include angelica root, basil, chamomile, cinnamon, clove, ginger, hyssop, jasmine, lavender, mint, nutmeg, patchouli, rose petals, sunflower petals, and yarrow. (For the magickal properties of these ingredients, see appendix II.)

The beautiful thing about teas and tisanes is that they can be easily blended. When you are just starting out making your own magical potions, you may choose to focus on just one herb for your brew, but as you get more experienced, you may want to blend herbs for combined intentions. When you brew a blend of more than one herb, speak to each of the herbs that you are working with individually and ask them to do their special work.

One very easy way to start this process is by looking at the herbs in the herbal tea blends in your cupboard. Research what these herbs are used for magickally and then get brewing! Making magic doesn't have to be hard and, as this chapter demonstrates, can be quite tasty too!

Madame Pamita is a professional tarot reader/scholar and rootworker and the author of Madame Pamita's Magical Tarot. *She is the owner of Madame Pamita's Parlour of Wonders, an old-time spiritualist's shop in Los Angeles, where she offers tarot readings in her salon, teaches classes in tarot and magic, and creates spiritual-magical tools for transforming lives. Visit Madame Pamita online at www.parlourofwonders.com.*

Putting Down Roots: A Spell for Moving to a New Location

Moving to a new house, especially one in a new city or state, can be a challenging experience. Making new friends and finding places and establishments where we feel a sense of belonging can take years to bring to fruition. And once we begin to settle into a new life in a new place, we often lose track of old friends and see previously established relationships begin to wither. This spell is designed to help us grow roots in a new space while retaining older, familiar connections.

This spell requires only four things: some seeds, an offering to the land (we suggest clean water, a coin, or some sort of alcoholic beverage), and two places to plant (or at least leave) your seeds. If you have a garden, you'll want to collect your seeds for this spell from it. If you are not a gardener, you can still cast this spell, but it will be a little bit different. Because of the differences, we've split the two ways of enacting this spell into separate sections. This spell starts in your old home and finishes in your new one. For those who don't have a garden, we suggest using wildflower seeds for this spell. If you live in the continental United States, flowers such as blue sage, white trillium, primrose, black-eyed Susans, and sunflowers are ideal. Not only are all of these flowers beautiful, but they are also noninvasive. (Before planting seeds in a new place, make sure what you are planting is not invasive to that area.)

If You Have an Existing Garden

If you are a gardener or can visit a sacred spot where you can harvest a seed (like a park), approach the plant or tree from which you will be gathering your seeds. As you approach it, think of the time you've spent in this place and the joy it has brought you. When you reach your plant or tree, put your hand on it and feel its energy. Follow the energy of your plant or tree to its powerful roots stretching down into the ground. Those roots are similar to the energy you've put into your soon-to-be-old home.

As you harvest your seeds, say:

> *I have put roots down in this place, and those roots will not be forgotten. Friendships and relationships have been built in this soil and under this sky. I now harvest that energy so that I may take it with me to my new home. A piece of me shall always reside in this place, and a piece of this place will soon find a new home with me.*

After you've harvested your seeds, leave your plant or tree an offering while saying:

> *I honor you for your gift. May some of your energy move with me to a new home, and may your power continue to resonate in this place.*

Take one more moment to appreciate the space around you and what it has meant to you over the years. Clean up your seeds and put them in a secure place so they will be readily available after you move.

After you have moved and set aside a place for gardening and/or growing things (even if it's just a pot!), take out your seeds and place them in your hand. Feel their energy and their connection to where you came from. As you approach the place where you will bury your seeds, find something to appreciate about it. It could be something as simple as a blue sky or a bird singing in a tree. Moving can be hard, but find joy and promise in this new beginning.

When you are ready, place the seeds in the soil while saying:

> *Today I put down new roots in this space. May it be more than just a place where I live, but a home. With this planting I hope to cultivate new friendships, new experiences, and new adventures. May my magickal roots continue to thrive in two places, and may both places always welcome me and those I love.*

As your plants take root in the soil of your new home, your magickal roots will start to grow in your new community. Relationships will bloom. New spaces will start to feel like familiar friends. With your new roots in the ground, you will soon thrive!

No Garden, No Problem!

If you aren't a gardener, don't worry, we've got you covered! For this version of the spell you'll need a package of wildflower seeds. Be very careful here, as you'll want to choose something that's not invasive where you currently live or where you'll be moving to! A mix of wildflowers from a gardening or home improvement store will most likely be pretty safe.

If you have your own yard, you can do the first part of the spell there, or can you visit a favorite spot. Wherever you choose to enact this spell, make sure the place has special resonance for you. Think about what has made that spot a happy one and how you will cherish the memories from it. Now think about the community you are a part of in a broader sense.

Take a second to think about what you are leaving behind and sprinkle half of your seeds while saying:

I have put down roots in this place. It has been home, and a part of it will always be so. I leave these seeds behind in this special place because I also leave a piece of myself behind. I will never be completely gone from this space, and the relationships I've cultivated will continue on.

Be sure not to sprinkle all the seeds; the other half of the seeds should be shared after you move.

Once you move, find a space to sprinkle your seeds either in your own yard or in a place that you believe will resonate with you in the long term. Hold those seeds in your hand and imagine yourself putting down roots in your new home. Think of restaurants and shops where you might become a regular. Visualize new friendships and new opportunities and a positive new beginning.

As you picture this bright future in your mind, sprinkle the second half of your seeds while saying:

Today I put down roots in this new space. May it become a home and a place that nurtures me to become more than I already am. May the seeds sprinkled here connect with their counterparts elsewhere, connecting me to both spaces. Let my heart always have room for what has come before and what will come to be.

As your seeds become one with the new place you've moved to, you will also become one with your new space. New friends and new opportunities will emerge as you explore your new place of residence. And what you left behind will always have a little piece of you within it.

Ari's Self-Esteem Rose Water

This is a simple spell to increase your self-esteem. You can use this spell anytime you need a dose of self-confidence, but it's especially useful before a job interview or date.

For this spell you will need:

- A pot of boiling water
- Rose petals, preferably pink or red

Boil the water and add your rose petals to it. As you add the petals, visualize your intention. Picture yourself strong and confident and up to any task or challenge before you. As you add the rose petals, say something like:

> *I can overcome anything in my way.*
> *In all this life of mine I hold sway.*

Let the rose petals boil in the water for at least fifteen minutes. Remove the pot from the heat and allow to cool for two hours. Don't remove the rose petals.

Once the water is cool, use it to wash your face, preferably in front of a mirror. Splash the water on your face, and as you do so, picture all of your self-doubt falling away. The rose water will remove any negative energy on your face and replace it with positive, loving energy. As you wash your face, look at yourself in the mirror and like the reflection you see there. Continue to wash until you are happy with how you look in the mirror.

When you are done, bottle up some of the water and store it in a small vial so you can carry it with you. When you need a burst of confidence, dab some of the water on your face or on the insides of your wrists.

Throwing Out the Trash: A Protective Potato Spell

Potatoes aren't just great for mealtime; they're also an effective way to rid yourself of negative influences or people. This is a simple spell that doesn't require much more than a potato, and possibly an athame or a marker. If you've got a semi-rotten potato, all the better! The problem you want to leave behind is probably more rotten than your potato!

To begin, hold the potato in your dominant hand and think about the person or thing that is causing you trouble. Envision that problem never bothering you again or causing you trouble. Picture them leaving your personal orbit and you living your life free from the problem instigated by them.

Once you've juiced up your potato with your intent, carve or write the name of the person or problem troubling you on the potato. My personal favorite here is to use my white-handled knife (if you use your athame, that's also ideal) to carve the name into the potato. A marker will also work, but you'll transfer more of your intent into the potato if you use a magickal tool.

The easiest way to discard your potato is to put it in a garbage can, a compost pile, or a hole in the ground. When we dispose of our potatoes, we say the following petition to the Goddess of Witches to ensure success. If you don't honor deity, no sweat; simply replace the words "Great Lady" with the place where you are depositing your potato, such as "bin of rubbish" or "heap of compost." Recite this petition as you discard your potato:

> *Today I cast (person or problem) away from me,*
> *Where they shall no longer trouble me!*
> *Leave me to live my life in peace,*
> *And with your irritation decease!*
> *Great Lady (or name of place), take away this pain,*
> *And allow all to be happy again!*
> *With harm to none I cast this spell,*
> *In my life may all be well!*
> *So mote it be!*

By placing your potato in the garbage (or a similar space), you are symbolically throwing that person or problem out of your life. Putting them in the trash will take the troublesome thing or person even further out of your life since they will then be headed to the local garbage dump. As the potato rots or is eaten, your intention will be magickally released into the world, your will be done!

Amanda's Herbal Bath for Spiritual Cleansing

When you need some serious spiritual cleansing, this bath will be sure to help.

For this spell you will need:

- 3 sprigs each of any combination of the following herbs: basil, bay, cedar, peppermint, rosemary, sage, or thyme (You can use all of these herbs or just one, but for best results use at least three.)
- 3 handfuls of salt
- A lemon cut into nine slices (Make sure to keep the ends of your lemon intact.)
- A small glass bowl or jar

Speak your intention aloud as you draw your bathwater. You might say something like, "These magickal waters will remove all unwanted negativity clinging to me," or "May these waters cleanse and renew for the journeys yet to come." As the water pours out of the spout, envision its water cleansing you and pulling away any negativity that is surrounding you. When your bath is about halfway full, gently toss in the sprigs of herbs and two of your three handfuls of salt. Place the remaining salt in your small bowl. Continue to let the tub fill up, and place the seven inner slices of lemon in your bath, leaving the two end pieces off to the side with the remaining salt.

Step into the warm bathwater, take a deep breath, and inhale the aroma of the herbs and lemon as they pull out any toxic energies from your body, mind, and spirit. Feel them gently releasing anything that no longer serves you from your physical body. Lose yourself in the warmth of the water and notice how the salt dissolves your unwanted stress.

If you feel so inclined, take some of the herbal sprigs and gently brush them along your skin, moving from your head down to your toes. As the herbs touch your body, envision them collecting all the negative energy from your body. When you are done, hold the sprigs up to your nose and inhale deeply, noticing their scent. Let their cleansing energies enter your body, bringing a sense of peace, clarity, and purity.

When you are ready, take one of the lemon end pieces and dip it in the salt in your small bowl. Starting at the top of your head, gently scrub your skin with the lemon and salt using a descending motion. (Keep the salt and lemon away from your eyes and mouth.) Feel the lemon and salt draw out all the unwanted energy in your psychic aura. Repeat this as many times as needed. You will need to refresh the salt on your lemon periodically, and if your lemon piece becomes unusable, replace it with the extra end piece you've held in reserve. Be sure to scrub the bottoms of your feet, where negative energy often gathers.

When you feel as if all unwanted energies have been removed, gather your herb sprigs and lemon pieces and set them aside. Release your used bathwater and watch as it washes down the drain. As the water moves away from you, visualize it carrying everything that's unwanted in your life away from you. When you are ready to leave the tub, stand up and exit from the back end, away from the drain, so you can continue to watch the bathwater move away from you. Do not rinse yourself off; let the energies of the herbs, lemon, and salt stay on your body.

Towel or air-dry yourself (don't use a hair dryer) so the energies of the herbs remain on your person. The sprigs and lemon can be disposed of in the trash can, placed in the compost, or buried in the ground.

Shared Spellcraft: An Apple Spell for Health and Protection
by Gwyn

The apple has had a revered place in human life as a food and as an offering to deities and the dead for centuries. Apples have also played a prominent role in divination, harvest celebrations, and more. They even have a pentagram in the center when you cut them in half. You cannot get more witchy than that!

In mythology, the apples tended by Iduna (a goddess of spring and rejuvenation and the wife of Bragi, the god of poetry) brought long life to the Norse gods. In Greek lore, a similar task belonged to the Hesperides (the nymphs of the west who guarded the golden apples) for the same reason.

Herbs, flowers, resins, and other corresponding ingredients are available for use in various forms of Witchcraft. As a Green Earth Witch, I ask plant spirits to assist me in my work. And when apple pairs with other plant spirit allies such as eucalyptus, rosemary, and lavender in nature-based magick, a Witch or magickal practitioner can create potent magick. What I'm going to share with you now is a spell I've worked with great success for healing and protection.

To enact this spell you will need:

- A piece of paper
- A writing utensil
- Salt
- Lavender sprigs and buds
- Water in a small dish
- A lighter
- A small cauldron or heat-safe vessel
- Rosemary sprigs and leaves
- A mortar and pestle
- A small plate
- Juniper essential oil
- Coconut oil
- A blue or white chime candle
- Eucalyptus sprigs
- A medium or large apple
- Incense, candles, and music for ambience (optional)
- A small paring knife (if needed)

Write down your intention on a piece of paper. Be specific—narrow your will down to a couple of sentences for healing or protection. For a spell cast on behalf of someone else, include their name as you write the intention. Here are some examples:

> *My immune system is strong and healthy and warding off all harmful viruses and bacteria, protecting me from becoming ill.*

> *Mary is protected from negative energy and unwanted presences in her home.*

Prepare your altar or spellcasting space according to your tradition or magickal path. Add a pinch of salt and some of your lavender buds to the water dish, then lightly asperge the area in which you will be working. Set the water dish aside.

Light a rosemary sprig over the cauldron with a lighter. Blow out the flame to create smoke, wafting the herb smoke over your head and then passing your candle through it. Relight the rosemary sprig and blow it out to create more smoke, then place it in the cauldron.

Add a few pinches of lavender buds and rosemary leaves to your mortar and pestle, grinding the herbs together. Pour a thin layer of salt onto the center of the small plate and add the ground herbs over the top. Concentrate on your intention throughout this process.

Put 2 drops of juniper essential oil and 4 drops of coconut oil in your hand. Rub your palms together, visualizing the healing and protective energy of juniper. Then take your chime candle in your hands and dress the candle with the oil from bottom to top, slowly rotating the candle until it is covered in the oil.

Now hold the chime candle at both ends and roll it in the herbs and salt until it's lightly coated from bottom to top. Set the candle and a sprig of eucalyptus beside the plate. Place the apple in the center of the plate on top of the remaining herbs and salt.

Wash your hands. Light some incense and candles for ambience if desired. Add whatever music might be useful to have in the background while you do spellwork.

Sitting in front of your altar or in your sacred space, meditate, ground, and center as needed. The plate with the apple, eucalyptus sprig, and prepared spell candle should be in front of you, and the lighter and a small paring knife should be beside you or within easy reach.

Focus your intention on the apple. Reach out and hold it in your hands, envisioning the outcome of your spell and asking the Spirit of Apple to assist you in your work. Then return the apple to the plate. Now gently pick up the eucalyptus sprig, cradle it in your hands, and breathe on it. Ask the plant spirit to assist you in healing or protection work. Then carefully stick the sprig into the top of the apple beside the stem. If the sprig's end is not strong enough to pierce the fruit, use the paring knife to create a small space and push the eucalyptus sprig into the hole.

Grasp the candle in your dominant hand and speak its work (healing or protecting) out loud, adding an incantation if that feels appropriate, or recite your written intention. Breathe these words into the candle. When you are ready, place the candle beside the eucalyptus sprig on the top of the apple. Use the paring knife to widen the space or gently rotate the candle until the base of the candle is secure (about the depth of a standard chime candleholder).

Light the candle. Allow the candle to burn down into the top of the apple. (Keep an eye on the candle; do not leave it unattended.) Once the flame is extinguished, the spell is cast. So mote it be!

Allow the apple to hold space on your altar or in your magickal workspace until it feels right to return it to the earth or dispose of it in your usual manner.

Gwyn is a Hekatean Green Witch and devotee of the Covenant of Hekate, a clairsentient medium, and a Tarot reader. She cohosts the podcast 3 Pagans and a Cat *and is a teacher/presenter at many Pagan events.*

Chapter Eleven
Stones and Crystals

Crystals and stones for personal transformation are experiencing a bit of a renaissance. Once strictly the province of Witches and New Age practitioners, crystals and stones for magickal purposes are now nearly inescapable. You can find crystals advertised with their magickal attributes in a variety of discount and chain stores. The current popularity of crystals also has a downside, with "wellness" experts advising people to put stones in their water bottles for extra energy and in room sprays, dangerous practices that can result in sickness and even death.[21]

The smart Witch knows, however, that magick is everywhere, and that two-hundred-dollar crystals aren't necessary in spellcraft. Do you feel a strange affinity toward that rock you kicked down your driveway? Then it's probably a good stone to use in your magickal work. Every stone has a bit of energy in it, but some are more suited to specific tasks than others. It can be fun to track down a more exotic (and expensive) stone like moldavite (formed by a meteorite impact 15 million years ago), but because there are hundreds of different types of stones, you can easily stock your cupboard affordably if you are smart about it.

Before we get started, it's important to point out that stones and crystals are a gigantic magickal category. There are very long books dedicated exclusively to the subject, and we recommend a lot of them (check the bibliography). Also, "stones and crystals" is a bit of a misnomer because we will be including materials in this chapter that aren't technically stones or crystals. Amber is fossilized tree sap, but because it's hard like a stone, it's generally included in books on crystals and rocks. Metals aren't technically stones either, but gold and silver have their own power and, like amber, are more like stones than any other substance. When writing about

---

21. Maggie Fox, "Mystery of Exotic Infectious Disease Traced to Aromatherapy Room Spray," CNN, updated October 24, 2021, https://www.cnn.com/2021/10/23/health/aromatherapy-melioidosis -mystery/index.html.

these various substances, we will usually use the word *stone* for simplicity's sake, but keep in mind that the use of that word here includes crystals, metals, and amber.

In many ways stones are quite similar to herbs when it comes to magickal use. Stones have their own innate energies and, unlike candles, they don't have to be charged to effect change. Stone magick might be more popular than ever these days because it's easy. Stones fit nicely on earrings, necklaces, and bracelets. Unlike herbs, stones are also close to indestructible. Even without trying, it's easy to turn a sachet of herbs into a small bag of dust. Herbs and plants can also rot and won't survive an accidental trip through the washing machine. Most stones don't have any of these issues.

Every type of stone has its own particular energy, but a stone's color also plays a role. Amethyst is a purple stone often used for healing and to overcome addiction. However, amethyst will turn green when subjected to intense heat, and if you associate the color green with money, then using green amethyst in a job or success spell would be appropriate. If that sounds contradictory, remember that most stones are at least a million years old.[22] It's not surprising that a 500-million-year-old object would contain a wide variety of energies!

People love to associate stones with long lists of correspondences. Stones are often connected to chakras, zodiac signs, particular months, planets, elements, vibrations, metals, deities, and angels. These types of correspondences might be important to some, but for us what's most important is what a particular stone does! We are much more interested in sharing how to use stones in magickal work and what types of energies are specific to certain stones. Ari shares a list of her favorite stones to use in magick at the end of this chapter. For anyone interested in long lists of correspondences, check the bibliography for further resources.

When using stones in magickal work, there are various options. The easiest one is to simply carry a particular stone in your pocket or purse or wear it on a piece of jewelry. Garnet has a fierce energy that enhances strength and virility and also contains healing and protective energies. When someone wears garnet (or carries it in their pocket), the energies of the stone will surround and affect them. If you've got a big day ahead of you and need a little extra *oomph*, garnet will help take care of that.

The most direct way to feel the energy of a stone is to hold it. If you find yourself really needing a little extra strength, touching the garnet on your necklace will

---

22. American Geosciences Institute, "How Can We Tell How Old Rocks Are?" accessed December 4, 2021, https://www.americangeosciences.org/education/k5geosource/content/fossils/how-can-we-tell-how-old-rocks-are.

have a direct and immediate effect. Today you see many people adding stones to their drinking water in order to absorb a particular stone's energy into their bodies. As noted at the beginning of this chapter, this can lead to serious illness and even death. And when buying a polished stone from a chain store, there's a good chance that the stone has some odd wax or chemical on it. We do not recommend adding stones to your drinking water, but if you think you must do such a thing (and really, you don't!), do so only after conducting an exhaustive search on the consequences of the practice, and for Goddess's sake, wash your stone first!

Placing a stone in a particular place is another easy form of magick. Tiger's eye is thought by many to attract wealth. You could wear tiger's eye to work to tap into its energies, but how about taping a small piece of it to the family checkbook or placing it on the dining room table where the bills are paid? Salt is well known for its cleansing and purifying powers, which is why candleholders and even lamps made of rock salt are increasingly common. A candleholder made from rock salt is ubiquitous and will quietly do its job absorbing negative energy while most people around you will remain blissfully unaware.

Stones can easily be added to other types of magickal work. A sachet filled with a few herbs and a stone or two and then anointed with oil and tied together with a magickal knot is some pretty powerful magick. When we're doing healing work as a coven, we often use a piece of aventurine as a focus and push our personal energy into it. As we do this, our energy combines with the energy of the aventurine, making our spellcraft that much more powerful before sending our magick out into the universe.

Cleansing, Charging, and Preparing Stones

While stones all have their own energies, they also absorb the energies around them. Unless you've gathered a stone yourself from some remote spot in the woods, you'll probably want to cleanse your stones and crystals before using them. It's not a requirement, but your magick will be all the better for it.

Crystal mining is often done in deplorable conditions. Human workers are exploited, the earth herself is abused, and the crystal you end up with has often been touched by dozens of human hands by the time it reaches you. The end result is that all of the negative energies from those encounters are a part of your crystal or stone. That negative energy then becomes a part of your spellwork if it's not removed.

Perhaps less dramatic but important nonetheless is cleansing a stone that comes from a fellow Witch. If a friend gives you a crystal they've been using for a few months, that crystal will be attuned to the energies of your friend, not you. In cases like this, cleansing acts as a reset for your stone so it can better attune itself to your energies. (More on this in just a bit!)

Cleansing a stone is much like cleansing a magickal space but on a smaller scale. Using some salted water or incense smoke is the easiest way to cleanse a stone of any unwanted energy. A word of warning here, though: salt is bad for a lot of stones. Some of our favorite stones do not react well to salt. That list includes moonstone, malachite, turquoise, and amber. A light sprinkling of salted water on these stones won't destroy them, but you'll want to remove the salt and water as soon as possible after you sprinkle it on them.

Incense or salted water usually take care of most cleansing needs, but sometimes they are not quite enough. If you pick up a stone and it feels icky or wrong or its energies feel out of sync with your own, it probably needs more cleansing. One of the easiest ways to do a little extra cleansing is to bury your stone in a small bowl of dry rice. Rice, unlike salt, won't hurt your stones, but it will absorb any negative energy emanating from them. In most cases, a day or two in the rice bowl will do the trick, but some unwanted energies are quite stubborn.

The most drastic—and effective—way of cleansing a stone is by burying it in the earth. Ideally, for magickal reasons you want to do your burying on a full moon night. The combined action of the waning moon and the earth's power will dissipate and absorb any negative energy in your stones. On the night of the next new moon, dig them up and they should be good to go. However, if they still don't feel quite right to the touch, you can put them back in the ground for another two weeks and then dig them up at the next full moon.

If this doesn't work … We're kidding—this should totally work. To keep your stone safe while it's underground, place it in a plastic bag so it won't be harmed by the elements. The bad energy will still radiate out of your stone, through the bag, and into the earth. If you don't have access to a yard for burying, you can bury your stones in a pot of earth or even just sand.

If playing in the dirt isn't your thing, there are a few other alternative ways to cleanse your stones. You can place them in the sun and let the power of sunlight eat away the negativity they contain. The downside to this is that if your stone is polished with wax, the wax will melt away. The sunlight might also dull your stones. Placing stones out in the rain or leaving them in the grass overnight to be cleansed by the morning dew are other options. But be careful: some stones such as calcite, lapis lazuli, and malachite are water-soluble, and metals like hematite will rust if they get wet. For these reasons, sand, rice, and earth remain the safest options.

Certain stones can be used to absorb negative energy. Quartz crystal points are commonly used for this type of work and sometimes will grow hot to the touch or even change color when filled with bad energy. When using a stone for this purpose, you will need to cleanse it before it can be used in future magickal work. If the energy is especially bad, the stone might be beyond cleansing and may have to be buried or thrown into a body of water such as a river or ocean.

Once your stones are cleansed, there are some additional steps you can take to get the most out of them. Most books on stones and crystals will list half a dozen energies associated with each stone. This is not because the authors have no idea what they are writing about but because we all interpret the energies of stones differently. To get maximum value out of your stones, you need to figure out what they mean to you and then attune yourself to their energies.

To attune to a stone, ignore what books like this one say about certain stones and begin by picking up the stone you want to attune with. Hold it in your dominant hand. If the stone is small, grasp it in your fist, feeling every curve and contour. If the stone is too big to hold, touch it with as much of your hand as possible. Feel the energy that comes from it. What does it feel like to you? How do you interpret the energy that the stone is emitting? When you've got a good sense of that energy, write down your observations so you won't forget them.

Once you've recorded your observations about the stone, go back and hold it once more. Feel its energy and find the rhythm of just how that energy is being released. It might be a steady hum, or perhaps the energy is released in waves, ebbing and flowing with varying intensities. However that energy is released, feel it and move with it. Connect your energy to the stone's, emitting your own personal energy with the same rhythm as the stone's. By doing this, you are attuning to the energy of the stone and teaching your body's energy how to better work with your stone.

Now that you are attuned to the stone, charge it with intentional purpose. Remember how you felt about the stone when you first held it and felt its power? Whatever your observations were, place that particular energy into the stone. If you felt protective energy, push a bit of your own protective energy into it while saying, "I charge this stone for protection." With this step, your personal protective energy will find itself in sync with the stone. Every time you use that stone for protection, your body will know how best to maximize the stone's energy. In a sense, you are telling the stone what to do with its power.

If you felt several different energies when you first held your stone, that's completely natural. You can attune to all of those different energies in your stone. Just add some of your own energies related to those various qualities. A stone can be charged with our own protective, loving, and healing energies.

Shapes of Stones

When visiting a stone and gem shop, you'll probably find crystals and stones in a wide variety of shapes. Today, spheres, points (resembling a pointed tower or obelisk), and natural pieces are all readily available. While many people probably don't give a lot of thought to the shape of the stone they are using, certain shapes are better than others for various kinds of magickal work.

The most common shape for a crystal or stone is probably a small chunk. We realize that the word *chunk* is not particularly elegant, but it's accurate. A chunk is either a small piece removed from a larger stone by human means or a naturally occurring smaller piece of a particular stone or crystal. These are the most inexpensive shapes of store-bought stones and are generally what we find out in nature.

Chunks are great for a variety of purposes. Because of their compact size, they fit well in sachets and can be conveniently tucked under a pillow or into a pocket. They are also inconspicuous and are unlikely to attract much attention if you leave them on a fireplace mantel or desk.

The energy from a chunk of stone (one without a defined point) will radiate from the entirety of the stone, which makes it harder to direct its energy from a specific spot, but in most magickal operations that's not necessary anyway. Using a chunk of stone is not a good way to project a blast of aventurine magick at someone, but it is a practical way to bring aventurine to a job interview and have it fit comfortably in your pocket.

There are many people who use crystals (especially) as wands to direct magickal energy, and when they do, they generally use a point. A point resembles an obelisk and most often has a sharp point at the top. Points can occur naturally in nature, though most of the ones for sale in stores have been shaped by human hands. When a crystal has a point, the energy from the crystal or stone will naturally flow toward the point. This is good for us because it allows points to be used in a variety of ways magickally.

A stone with a point can be used as a wand to wield magickal energy. This energy can be used to do things like create a magick circle, or it can simply be directed to a specific target. The energy that is emitted from the point of a crystal is like a laser beam; it's much more precise and targeted than the energy that is emitted from a chunk of stone, which radiates in all directions and doesn't have any particular place to go.

When we hold on to a crystal point, we can direct the energy to release faster by pushing some of our own energy into it. Our personal energy "tells" the stone to release its energy more quickly, and it helps target the stone's energy, too. If we aren't touching the stone, we can still push our personal energy into it and direct that power up and out of it. For this reason, crystal points are one of the most effective ways to perform magickal work targeted at a specific person or place. When we push energy up and out of a crystal, that energy is also super concentrated and more powerful than what we'd normally get from just having a piece of malachite sitting on a shelf.

Points are also great places to focus energy, especially when working with others. In our coven we will stand around our altar raising energy and sending it into whatever crystal point we are using during our working. When we've reached the pinnacle of our energy raising, whoever is in charge of releasing that energy will use the crystal's point to direct all the power we've gathered to the specific spot where it needs to go. The energy from the point of the crystal projects up and out of our circle, shooting out like a laser beam.

Spheres are almost entirely human-made but are still a valuable shape for magickal use. Most spheres are small, about the size of a little bouncy ball, while others are the size of a baseball or larger. Without a specific point, a stone sphere will radiate its energy outward evenly. This makes it effective if you are trying to send magick to a number of different people or places instead of focusing on a specific individual or place. Spheres also make useful focal points when doing magick in a group setting.

Increasingly popular are tall, thin slabs of stone that resemble a door with a rounded (arched) top. Stones of this shape usually taper slightly as they reach their rounded top. Because of their size, these cuts of stones, when laid flat, can double as an altar for magickal work and can be used as a charging station for tools. When highly polished, slabs resemble a mirror and can be used for divinatory work, depending on the energy that emanates from the particular stone.

One of the great things about the magickal energy of stones, crystals, and metals is that we can wield their power when they are a part of the jewelry we wear. Any small stone can be fashioned into a necklace, and when that stone touches our skin, we more readily absorb its energies. The shape of a stone in our jewelry is not a big factor in the stone's effectiveness, but where we wear a stone can have some effect.

If you are trying to utilize a stone's protective energy, keeping it near your heart (like on a necklace) will serve you better than wearing it on an ankle bracelet. If you are trying to improve your concentration with a stone, wearing it as an earring would be ideal. When writing, Jason has been known to slip on a malachite bracelet to increase the number of words he types per minute and to stay focused on whatever he's writing. Malachite works like a battery, and we can tap into its energy when we find our concentration faltering, such as when writing a long chapter about stones.

Warnings about Stones

It has become increasingly common in many circles to add stones and crystals to drinking water. We do not recommend this practice. Many stones and gems are toxic to the human body and can cause serious problems, even death. The sourcing of stones remains troubling, and many unscrupulous retailers mislabel their stones for maximum profit.

Many self-help books featuring stones and crystals recommend tossing those items into your bathwater so you can soak up their energies. Setting your stone on the side of your bathtub will have the same effect as adding it to the water, and without the risk involved. Not only can certain stones release toxins such as arsenic or lead into your water (which can be deadly!), but some stones are water-soluble and will actually break down in water, releasing dangerous shards in their wake. Water can also simply be bad for many stones, so why take the risk?

In addition to keeping your stones nice and dry, you may want to learn the history of how your stones were mined and polished. Many stones come from large-scale industrial mines with long histories of both labor violations and environmentally destructive practices. Finding out where your stones came from can be challenging—a stone might change hands half a dozen times before arriving on your altar—but it never hurts to ask.[23] Many Witch and metaphysical stores attempt

---

23. Emily Atkin, "Do You Know Where Your Healing Crystals Come From?" The New Republic, May 11, 2018, https://newrepublic.com/article/148190/know-healing-crystals-come-from. This article also includes a few stone shops that attempt to ethically source their wares. The whole thing is worth reading.

to buy their stones from earth-friendly mines and distributors, and the stores that do so are generally more open to questions.

Ari's Favorite Stones

There are literally thousands of stones, crystals, and metals that can be used in magickal work. Every stone, no matter how common it might look, has energy within it that you can use. However, certain stones are prized more than others for use in spellcraft. What follows is a list of Ari's favorite stones. When we are working together as a coven and putting together a spell, we often stand back and let her gather whatever stones her experience and intuition tell her to use.

You do not have to buy all the stones on this list or any of them to work magick. The well-stocked Witch's cupboard doesn't need every kind of stone and crystal in creation to be effective. All you need are the stones that you work best with. Bigger pieces of stones and crystals have more energy (which makes sense when you think about it), but you can work magick with a reasonably sized stone, too. No one needs a crystal point the size of their arm to be an effective Witch!

The following correspondences reflect the general feelings that Ari has when working with her favorite stones. Other sources will suggest different interpretations, because we all process energy differently. These are general guidelines for certain stones, not absolutes. If your interpretation of a stone's energy is different, use that interpretation because it's just as valid!

Amber

It's worth pointing out again that amber is not a stone or crystal; it's fossilized tree sap, generally from trees similar to modern pines. Because of its uniqueness, amber has been used in religious and magickal rites for thousands of years, and the traditional necklace in many Witch traditions is one made of amber and jet. Amber has a multitude of magickal uses, but first and foremost we find amber to be empowering. This sense of empowerment can be used to increase strength, feelings of worth and beauty, and protection. When held, amber can also have a calming effect, most likely because it makes us feel in control of the situation.

Many pieces of amber contain pieces of insects or even whole ones. When using amber with an insect in it, you are getting two forms of power in one charm. It's worth exploring just what might be in your amber and how that affects its energy. An ant stuck in a piece of amber might lend industrious energies to it, while a spider might add predatory energies.

Amethyst

Amethyst can promote good feelings between people; it's not quite love, but more like a stable, solid friendship. Amethyst is also useful for emotional healing. Sleeping with a piece of amethyst under your bed won't just help heal a wounded psyche but will also help get you a good night's sleep!

According to Greek myth, amethyst the crystal was originally Amethyst the nymph. Enchanted by her beauty, the god Dionysus pursued the virginal Amethyst. Frightened by the god's advances, Amethyst cried out for protection to Artemis, who promptly turned Amethyst into a crystal. Dionysus then spilled a bit of wine on the crystal, creating amethyst. For this reason, amethyst is said to assist with sobriety. This quality can be extended to other behaviors and addictions you want to control. If you are trying to quit something that's bad for you, carry a piece of amethyst with you to help.

Aventurine

In our coven we primarily use (green) aventurine when doing prosperity magick. This might be magick related to a new job, a raise, or even a book publishing deal. For this reason, aventurine is popular with gamblers and anyone who engages in games of chance.

Aventurine is generally green but can be found in a variety of colors. The color of the stone will impact its magickal energy, so it's a good idea to spend some time with any pieces of aventurine you acquire that are not green to determine their magickal qualities.

Bloodstone

Bloodstone is especially useful in healing spells, specifically ones involving blood disorders. It's a stone that's best used when the body, and not the mind or spirit, is in need of healing. Bloodstone can be used in conjunction with other healing stones and will amplify their energies.

Carnelian

Carnelian has a variety of magickal uses. It's an excellent stone to use in spells for protection, but we don't suggest wearing it as jewelry for that specific purpose because of its other properties. Carnelian also has a lot of lusty energy. It's not a stone connected to deep emotional love, but instead is one that stimulates feelings of lust and physical desire. Ari describes its energy as "the friends with benefits kind of love."

In ancient Egypt, carnelian was known as "the blood of Isis," and an amulet made from the stone was thought to bestow the blessings of Isis.[24] Isis, both in the ancient world and today, is a goddess of just about everything, and wearing carnelian is a way to strengthen your relationship with her.

Citrine

Most books don't have much to say about citrine, but it's one of Ari's absolute favorite healing stones. Citrine gives energy to the body, which aids in healing. Because of its bright yellow color, citrine is also a popular crystal to use when doing magickal work to bring happiness and positivity.

Fluorite

Fluorite has become an increasingly popular stone in Witch circles, and for good reason. It is an excellent protection stone and also aids in concentration. When you're reading or studying, a piece of fluorite in your pocket will help you retain information more easily. Fluorite is increasingly used in healing magick and is thought to be an immunity booster.

Garnet

Garnet has been connected to a variety of goddesses over the centuries. Due to its red color, garnet is often associated with pomegranates, which connects the stone to the land of the dead and its queen, Persephone. This makes garnet an excellent stone to use at Samhain and to help facilitate trips between the mortal world and that of the dead. Its color is also like that of blood, further connecting it to the mysteries of life and death.

Because of its lustful energies, garnet can also be connected to the goddess Aphrodite. Garnet is one of Ari's favorite stones because of this connection. Garnet can be used in spells to find both lust and love. It's also a powerful stone that lends strength and vigor to magickal work and everyday situations.

---

24. Nicholas Pearson, *Stones of the Goddess: Crystals for the Divine Feminine* (Rochester, VT: Inner Traditions, 2019), 204–5.

Gold

In the modern world, gold is one of the most common symbols of wealth and power. Utilizing the concept of "like attracts like," gold is most often used in spells focused on money. For Witches, gold has another association that might be even more important, and that is its connection to the sun. Gold symbolizes the power of the sun, which means it can be used in magickal work focusing on both growth (from Yule to Midsummer, while the sun is waxing) and decrease (from Midsummer to Yule, while the sun is waning).

Hematite

Hematite is one of the most popular stones used by Witches today, and for good reason. It's a great stone to use for grounding and can also be used for healing and to tap into your psychic and divinatory powers. But hematite is a very strange stone, because it seems to affect everyone differently.

Ari swears by hematite as a battery. When she needs a bit of extra energy, she goes to her hematite jewelry and stones, and she's not alone. For many people, simply touching hematite makes them feel energized. However, for a lot of people, hematite has the exact opposite effect. There are many who feel as if hematite actively pulls energy from their body, storing it until the stone is handled by someone who draws energy from the stone. When working with hematite, take some time to figure out just what sort of effect it has on you.

Jet

Jet is much like amber in that it's neither a stone nor a crystal; instead, it's fossilized wood and, technically, a form of coal. Jet is an especially good stone to use for protection, as both its color and its origin as wood allow it to easily absorb negative energies. It's also handy if you are trying to break a curse or hex.

There's something comforting about jet, most likely because it absorbs our own personal negative energies, taking them away from us. When you're feeling sad, grab a piece of jet and set your emotions free. The jet will absorb your tears and pain and shield you from them. If you do this with frequency, your stone might fill up with the sad energy you've poured into it. You can renew your jet by burying it in the ground under a full moon for a twenty-eight-day cycle. Be careful with a piece of jet that is full of sad energy, because letting it fall into someone else's hands will transfer your sad energy to whoever picks it up.

Lapis Lazuli

Lapis lazuli is one of the prettiest stones used by Witches, and when it's turned into a sphere, it sort of resembles the planet Earth. This resemblance enhances lapis lazuli's energy, which often invokes feelings of earth goddesses like Gaia. Like most blue stones, lapis lazuli helps stir up psychic energy in the body.

In the story of Inanna, the goddess travels to the land of the dead wearing a necklace made of lapis lazuli. In myth, Inanna is required to set aside all of her garments and jewelry one by one in order to pass through the various gates of the Underworld. Near her journey's end, the only thing on her person is her necklace of lapis lazuli. Because of this, lapis lazuli is often used for protection and to cultivate courage.

Lepidolite

Lepidolite is not particularly well known but has qualities not often found in other stones. It is a stone of peace and can be used to help end conflicts with others. Lepidolite is a soothing stone, bringing energies of balance and steadiness to whoever uses it. Because of this, it's a useful stone to keep nearby when going through a major life change. Whether you're changing jobs, living situations, or romantic partners, keeping a piece of lepidolite in a drawer or a pocket can make such transitions smoother.

Malachite

Once a year our coven does a jobs spell focused on finding new employment for those who need it and acquiring raises and promotions for those who deserve them. One thing included in this spell every year is a big chunk of malachite. Malachite is *the stone* for job spells and to bring business success. It's a stone that can be used to attract wealth when carried on one's person.

In the course of researching this book, we were surprised to find that our understanding of malachite was quite different from what's in many books. Many Witches also use malachite in love spells and as a form of protection, especially for children.

Moonstone

Moonstone is useful for a variety of lunar-related activities. When placed under a pillow, it induces sleep and ensures good dreams. The Witchcraft rite known as "drawing down the moon" can also be more easily accomplished when holding on to or wearing moonstones. The moonstone actively emits goddess energy and helps put the mind into a trancelike state. It's the perfect combination if you are looking to invoke a goddess into the body of a covenmate.

Pyrite (or Fool's Gold)

Pyrite is often used as a substitute for gold in both jewelry and magickal work. Others see pyrite as quite different from gold and believe that magically it's best used to confuse, trick, or obfuscate. How you feel about pyrite should determine how you use it in magickal work. (Amanda, for instance, uses it in money magick. Jason does not.)

Quartz

If we had to choose just one stone or crystal to use in magick, it would be quartz. Quartz is literally good for everything, whether it's protection, love, prosperity, passion, or happiness. It can be used for all these purposes and more. Quartz also amplifies nearby energies and can be used to store excess energy until it's needed. If you've got a place in your home dedicated to magickal work, place a piece of quartz in it to store any unused energies. Ari and Jason keep a piece of quartz in their car at all times, just in case of a magickal emergency.

Quartz often has lines running through it. The type of quartz with golden or red lines in it is referred to as *rutilated quartz*. (Rutile is the name of the mineral that creates those lines.) When we work magick, the lines in rutilated quartz carry our energy to its target. This is useful when doing a job spell. Rutilated quartz is also useful when targeting specific individuals, but even better is *tourmalinated quartz*, which has strands of black tourmaline running through it. When doing magick for a specific person, such as a healing spell, the pathways in a piece of tourmalinated quartz will take your energy directly to that person. Like quartz, tourmaline is an "everything" stone, which makes tourmalinated quartz ideal for a variety of magickal endeavors.

Rhodochrosite

There are many stones that are useful for finding love, but because love is such a multilayered energy, it comes in a variety of forms. Rhodochrosite works best for drawing peaceful, deep love. It's not a stone of passion, but a stone to attract love built on a solid foundation of trust and care.

Rhodochrosite is also a calming stone, and when held during anxious moments, it can soothe the body and mind. Like malachite, rhodochrosite has different effects on different people. Some individuals find it energizing, while others find it so relaxing that it can lead to an unscheduled afternoon nap.

Rose Quartz

Rose quartz is a must for any Witch's crystal collection and is popular in love and friendship spells. Like regular quartz, rose quartz contains a variety of energies, and wearing jewelry containing rose quartz is an effective way to attract love. For those who are already partnered up, rose quartz deepens feelings of connection and helps ensure peace on the home front.

Rose quartz is also good for general happiness and can be used in spells to overcome depression or worn in stressful situations to help keep a positive attitude. Like moonstone, rose quartz is useful for initiating interactions with female deities.

Sapphire

Because of its cost, sapphire isn't commonly used in spellwork, but it has a great deal of energy that can be utilized when worn as jewelry. In ancient Greece, sapphires were sacred to the god Apollo, a god of prophecy. When reading tarot or doing other divinatory work, sapphire will enhance prophetic energy. Sapphires are also a source of wisdom and are thought to reveal truth.

Over the centuries, sapphire has been associated with love, but generally deep contented love; it is not a stone of passion. Sapphires can also be worn for protection. They help deflect negative magick and help the body ward off disease.

Smoky Quartz

Before you begin any magickal work or when you are faced with a vexing problem, hold a piece of smoky quartz and think about what you are about to work on or what you are dealing with. Smoky quartz encourages clarity of thought and can help reveal answers and provide focus. After absorbing the energies from the smoky quartz, you will have formulated a good plan and be ready to proceed.

Chapter Twelve
Spells by Stone and Crystal

While we suggest using specific stones in most of the spells in this chapter, it's worth noting that if a certain stone or crystal doesn't resonate with you, you should replace it with something else. Also worth mentioning is that if you don't have a large crystal/stone collection, quartz is an easy and effective substitute for nearly everything. While there are some exotic stones listed in a few of the spells in this chapter, use what you have and feel free to improvise! Ari has been building her stone collection for twenty-five years. Most of us can't say that!

Spell to Attract Customers to Your Business

This spell is designed to bring more customers to your business and increase the amount of money you bring in.

For this spell you will need:

- A business card (or a small piece of paper with your business's name on it)
- Pyrite or a small piece or flake of gold
- Aventurine
- Citrine

The pyrite or gold will bring prosperity and the aventurine will attract success and wealth. The citrine will provide happiness, prosperity, and a level of protection.

On your business card (or piece of paper), write the words *success* and *wealth* and place the card in your store's cash drawer or near where you do business. (If you have an online store, for instance, you could put it near your computer.) Place the stones on top of your card while articulating the energies that each stone will bring to your business:

Pyrite/gold for prosperity!
Aventurine for success in my endeavors!
Citrine for happiness and protection!

If the pieces of stone you use are small, you can tape or glue them to your business card so they won't be displaced.

Spell to Increase Your Sense of Self-Love and Self-Worth

We all have moments of doubt when we feel unworthy of love. This spell counteracts those feelings and reminds us that even in our lowest moments we have value.

For this spell you will need:

- Snowflake obsidian
- A small shovel/spade
- Rose quartz
- Carnelian
- A shower or bath
- A tall mirror

Snowflake obsidian is a type of obsidian that is speckled with the white mineral cristobalite and looks a bit like snow. It helps remove self-doubt and clears feelings of unworthiness. Carnelian is a stone of confidence and helps with moving forward. Rose quartz is a crystal that represents unconditional love both for ourselves and for others.

Begin by taking the snowflake obsidian in your dominant hand. As you hold it, think of all the negative self-talk, self-doubt, and lies that you routinely tell yourself. Also dredge up the lies told about you by others, no matter how painful it might be. Send all that energy into the snowflake obsidian. This will take some time, so don't rush the process.

Eventually the stone will begin to feel heavy or "full." When your stone reaches this point, bury it using a small shovel or spade. This will require you to leave your ritual space and take a walk to a park or perhaps a spot in your backyard. As you walk, feel the negative energy within the snowflake obsidian heavy in your hand. Fill your mind with happy thoughts of burying that negativity. When you find a suitable place, bury your stone, knowing that the negative energy you're ridding yourself of will be recycled and turned into something positive thanks to the power of the earth. After burying your stone, take a few steadying breaths and return home.

Once you've arrived back home, take a relaxing shower or bath. Wash away any negativity that might be clinging to you. Enjoy the water; *feel good* while the water washes over you.

When you are done with your shower or bath, take your rose quartz and carnelian in your dominant hand and stand nude in front of a tall mirror. (If you don't have a full-length mirror, a handheld or even bathroom mirror will work.) Look your reflection in the eyes and speak positively! Say these words out loud:

> *I am worthy of love.*
> *I am deserving of all the great gifts life has to offer.*
> *I am successful.*

Feel free to add anything else that you think is important. Place your rose quartz and carnelian in a place where you will see them every day, such as where you keep your jewelry or cologne. For the next seven days, repeat the affirmations in front of your mirror while holding your stones. Your self-worth will grow daily while doing this spell. If you feel your magick start to wane after the initial seven days, repeat the mantra above while holding your stones and let their energy wash over you.

Finding the Possibilities Spell

For this spell all you need is a piece of rutilated quartz. The lines in the crystal (rutile inclusions) should be clear to the naked eye. Many Witches like to work in the shadows, but for this spell the area where you keep your quartz should be sufficiently illuminated so you can easily see it.

This spell was originally designed for a first date but can be used for any life experience that will result in new possibilities. Some examples of that include starting school, having children, or changing careers.

Start by taking your rutilated quartz in your hand and feeling its energy. You should be able to feel a slight pulse in your hand as you hold it. Find the current of the stone's energy and connect with it. Be open to the pathways that run through it. Once you've felt the stone's energy, say:

> *Open up the possibilities that are before me.*
> *May I see just a glimpse of what lies ahead.*
> *Prepare me for what this journey will bring.*
> *Let my vision be clear and show me where I might tread!*

Take a deep breath, hold for a count of three, then release. Repeat this process six more times, and every time you exhale, push all of the tension and anxiety occupying your mind out of your body. When you start this magickal work, you want your mind to be blank, without any preconceived ideas. After breathing and exhaling, you should find yourself in a peaceful state. If you are not in a peaceful state, repeat the deep breaths until you reach one.

Now that you are free of any preconceived ideas and tension, look deeply into your piece of rutilated quartz. As you look at the quartz, imagine your current opportunity before you. Is it a first date? Imagine that partner and what you know of them. While focusing on your ideal mental image, look again at the rutilated quartz, and let your mind wander and your eyes lose focus for a few moments. Notice any images you see in the quartz and file them away in your mind.

Breathe deeply and let your gaze sharpen once again. Find the first line in the rutilated quartz and follow it through the stone. Where does it end up? Open your mind to where the line takes you. Follow this by going through every thread in the rutilated quartz until your curiosity about the future is satiated.

Moonstone for Good Sleep and Pleasant Dreams

Moonstone gets its name from its deep connection to the moon. Because of this, people have been using moonstone in spells for sleep and good dreams for centuries. For this spell all you need is a small piece of moonstone.

This spell requires two nights of work. On the first night, situate yourself in a place where you can see the moon. The night before a full moon is ideal but not necessary. The best place to work your magick is one where it will receive the light of the moon most of the night.

Hold your moonstone in your hand and look up at the moon. Think of it up there in the sky, shining its light and radiating an energy that supports a restful sleep and a night of positive dreams. The moon has been guiding Witches for millennia, powering our magick and spellcraft.

Place your moonstone in a spot where the light of the moon is shining upon it and say:

Dear moon, bathe my stone in your light.
Let it harness the power of the night.
Gather here energies of peace and rest,
So that my future slumbers may be blessed!

Leave your moonstone in this spot overnight to absorb the energies of the moon and the night.

The following night, as you go to bed, hold your moonstone in your hand and say:

Restful and deep,
A good night's sleep.
Only pleasant dreams
From my moonstone's beams!

Place the moonstone under your pillow and let its energy lull you to sleep and protect you from unwanted dreams. Repeat the words of the spell and place your moonstone under your pillow any night when you need an especially restful slumber.

Animal Companion Bonding Spell

This spell is designed to develop a strong bond between you and a new animal companion. It can also be done when introducing an animal companion to a new lover or roommate. This is an especially good spell to do when bringing a new furry friend into your life to get them attuned to your personal energy.

For this spell you will need:

- A leopard skin jasper stone
- A small wire cage that can be placed around a collar (optional)

Hold the leopard skin jasper in your dominant hand and think about your animal friend. Imagine the two of you loving and caring for each other. Picture yourself doing all the things necessary to take good care of them; hear the purrs of your cat or the excited pant of your dog in your head. Push your loving energy into the stone until the jasper is warm to the touch. The love you have for your animal companion is what's most important here; it's love that builds the bonds between us and our animal friends.

Once your stone has been charged, you can place it on their collar or in a place they frequent. Ari and Jason's cats are indoor-only kitties and don't wear collars, so the two of them wrapped the piece of jasper up in a soft towel and placed it on their cats' bed. If your animal friend is a creature in an enclosed area, you can simply add the stone to their space.

A Spell for Patience

Waiting is not always easy and is often anxiety-inducing. This spell is designed to ease the worry and stress that often comes with having to wait for something you really want (or want to happen). For this spell you'll need either a piece of amber or a piece of petrified wood. Both materials are formed from organic materials, making them different from the other types of "stones" we generally use in magick. They both also take millions of years to form, which is most certainly an example of patience.

Take your amber or petrified wood and hold it in your dominant hand. As you hold it, let its energy enter your body and then allow your mind to wander. As your mind wanders, you might see images of the tree that your petrified wood or amber came from. Think about that image and about the millions of years it took for nature to form the object you hold in your hand. To us, this energy is generally soothing since it was formed very slowly over time.

When you are in tune with the energy of the amber or petrified wood, think about what it is you are waiting for. Visualize your stress, worry, and lack of patience. Picture yourself fretting and being consumed by the wait ahead of you. Grip the amber or fossilized wood more tightly in your hand, allowing all that worry and stress to flow out of you and into the piece. As you release that energy, say:

Take my stress and anxiety away.
What I will shall come my way.
May I be free of all concern and worry,
And not be in such a big hurry!

Take a deep cleansing breath after the last line of the incantation and notice the energy of the amber or petrified wood. You may notice heat coming from it; this is the stress you've put into it. Wait a second and let that energy pass. What you should feel after that is something calm and soothing, an energy that has developed patiently over millions of years. Absorb this energy and let it relax you as the anxiety of your wait drifts away.

Over the next few weeks, days, or hours, or however long you have to wait, revisit your amber or fossilized wood when you are having trouble being patient. Pour your unwanted anxious energy into it when you need to. And when you just need a bit of assurance that you can be patient and get through this obstacle, touch your amber or fossilized wood lightly and notice its calming energy. Carry the piece with you if necessary.

If you've used your amber or petrified wood to soak up a lot of unwanted energy, place it on your altar or in a small dish of salt or soil at night to rid it of your anxious energies. The next morning, it should be cleansed and ready for use again.

A Traveler's Spell (for People and Luggage)

This is an easy spell that only requires two pieces of malachite. As you stand in front of your travel luggage, hold your two pieces of malachite in your dominant hand and say:

> *May my bag come back to me.*
> *As I will, so mote it be!*

Place one of your pieces of malachite in the bag and the other piece in your pocket or purse. Your luggage should now arrive to you at your destination safe and sound!

This spell can also be done on human beings. When Jason travels for work, Ari will place a picture of him on the refrigerator and attach a piece of malachite to it. As she places the malachite on the picture, she says:

> *May my husband (partner/wife/etc.) come home safe and sound to me.*
> *By the power in this stone, so mote it be!*

She'll then repeat the cantrip above before placing the second piece of malachite in his luggage (she doesn't trust him not to lose the malachite if he keeps it in his pocket!) to make sure he returns home safely from his travels.

Shared Spellcraft: Hagstone Divination Spell
by Katie Gerrard

Hagstones (also known as adder stones, Witch stones, holey stones, or Odin stones) are pieces of rock or pebble that have formed naturally to feature a hole. The hole is usually created by water, which means these stones are often found on a beach or near a running stream.

Hagstones can take many forms: large or small, rough or smooth. Some have multiple holes, whilst many have just one, or one hole and a few indentations that will eventually become holes. You might find a hagstone that has a smaller pebble trapped inside it. These stones can have significant meaning in magic, too.

Hagstones are often fixed to a cord and worn round the neck or hung in a doorway for protection. But they can also be used for divination, which is the subject of this particular spell.

Hagstones have been linked to the Norse god Odin, who sacrificed his eye to drink from the Well of Mimir. This process gained him much wisdom but left his eye separate from him and forever living in the bottom of the well. When I see a hagstone shimmering in the water, I always think of Odin's missing eye.

Before you begin this spell, you'll need to find a hagstone. You'll also need a candle and some incense.

Not all beaches are good for finding holey stones, so do a little research online and see if any near you are known for them.

I live near a chalk cliff beach, and many of the chalk rocks found on the sand have holes in them. These can be very delicate, however. Flint is another material that often has naturally forming holes. Flint is much more durable, but because of this, holes take longer to form in it, and you will find fewer of these than the more common, softer chalk alternatives.

If you can't find your own holey stone, try buying one online. There are plenty of people who live near beaches and love collecting more bits of shell and rock than they personally need.

Like all good spells, start your rite by purifying your working space. I chant the runes Kenaz and Laguz to achieve this, but you can easily cast a ritual circle or maybe use a tuning fork to cleanse the air.

Take your holey stone and hold it in the palm of your hand. Ask Odin to bless the stone, and promise to dedicate this individual hagstone to him from this point onward.

Light the candle and the incense.

Hold your hagstone so it's between your eye and the candle. You should be able to see the flame through the hole. Focus your eye on the candle flame as you chant this rhyme:

> *Seeing stone, knowing stone,*
> *Odin's missing eye;*
> *See for me, know for me,*
> *Work with me to scry.*

Chant this a few times to build up energy, then silently focus on the candle flame.

When your eyes start to feel heavy, close them and allow your mind to visualize and wander.

Use this spell at the beginning of a meditation session during which you receive visions and wisdom.

This works even better if, as with other forms of divination, you start with a specific question as your intent.

Good luck!

Katie Gerrard is a Heathen Witch and author who lives in London, England.

Chapter Thirteen
Essential Oils and Incense

Oils are concentrated energy in a bottle. If you want to use the very essence of a particular flower, tree, or herb, use an essential oil. Despite all the power they contain, oils usually play a complementary role in magick and Witchcraft.

Magickal oils are available in a variety of formulations. The most familiar are essential oils, which are typically extracted from a single plant source, such as jasmine or lemon. Most essential oils are "pure," meaning they have no additives or fillers, but pure essential oil is not easily obtained. For example, it takes over fifty thousand roses to produce just one ounce of rose oil. Such astonishing numbers explain the high price tag that accompanies many essential oils.

The more expensive essential oils are often diluted with a carrier oil (such as olive, jojoba, or sunflower) to create a more affordable version. The carrier oil acts as a base, often with just a few drops of the pure essential oil added. If you've ever wondered why some bottles of rose oil are fifteen dollars and others are eighty, it's because the fifteen-dollar bottle has been diluted.

We are sacrificing a bit of magickal power when we use diluted oils, but adding a pure essential oil to a carrier oil serves a few purposes. For one, it makes the oil more affordable. A tiny bottle of pure lavender oil at twenty dollars is not going to last very long. A twenty-dollar bottle of pure lavender oil mixed with a carrier oil will give you lavender oil for years! The second reason to dilute an oil is because most essential oils are harmful to the human body in concentrated amounts. If you've ever had pure cinnamon essential oil applied to your forehead in a ritual, it's a painful moment you are not likely to ever forget.

Oil blends are increasingly common in Witch and metaphysical stores (and are created by many Witches at home, too) and are usually made with a variety of essential oils and a carrier oil. Some of these formulations have been used for hundreds of years, while others are of a more recent vintage. If you are buying from a reputable store or brand, you are probably getting an effective magickal oil. If you are buying at a big-box store and your oil blend has a price point that's too good to be true, there's a good chance your oil is synthetic. Synthetic oils contain artificial fragrances made in a laboratory from chemical compounds.

Are synthetic oils bad? Yes and no. Certainly there's going to be far more magickal power in an oil extracted from a living (or once living) plant. The oil is going to contain much of the energy the plant had during its lifetime. There's certainly more energy radiating from a living thing than from something created in a test tube. But…

While we don't believe that a synthetic oil will have quite the same punch as a natural one, it's not necessarily devoid of energy. If you use a synthetic jasmine oil, the scent of that oil is going to conjure up feelings of jasmine's normal energy in you. Its power on your olfactory senses will probably be enough to affect you in some slight way. Synthetics allow many people to enjoy certain scents when they otherwise might not be able to.

Oils are used primarily as an accompaniment or accessory in magickal practice. The most common use for oil is probably in the anointing of candles. When you rub a candle with oil, you are adding the power of that oil to the candle, and the more power the better! But oil can be used for more than just candles.

Just about anything can be anointed. You can add to the power of your stones and crystals by anointing them with oil. (A word of warning: oil can be harmful to certain crystals, so do some research first. Most stones will be just fine, though.) Books and written spells can be anointed with oil, too. Drawing a large invoking or banishing pentagram on such items with oil will add a lot of extra power to your magickal work.

Anointing ritual tools is an easy way to add the power of essential oils to your magickal workings. As a double bonus, a bit of oil on an athame or sword will also protect it from rust! We generally anoint all of our ritual tools and then redo them every year to keep the essential oil's energy in them strong.

Oil can be used in ways beyond simply anointing, too. An oil diffuser will put the energy of the oil you are utilizing directly into the air, where it can be directed into your magickal work. Oil in a diffuser can also be used to create a magickal atmosphere. Having a party that you want to sizzle with energy? Diffuse some rosemary oil. An oil diffused in the air will share its energy with anyone it comes into contact with and subtly change their consciousness. (If you share your home with a bird or other small creature, be cautious when using a diffuser; their small bodies have trouble metabolizing some oils.)

If diffusing an oil with a diffuser is too much work or you aren't in a position to tend the flame, a spray bottle with a few drops of essential oil added to some water can work wonders. When our coven is a little too boisterous for our High Priestess, she'll spray some clary sage water in our ritual space. Clary sage promotes focus and clear thinking, which is something we desperately need at times.

In our coven, before beginning ritual we add a few drops of rose oil to a large pitcher of water and use that to ceremonially wash the hands of everyone present. The rose oil promotes energy in line with "perfect love and perfect trust," which is an ideal many covens strive for. A couple of drops of a cleansing oil such as ylang-ylang in a large bowl is perfect for some self-cleansing before beginning magickal work. (There's a lot more space dedicated to the blessing bowl back in chapter 2.)

Essential oils are also used in bath salts. The combination of the salt and the oil is a great way to remove negative energy, pamper your skin, and infuse your bath with a little extra energy. Plus, you'll smell amazing when you get out of the tub!

Oil can be used in dozens of ways and is a powerful ally in magick. The only limit to how oil can be used is your imagination. If you can put oil on it, do it! Your magick will be all the stronger for it.

Amanda's Favorite Magickal Oils

Many of the magickal items highlighted in this book seem to have a multitude of uses, which can be confusing to a Witch who is just starting out. Because the energies of things like oils and stones affect all of us differently, most magickal accessories have many associations. When using a particular oil, it's wise to figure out how you personally react to its energy and make a note of it. Your reactions to the essential oils in this section might be completely different from what is described here.

Allspice

Allspice is for more than just pumpkin pie; it's also a great magickal oil. Generally associated with prosperity and abundance, allspice is also useful for consecrating sacred items. When dedicating a new altar for the Craft,[25] anoint each of the altar's corners (or its circumference, if your altar is round) with allspice. This will help cleanse your altar and will magnify the magick you create on it.

---

25. You can read more about altars in *The Witch's Altar*, cowritten by Jason and the amazing Laura Tempest Zakroff and also published by Llewellyn in 2018.

Angelica

Angelica lives up to its name! It's especially useful when attempting to connect with angelic spirits (there are a lot of Witches who work with angels) or other higher powers or when you are seeking some divine intervention in your life. Like angels in magickal practice, angelica is also a source of protection and guidance. When attempting to connect with angelic energies during meditation, rubbing a bit of angelica on your temples will give you a greater chance of success.

Angelica has also been used in exorcisms over the centuries. If there are hostile forces or spirits in your home, anoint the corners of your house with angelica to drive them away. A wand or athame consecrated with angelica oil will also help rid your home of negative entities. (Near the end of the next chapter, there's a complete spell for this called "Angelica Athame Spell.")

Anise

Because it smells like black licorice, anise is something that most people either love or hate. (One of us said "eww!" about it while working on this book.) If you are someone who enjoys the scent of anise, you are in luck because it has a variety of uses in magick. It's a source of protection, luck, and fertility. It's also a useful oil when engaging in divination or dreamwork.

Anise is also great for connecting with your emotions. When dealing with matters of the heart, drawing an invoking pentagram over your heart with anise will help to keep your heart from being broken.

Camphor

Camphor has been used in medicine for hundreds of years and is an antimicrobial. In addition to killing germs, it also provides strength and protection and clears negative energy. During stressful times, a few drops of camphor oil in an oil diffuser will keep your living space calm, cool, and running smoothly.

Cinnamon

Cinnamon oil is not for the faint of heart. While extremely useful in magick, it must always be diluted because it will cause burning sensations on the skin. Its burning properties are most likely the reason that it's a powerful oil to use in defense magick. Cinnamon also brings success, luck, and prosperity. To harness its advantageous properties, dab some cinnamon oil on a business card (or a piece of paper) and place it in your wallet to attract money.

Cinnamon is also a powerful sexual oil. Before making love to a partner, the two of you can anoint each other on the forehead with diluted cinnamon oil. Your love-making will be full of extra passion and lust.

Clary Sage

Ari loves clary sage because it's an extremely practical oil. It provides focus, increases intuition, and brings balance. It also promotes feelings of beauty, which is especially helpful if you're dealing with self-esteem issues.

Ari always keeps a spritzer bottle filled with water and a few drops of clary sage around the house. Spraying it helps her to center when dealing with difficult situations. When dealing with menstrual cramps and pain, a few spritzes of clary sage will help alleviate symptoms.

Cypress

Cypress is a powerful oil to use during meditation. It brings clarity to the mind and helps us to connect with spirit. To take full advantage of cypress's magickal qualities, use it to anoint your third eye before beginning divination work. It will not only make you more open to psychic and spiritual energy but also provide a bit of protection to keep away unwanted forces.

Eucalyptus

Most of us are familiar with the scent of eucalyptus because it turns up frequently in cough drops during cold and flu season. Because of the medicinal properties of eucalyptus, you can add a few drops to some water in a spray bottle and spritz it around the house or use it in an oil diffuser to help with breathing problems and to promote health and mental clarity. (It's also great in the bath when you're congested!)

Eucalyptus is used to bring balance and is a valuable ally in dreamwork. It can also be used for cleansing and purification.

Jasmine

Jasmine is one of our absolute favorite oils. Because jasmine blooms at night, the plant (and the oil) is traditionally associated with all things related to the moon and the night. To ensure pleasant dreams, place a drop of jasmine oil on your pillow or add a few drops to some water in a spray bottle and lightly spritz your pillows. Jasmine is also seductive and promotes love, which is another great reason to put it on your pillows!

Jasmine oil applied to the crown chakra will help initiate contact with lunar goddesses. It is also associated with mystery, which makes it a great oil to use when conducting an initiation or elevation ritual. Jasmine is a must-have in the well-stocked Witch's cupboard!

Juniper

Juniper helps to cultivate psychic ability and promote the powers of prophecy and divination. Before doing a tarot card reading or engaging in other forms of divination, spray the table you're using with a spritz of juniper to make your readings more accurate. You can also add a drop or two of (diluted) juniper to your fingertips and then shuffle your cards, infusing them with its power.

In addition to its usefulness in divination, juniper also helps us overcome obstacles and is a great oil to use in defensive magick. For this reason, it's one of the main ingredients in Van Van oil, one of the most popular oil blends found in Conjure traditions. (We'll get to Van Van oil in a little bit!)

Lemon

Like most citrus oils, lemon is full of positive energy. It can bring clarity, abundance, and happiness into your life. It's also an excellent oil to use in uncrossing spells to remove blockages in your life. Lemons (and most other forms of citrus) absorb a great deal of solar energy, making them great for growing closer to sun deities or bringing a little bit of sunshine and abundance into your life.

When added to a salt scrub, lemon oil will not only remove any negative energy clinging to you but also leave you feeling happy and refreshed.

Marjoram

Marjoram is one of the most effective protection oils. It provides security and can act as a barrier when negative energy is being sent your way. Most Witches are pretty cool toward fellow Witches, but there are some petty Witches who will hex and curse anyone who disagrees with them. Marjoram is a go-to oil when that sort of thing happens.

Marjoram also provides comfort when mourning. If you have to go to a funeral and need some support, put a few drops of marjoram on some tissues or a hand-kerchief to help you power through your grief. If you're hosting a wake or a post-funeral gathering, putting some marjoram on a diffuser will help your guests deal with their pain and sadness.

Neroli

Neroli is another "positive" oil and is known for bringing joy, beauty, love, and happiness into our lives. It's also associated with fertility, which means it should be used anytime you are looking to increase something in your life.

To bring a bit of extra joy and happiness to your day, add a couple of drops of neroli oil to your shampoo or conditioner. Not only will you leave your shower with a bit of a pick-me-up but you'll also smell great for the entire day. Neroli can also be added to body lotion for a similar effect.

Oakmoss

Oakmoss is a lichen that grows on oak trees and smells like a forest after a rainstorm. Its energies facilitate contact with woodland spirits. Applying a few drops of oakmoss above the third eye (the middle of the forehead) will help you spot the fey while out in the woods.

The earthy scent of oakmoss also helps when working with our ancestors. Because of its association with death, oakmoss is the perfect anointing oil to use at Samhain or with any other ritual honoring the dead.

Peppermint

Peppermint has a myriad of uses in magickal practice. It can be used to banish unwanted energies and habits, and it also attracts abundance and prosperity. Its best use, though, might be in providing clarity and focus.

When studying, add a few drops of peppermint oil to a spritzer bottle or an oil diffuser. Peppermint will help you retain the knowledge you are gathering. When planning a party and sending out invitations, put a few drops of peppermint oil on your fingers and apply it to your invitations. This will help your guests remember the details of your party. In a similar fashion, you can anoint your calendar with peppermint oil so you remember your own schedule!

Thyme

Strength, healing, purification, and divination are all energies present in thyme oil. Because thyme is great for both divination and purification, it's an especially useful oil to use when breaking in a new set of runes or tarot cards or a scrying device. A few drops of thyme placed in a spray bottle with water can be used to clear unwanted energies from a room you're using for divination and to enhance your psychic powers.

To cleanse your tarot deck after you've let someone else use it, place a few drops of thyme oil on your fingers and then shuffle your cards. The thyme will help remove any unwanted energy from the cards.

Vetiver

We aren't going to tell you that vetiver is the perfect oil for gamblers, but if you want to increase your luck at the blackjack table or while playing slots, rub a few drops of vetiver on your hands before hitting the casino. If you are hosting some in-house poker and want to give yourself a bit of a magickal advantage, bless and anoint your cards with vetiver oil.

In addition to its use in gambling, vetiver attracts luck and money and can break an especially strong hex or curse. It's also a strengthening oil, which can come in handy when dealing with difficult situations. Massage a few drops on the insides of your wrists to help power through such moments.

Yarrow

When you're trying to find a solution to a vexing problem, a spritz or dab of yarrow oil on your pillow will help bring clarity, grounding, and pleasant dreams. Yarrow also has protective properties and can be used to guard against nightmares.

Ylang-Ylang

We all really love ylang-ylang, and not just because it's fun to say. Add ylang-ylang oil to lotion or your bathwater to feel more beautiful and to help attract a lover. Ylang-ylang oil contains a quiet confidence that will also help you find inner peace and balance.

If your household is full of arguments and conflict, put a few drops of ylang-ylang in an oil diffuser to help calm the situation. Its energies will put everyone in the right frame of mind to resolve conflicts and find some harmony.

Carrier Oils

Carrier oils are body-safe oils that are used to "carry" expensive and often physically irritating essential oils, especially if you are using that oil to anoint a candle or are planning to place it on your skin. Most essential oil blends contain essential oils that are added to a carrier oil. If you wanted to create an oil formula to help you feel more desirable, you might add a drop of cinnamon oil, a drop of neroli, and a drop of jasmine to an ounce of jojoba oil. This way, you could utilize the combined energies of the three essential oils and safely apply them to the body.

What is the right level of dilution when adding an essential oil to a carrier oil? That probably depends on you, but a good rule of thumb is three or four drops of pure essential oil per ounce of carrier oil. However, ultimately you should use what works for you. If that level of dilution interferes with the scent of the oil you are trying to use, you might want to add more.

While there is no right or wrong carrier oil to use, there are some additional factors to consider. Carrier oils have their own magickal associations, so keep that in mind when picking a carrier oil. Certain oils also last longer than others. Oil is a natural product, so it can and will go rancid over time.

To make the most of your oil blends, store them in dark-colored vials away from sunlight. Ideally you should try to store any blend you create in the refrigerator. Blends kept in the refrigerator will last longer and are less likely to go rancid.

There are dozens of different carrier oils. The following are some of our favorites.

Apricot

Due to their sweet flavor, apricots have a long history in love magick, and apricot oil can be used for this purpose all on its own. Because of its lightly sweet scent, apricot oil is a great carrier oil when creating magickal oil blends to be placed on the skin. Apricot oil is generally edible, but be careful: certain blends of this oil are designed for "cosmetic use only," which means they are harmful if ingested. Apricot oil has a shelf life of about a year.

Avocado

If you are creating an oil blend to apply to the skin, avocado oil is another good choice. Avocado oil will help hydrate dry skin, but on the downside, it can exacerbate acne problems. Avocados have been associated with love and beauty for thousands of years, making avocado oil an excellent carrier oil for blends focusing on sex, desire, and romance. In the refrigerator, avocado oil will solidify and has a shelf life of about a year.

Coconut

Generally solid at room temperature (anything over 75 degrees Fahrenheit), coconut oil is an ideal carrier oil when creating oil blends to be used on the body. It's easier to work with than jojoba wax because it liquefies at a fairly comfortable temperature, making adding other oils to it a breeze. Coconut oil has a reasonably long shelf life of two years, and since most people keep it in their refrigerator, it often lasts even longer than that.

Commercially, there are two types of coconut oil available in most grocery stores: refined and unrefined. Unrefined coconut oil is ideal for magickal use. It contains no additives or chemicals and is generally 100 percent natural. The only downside to it is that it smells like coconuts. Depending on how you feel about coconuts, this could be a good thing. Refined coconut oil has very little smell but is created using a chemical process. Because of this, most magickal practitioners prefer to use unrefined coconut oil in their oil blends.

Magickally, the scent of coconut oil conjures up images of summer vacations and lazy days spent at the beach. Coconuts are traditionally associated with chastity and protection. That first one is kind of a surprise and is why we don't recommend using coconut oil as a carrier if you're trying to use essential oils to kick-start your libido.

Grapeseed (Grape Seed)

Grapeseed oil comes from grapes and is a by-product of wine making. It doesn't have much of a scent and is very lightweight. For these reasons it's a popular carrier oil. The downside to grapeseed oil is that it has a very short shelf life of only three months or so when not stored in the refrigerator. If you use grapeseed oil to make an oil blend, you should plan on using your oil quickly.

Grapeseed oil is rich in the energies of fertility and abundance—perfect for bringing more wealth into your life. When grapeseed oil is used as a carrier oil, it will add its attributes to any oil you combine it with.

Jojoba

Jojoba is sold commercially as both an oil and a wax, both of which come from jojoba seeds. (The jojoba plant is native to the American Southwest.) Other essential oils can be added to either form. Jojoba wax is especially handy if you want to create a balm using essential oils.

Jojoba oil has a very long shelf life, making it a great carrier oil. An oil blend utilizing jojoba will last for years without much fuss. Refined jojoba oil is odor-free, which is another reason it's such a popular carrier oil. (Unrefined jojoba oil has a slight odor to it.) In blends, jojoba is most compatible with oils whose energies are associated with love or healing.

Olive

One of the best things about oil olive is that most of us already have a bottle of it in our homes. The downside to olive oil is that its shelf life is less than many of the other oils on this list. In other words, if you are putting together an oil blend that you want to keep for a couple of years, olive oil is the wrong choice.

Olive oil also has its own scent, not powerful enough to overwhelm a pure essential oil but strong enough that you'll often be aware of its presence. Olive oil has a strong link to the gods of ancient Greece and can be used on its own to invoke energies related to protection, abundance, and knowledge.

Sunflower

Sunflower oil is another readily available oil that can be purchased inexpensively. Its energy is bright and sunny, and unless you are making an oil blend designed to contact the dead, sunflower is compatible with just about everything. Sunflower oil does not have a particularly long shelf life, normally about two years in an unopened bottle and one year in an opened one.

Sweet Almond

There are two types of almond oil, bitter and sweet, and each is made from a different type of almond. Bitter almond oil is hard to find and is not used by many magickal practitioners. As a carrier oil, sweet almond has some drawbacks. It has a relatively short shelf life, as little as six months in some cases. It also has a pretty strong scent, meaning it will mask some essential oils that have lighter scents.

On the plus side, almond oil is very good for the skin and smells nice all on its own. It's a great carrier oil if you are going to be anointing the body. It's also good on its own for magickal work dealing with money and prosperity.

Common Magickal Oil Blends

The most common types of oil blends for magickal use come from Hoodoo. The roots of Hoodoo are African, but the practice also contains some American and

European elements. Hoodoo originated in the American South, but during the early twentieth century it spread across the United States as the African American population moved around the country.

Most named Hoodoo oil blends have been commercially available for the last hundred-plus years, but the formulations used to make those blends vary from manufacturer to manufacturer. Most of the blends listed in this section began with traditional Hoodoo practitioners, but with the rise of mail-order catalogs, the sale of such oils began to be dominated by large companies whose links to Hoodoo (and the African American community) were often suspect at best.

In our own practice, we make extensive use of these oils and are lucky that Matt trained in the tradition. If you buy your oils from a reputable magickal store or manufacturer, it's likely that your oil blend has been infused with magickal energy. If you can't trace the origin of the oil blend you are using, your oil might not be as powerful. In the next chapter we include our own formulas for some of these blends.

Many oil blends have rather obvious names. An oil named Happy Home doesn't need much in the way of explanation. For that reason, we've only included oils with names that leave something to the imagination here.

Adam and Eve Oil (Adam and Steve Oil, Anna and Eve Oil, etc.)

Many practitioners of Hoodoo identify as Christians, and the names of many Hoodoo oils contain biblical references. Adam and Eve oil is one of the oldest traditional Hoodoo blends and can be used to attract a partner or mend fences between lovers after a fight.

As our world becomes more inclusive, the name of this oil is now known by variants such as Adam and Steve oil and Anna and Eve oil. The properties of the oil remain the same, but the new names break down the gender binary.

Altar Oil

If you are looking for an oil to consecrate your altar or your magickal tools, Altar oil is the oil for you! It can also be used to help facilitate a fresh start in business, relationships, or simply life as a whole.

Be Gone Oil/Keep Away Oil

There are dozens of different names and formulations for this type of oil, but all of them are designed to rid unwanted people and energies from your life. (Jason's favorite is Dorothy Morrison's Bitch Be Gone oil, and he can vouch for its effectiveness.) Be Gone oil can be used in any magick done for banishment. It's also effective at removing evil and vindictive energies.

Bewitching Oil

Another blend available in a variety of formulations, Bewitching oil is designed to entice others romantically. If you are looking to seduce a date, dab some Bewitching oil on your neck and wrists so it can work its magick on your prospective lover. Don't have a date? Bewitching oil can also be used to attract a partner.

Black Cat Oil

Black Cat oil brings luck and protection, the opposite of its namesake. Traditionally it was used by gamblers and is thought to reverse bad luck.

Blockbuster Oil

Similar to Road Opener oil but more explosive is Blockbuster oil, which is designed to remove major, deep-rooted obstacles that stand in your path. The removal of these obstacles will often have major repercussions, so such magickal operations should be done with care. (When we talk about major changes here, we mean things like cutting a family member out of your life or perhaps breaking up with a partner.) We think of Blockbuster oil as magickal dynamite, which is why it's effective but also why it can have major consequences.

Crown of Success Oil

One of the oldest oil blends, Crown of Success oil brings about victory in both the magickal and business spheres. Crown of Success oil can help make your hexes more effective and weaken the defenses of those working magick against you. Before heading out on a new adventure, add a few drops of Crown of Success oil to your shoes to ensure good fortune on your journey.

Road Opener Oil

After Van Van oil, Road Opener oil is probably the second most popular Hoodoo blend. It's designed to subtly create new opportunities in life. Matt describes it as "cutting your way through a jungle with a machete." Road Opener oil should be used when you are starting a new endeavor or looking to make a life change.

Uncrossing Oil

Another oil that comes in a variety of formulations, Uncrossing oil is designed to remove hexes and jinxes. It can also be worn on the body when entering an unwelcoming space. If you've got a lot of enemies at work or have to be around others who are jealous of your success, apply a dab or two of Uncrossing oil to keep unwanted energies away.

Van Van Oil

Developed in New Orleans, Louisiana, Van Van oil's first formulation was simply alcohol with lemongrass oil. As the popularity of Van Van spread around the country, various formulations arose. Van Van oil might be the most popular oil in Conjure, and that popularity has extended to many other magickal traditions.

Van Van oil is used for cleansing, to attract money and love, and to create new opportunities. It is an *everything* oil and will amplify whatever spellwork you are attempting. Van Van oil often smells like a cleaning product, and over the last hundred years it has been added to household cleansers and mop water to rid homes of negativity.

Incense

It's hard to imagine Witch ritual without incense. Not only do the various scents we burn in ritual enchant the olfactory nerves, but the coiling smoke that spills out from our incense is captivating as well. In a world full of cell phones, print-on-demand rituals, and electric candles, there's something romantic and timeless about incense. In many cases, today's incense is essentially the same as it was hundreds or even thousands of years ago.

Incense has a transformative power that's often overlooked. Our coven uses a proprietary incense blend created by Ari, and simply lighting that incense puts all of us into a ritual state of mind almost immediately. While working on the spells in this book, we'd often light that particular incense for inspiration and to activate our inner Witch. Doing so transformed work meetings (writing a book is hard work, no matter how much fun it might seem) into magickal gatherings where we simply lost ourselves in the spellwork and forgot about word counts and deadlines.

When we consider what incense does in ritual or magickal workings, the first thing we think of is *atmosphere*. Incense transforms mundane spaces into magickal ones. Most of us tend to reserve incense for specific occasions. In our case, those occasions are usually attached to our Witchcraft. We've tried alternatives to incense over the years, such as oil diffusers and scented candles, but nothing seems to work as well.

In addition to creating atmosphere, incense is often used for cleansing. If there's incense burning on our magickal altar, it's probably going to be used to purify the space we are working in and often the participants in that space as well. Incense is also frequently used to cleanse magickal tools and other items.

Incense is more powerful than many believe. In an initiation ritual in their book *A Witches' Bible* (originally published as *The Witches' Way*), Janet and Stewart Farrar list another use for incense: "to welcome and encourage good spirits, and to banish evil spirits."[26] We assume that good spirits are as enchanted by incense as we are and that its use encourages them to visit during ritual and spellcraft. The banishing aspects of incense are related to its purifying powers, and that power is why you see Catholic priests swinging censers before church services.

For most of us, incense is an *accompaniment* in spellwork. Most of us don't do spells with just incense, and in many cases we don't even really think about what we are burning, but that's shortsighted. Rose incense, assuming it's made from actual rose oil, contains all the energy of rose oil or dried rose petals. When burned, it releases energy that attracts love and makes us love ourselves just a little bit more. The incense is working magick, whether we realize it or not.

Generally, since a stick of rose incense contains more charcoal and wood than essence of rose does, the energy released by burning rose incense is subtle. It's not going to bring us love on its own, but when its energies are added to a red candle, rose oil, a piece of rose quartz, and our own wills, then we've got a super powerful spell. When doing magick focused on a particular goal or objective, it's a good idea to accompany that work with the right incense.

Traditionally, the most common substance used to make incense is resin, a dried plant secretion (most typically sap from trees). Incenses such as frankincense, dragon's blood, copal, and myrrh all come from trees, and tree incenses are by far the most popular types of incense. Resin is usually yellow to brown in color and is sold in small pieces. (Technically, anything that burns could be a form of incense, but that doesn't mean what you are burning will smell good!)

A lot of us still burn resin, but it's been eclipsed in popularity by ready-to-go forms of incense such as sticks and cones. There's nothing wrong with a stick or cone, but instead of resin, the active ingredient in these types of incense tends to

---

26. Janet and Stewart Farrar, *A Witches' Bible: The Complete Witches' Handbook* (Custer, WA: Phoenix Publishing, 1996), 20. Originally published in 1984 as *The Witches' Way*.

be essential oils. If you are buying twenty sticks of incense for a dollar, it's likely that the oil being used for that incense is synthetic, which means it will probably smell like whatever name is on the package but won't actually be made from that substance.

Are synthetic incenses effective? Maybe? The smell of frankincense will probably put you in a particular state of mind, but we doubt that the scent will contain all the power and energy of *Boswellia sacra*, the tree that frankincense resin comes from. If you are going to burn some incense to accompany some serious spellwork, we advise using natural types of incense. If you are using incense primarily to create a certain atmosphere, artificial incense is probably fine.

While incense is common at many Witchcraft rites, it's best to check in with folks before lighting it. There are many people who are allergic to incense, especially to the glues and other binders used to create cone and stick incenses. Even if the oil used to make the incense is natural, the glues are not.

Though most of us burn incense to utilize its magickal properties, it can also be added to sachets and spell bags in its whole form. This generally works best when adding a resin incense, or a wood incense such as palo santo. Carrying a small pouch with a piece or two of resin inside is also a great way to utilize the energy of an incense without burning it. We'll talk more about sachets in chapter 15.

Types of Incense

There are two basic types of incense. The first is *direct*, or *combustible*, incense. Direct incense is incense that does not require a source of heat. When you light a piece of direct incense, such as a cone or a stick, it will produce incense smoke until it burns out and requires very little supervision. *Indirect*, or *noncombustible*, incense requires a secondary source of heat, usually a piece of charcoal. With indirect incense, the raw material (generally resin) is placed directly on whatever is being used to generate heat and then must be re-added at periodic intervals to maintain the smoke.

Which type of incense is better? That's up to the individual Witch. There's certainly an ease of use to most types of direct incense. You simply light your incense and get a steady stream of smoke. One of the downsides to direct incense is that you can't control the amount of smoke being produced (outside of simply lighting more of it). If you are looking to produce billowing amounts of myrrh smoke, you can do that with indirect incense. When it comes to incense, what matters most is personal preference, though the varieties of incense available today do have some notable differences.

Sticks

The most common form of incense today is the incense stick. These sticks are generally made of bamboo and then coated with a paste containing both the burning agent and the desired scent of the incense. Most stick incense contains either sawdust or charcoal dust as the burning agent, with the aromatic materials composed primarily of resin, essential oils, or synthetic materials. Most stick incenses also contain saltpeter (potassium nitrate) to promote even burning.

Many of the companies that produce incense sticks use natural materials and avoid synthetic ingredients and scents. If you stick with natural-sounding types of incense, you'll probably have good results. If you buy "cotton candy" or "pina colada" scented incense, you are probably getting something that's mostly synthetic.

One of the nicest things about stick incense is that it can be picked up and moved around easily. For this reason it's an especially attractive incense to use when blessing tools, objects, and people. The ash collected from stick incense also has magickal uses. If you are burning an incense with protective energy, pick up the ash and sprinkle it around the outside of your home for extra security.

Stick incense can be messy, and the majority of incense holders available from commercial retailers are more decorative than effective. If you like stick incense but want to avoid the mess, place your incense in a seven-day candle that is mostly burned down. You can poke the non-burning end of the stick into the wax and then watch the ashes fall harmlessly into the candle jar.

Cone

Cone incense isn't much different from stick incense, though it absolutely requires a heatproof container to rest on. Like sticks, cones are made from sawdust or charcoal dust, some sort of glue (which can be natural or synthetic), and usually essential oils or some other form of aromatic. If you buy your cone incense from a reputable metaphysical or Witch shop, it's probably made from mostly natural ingredients. If you buy colored cone incense from a chain store, it's probably mostly made out of synthetic materials.

Over the years we've seen a lot of people burn incense cones in unsafe ways, which is frustrating because a container for cone incense is easy enough to make. All that's required is a small plate or bowl with some sand on it. Position your cone upright in the sand and you are good to go! The ash that's left over can easily be scooped out of the sand when the incense is done burning.

Coil

Coil incense is a lot like stick incense except there's no actual stick; instead, resin is added to an incense paste and some sort of combustible material, generally made of charcoal or a petroleum product. Coil incense is fragile, takes up a lot of room, and can be kind of messy, which is why it doesn't show up on too many altars. However, it is easy to light, typically burns for a much longer period of time than stick incense, and is purer since there is no burning bamboo mixed in with the incense smoke.

Powder

The type of incense we use in our coven work is a powder. Powdered incense contains finely ground resins and other materials mixed with some form of burning agent. Some incense powders contain charcoal or sawdust, but there are some far more clever solutions. The incense we use contains tree bark as the burning agent. The advantage to this is that there is no saltpeter, glue, or other binding agent added. Because there's not much filler used to make powdered incense, its energies are generally stronger than what is produced by stick, cone, or coil incense. The bark used in our incense actually adds to its scent in a positive way.

We use powdered incense because Ari is allergic to the binders used in most forms of combustible incense. This makes it a good choice if anyone you work with is sensitive to artificial ingredients. The only downside to many types of powdered incense is that they don't burn particularly well. Even the smallest amount of moisture can make them finicky about burning. Unlike most forms of direct incense, powdered incense usually requires a little bit of attention to keep it burning.

Indirect (Noncombustible) Incense

Indirect incense is the oldest type of incense and the most natural. There are no glues or binding agents in noncombustible incense; all you need is whatever incense you are burning and a piece of charcoal. Because you are burning nothing but pure resin or aromatic herbs, this type of incense generates the greatest amount of energy. If you are using incense as an offering to a deity or other higher power or want to use it to help power a particular spell, indirect incense is your best bet.

The most common type of indirect incense to burn is resin. Resin burns cleanly, and when it's done burning, all that will be left is the charcoal it burned upon. Many indirect incense blends contain aromatic herbs and other materials. This is certainly acceptable; however, after a while dried plant material will eventually just smell like burning. In small amounts it's probably fine, but if you buy an indirect incense that looks more like something for your herbal apothecary, you'll end up with a lot of charred (and smelly) material at the end of your rite.

Indirect incense has some other drawbacks as well. Resin burns rather quickly, and if you want to keep your incense going during spellwork, you may have to burn more resin than you'd like. Charcoal discs also don't have particularly long burn times, so a long rite might require the lighting of a second or third disc.

"Instant lighting" charcoal discs are increasingly popular, but they contain saltpeter, so they aren't completely natural. You can still buy 100 percent natural charcoal discs (generally made from bamboo), but such discs are more difficult to light. It goes without saying that charcoal should only be used with an incense burner or when placed upon a plate covered with sand. (Charcoal discs are not the same as the charcoal briquets used on a grill. Briquets should never be used indoors, while charcoal discs are designed for in-home use.)

When choosing an incense, pick what bests suits your needs. Do you require convenience and ease of use? Sticks of incense are probably best. Do you want a lot of smoke or are you trying to avoid unnatural ingredients? Then indirect incense is probably for you. Whatever you do, try to buy incense that's as natural as possible and avoid the chemicals.

Common Incenses

Here are many of the more common resin incenses, along with a few that frequently show up in cone or stick form. In addition to what we list here, there are a variety of herbs that are used as incense, too. Before burning anything, do some research and make sure what you are burning is not poisonous.

Benzoin

Benzoin has a slightly sweet scent, like vanilla, and is burned for protection and prosperity, making it a great everyday incense.

To bring a little extra financial and physical security to your home, start every month by purifying your house with benzoin. This is most easily done with incense sticks but can be done with the resin version, provided the benzoin and charcoal are burned on a sturdy dish lined with sand. Benzoin is also used by many to promote psychic ability, making it the perfect incense for tarot card readings.

Copal

Copal is native to Central America and was originally used by both the Aztecs and the Maya. For this reason it's sacred to the folk saint Santa Muerte and can be burned as an offering to her. Copal has a slightly woody smell, like pine.

Traditionally copal was used for healing, so it's a great accompaniment to healing spells. It's also an excellent smoke to use for cleansing and purification, and its ability to clear away negative energy makes it useful for protection. There are many Witches who use copal when cleansing stones and crystals.

Dragon's Blood

Dragon's blood gets its name from its dark red color. The resin comes from dragon trees, which are native to Europe and Asia. Dragon's blood has been used for spiritual and medicinal purposes for thousands of years. Because of its use in healing, it's often sold as a health supplement.

Not surprisingly, dragon's blood is burned during healing spells, but it's equally common in love and relationship spells. A potent incense, it can also be used to increase the libido. We recommend burning dragon's blood during lovemaking to spice up your sexual encounters.

There are many who find the smell of dragon's blood pleasant, but there are also those who actively dislike it. Descriptions of the smell of dragon's blood range from musky to sweet.

Frankincense

Having grown up in the Catholic Church, Ari often describes the smell of frankincense as "church." The pungent scent of frankincense has made it one of the most well-known incenses in the world, and it's used by a wide variety of religious practitioners. There's something very authoritative and focused about frankincense, making it a great incense to use during "serious" rituals, such as at Samhain.

Frankincense smoke is cleansing and purifying and is perfect for getting rid of unwanted energies and entities in the home, such as a spirit trapped in this world. Frankincense was traditionally associated with wealth, and because of this it shows up in a well-known (New Testament) Bible story. This categorization is still one we use in our magickal work, and we often burn frankincense when working on job or money spells.

Gum Arabic

Gum arabic comes from the acacia tree, which has been used for various magickal and spiritual purposes for thousands of years, from India to Egypt. Gum arabic is probably best known today as a binder (hence *gum*), which makes it a useful incense to burn when looking for a relationship or trying to get a new habit to "stick."

Gum arabic is frequently used for protection and for increasing psychic powers. It has a light fruity and/or nutty scent.

Myrrh (also Sweet Myrrh)

Myrrh is an exceedingly common form of incense but is generally burned in conjunction with something else. This is probably because many people find the smell of myrrh unpleasant. (Its scent is often described as "medicinal.") Myrrh is traditionally burned during meditation or when greater clarity is needed. Because of its scent, it's also useful in healing spells. Like most of the incenses in this list, myrrh is also used for purification and protection.

Sweet myrrh, or *opopanax*, is myrrh's more aromatic cousin. Because of its pleasant scent, sweet myrrh can be burned to inspire good feelings and a sense of calm and to promote feelings of hospitality. It can also be used to attract positive energy, whether in the home or in ritual space.

Nag Champa

Nag champa is one of the most common incense blends and is made from two main ingredients: sandalwood and frangipani. It comes from India, where it's been used in Hindu and Buddhist rituals for centuries. Nag champa can be found in magickal supply stores and head shops around the world.

How nag champa influences magick probably depends on what you associate it with. Back in their college days, Jason and Ari came to associate the scent of nag champa with friends who listened to jam bands and wore hemp shoes (not that there's anything wrong with either of those things). Traditionally nag champa is burned for protection and to aid in spiritual enlightenment.

Palo Santo

Palo santo is a tree native to South America whose name translates as "holy wood." It's traditionally used for healing and to rid spaces of negative energy, and it's usually burned as a piece of wood, much like one would burn a bundle of sage. However, unlike sage, palo santo does not stay lit for long periods of time and typically requires frequent relighting.

Palo santo has become increasingly popular over the last ten years and is used by a wide variety of wellness practitioners. Because of its current popularity, *where* your palo santo comes from is a big concern. Is it being harvested ethically and in a sustainable way or are people clear-cutting trees? Using palo santo from an ethical source will make your magick that much stronger.

Patchouli

Unlike most of the incenses in this list, patchouli incense is derived from oils extracted from the leaves of the patchouli plant, which is native to tropical parts of Asia. Patchouli has a wide variety of magickal uses but is primarily used to attract abundance. It can attract lovers (it's a lust scent, not a love one) and help bring wealth and prosperity.

Patchouli has a sweet, musky smell, but, like nag champa, its presence in metaphysical stores and head shops causes many people to associate the smell with marijuana. (Patchouli has long been used to cover up the smell of burning marijuana.) If the smell of patchouli makes you giggle or think of the Grateful Dead, you should probably burn something else during your magickal work.

Sandalwood

Sandalwood is generally burned as powdered wood, though it's also available in chip form. It is often used for protection but can also be used to facilitate interaction with higher powers such as deities or angels. Because of sandalwood's popularity, it is often harvested unethically and is endangered in many of its traditional Asian habitats.

Sandalwood chips are especially useful in magickal practice. If you write an intention on a piece of sandalwood and then burn it in small censer or cauldron, not only will your intention be released out into the world but your ritual space will also be blessed with the earthy scent of sandalwood smoke.

Chapter Fourteen
Spells by Scent and Smoke

Oil and incense are generally accompaniments to magick. Unlike candles or even stones, they rarely take center stage on their own. Because of that, this chapter includes a few formulations and ritual techniques that fall outside the realm of general spellwork.

Egyptian Ritual Anointing Oil

Several different sets of Egyptian hieroglyphs make mention of "seven sacred oils" named *setji-beb, hekenu, seftji, nekhnem, twat, hatet-ash,* and *hatet-tjehenu.* Of those seven oils, there is only one whose identity can be confirmed: *hatet-ash* is cedar or pine oil. Despite the fact that we do not know exactly what the other six sacred oils were, we do know what they were used for in ancient Egypt. The oils were used to anoint the bodies of the dead as the deceased prepared to move into the afterlife.

This recipe utilizes some of the most popular scents in ancient Egypt, along with oils found on the mummies of the dead. This version of Egyptian anointing oil contains seven different oils blended together to honor the idea of the seven sacred oils. The best part of this oil is that we are using it here for the living. It's designed to be used for any situation that calls for "walking between the worlds," such as sabbat rituals or initiation and elevation rituals.

To make this oil blend you will need:

- Cardamom oil
- Cassia oil
- Cedar oil
- Chamomile oil
- Cinnamon oil
- Frankincense oil

- Myrrh oil
- A 15 milliliter brown bottle (about one ounce), clean and sterilized
- A dropper
- Olive oil (as a carrier oil)

Most essential oils are sold with a dropper included or are designed so that only one drop of oil can be shaken out of the bottle at a time. One drop is generally about one-twentieth of a milliliter, though the size will vary from dropper to dropper.

For this oil blend you want to add two drops each of the seven essential oils (cardamom, cassia, cedar, chamomile, cinnamon, frankincense, and myrrh) to your clean and sterilized brown bottle. Top off the bottle with olive oil (approximately 14 milliliters) and shake. Alternatively, the oils can all be mixed in one bowl and gently swirled together, but shaking the bottle to mix generally works well enough.

At the start of ritual, anoint each participant by drawing an invoking pentagram with the oil on their forehead. The oil will help facilitate travel between the worlds and make your magick stronger. When you are done with the oil, store it in the refrigerator to keep it from going rancid.

Matt's Van Van Oil

Formulas for Van Van oil vary, but nearly every formulation is heavy on sweetgrass and citronella oils, and Matt's formula is no different. For extra potency, this formula includes more than just oils. To make your own Van Van oil you will need:

- Dried lemongrass
- A 1 dram bottle
- At least one pyrite chip
- A dropper
- Lemongrass essential oil
- Citronella essential oil
- Palmarosa essential oil
- Vetiver essential oil
- Sweet almond oil (as a carrier oil)

Begin by adding a pinch of the dried lemongrass to your bottle, followed by the pyrite chip(s). The lemongrass adds extra cleansing power to your Van Van oil, while the pyrite is used to attract good fortune.

Formulations for Van Van oil are often a matter of personal preference. Matt suggests using seven drops of lemongrass oil, one or two drops of citronella, one drop of palmarosa, and a drop or two of vetiver. Start with the lemongrass before moving on to the other scents. Before adding a second drop of citronella or vetiver, check to make sure your first drop did not mask the scent of the lemongrass. No matter the exact formulation you use, lemongrass should be the dominant scent in your blend.

Once you've added all your essential oils, top off your bottle with the sweet almond oil and shake. Store in a refrigerator or a cool spot free of excessive sunlight. Van Van is a multiuse oil and can be used for just about everything!

Protection Oil

This is an easy-to-make protection oil that you can use in spellwork and apply directly to both yourself and any items you want to keep safe. If you dab it on your own skin, we suggest applying it to your temples or wrists.

To make this oil you will need:

- A small piece of dragon's blood resin
- A 1 dram bottle
- 13 drops frankincense oil
- 9 drops myrrh oil
- 7 drops dragon's blood oil
- 3 drops rue oil
- Sweet almond oil (as a carrier oil)
- A fingernail clipping (optional)

Place your small bit of dragon's blood resin in your bottle and then top with the recommended amounts of oil. If there are certain scents you like more than others, it's fine to adjust the number of drops accordingly. After the essential oils have been added, top off the bottle with sweet almond oil and shake.

If you are using the oil primarily to protect yourself or your home, add a fingernail clipping to your blend so its energies will more closely align with your own.

Moon Oil

This oil blend is especially useful when trying to harness the power of the moon or working with moon goddesses or gods. If you are trying to invoke a goddess, anoint yourself with this oil to increase the chances of her fully showing up.

To make this oil blend you will need:

- A chip of moonstone (optional but recommended)
- A 1 dram bottle
- 8 drops jasmine oil
- 4 drops rose oil
- 4 drops sandalwood oil
- The carrier oil of your choice

Place your moonstone chip in the bottle, then top with the jasmine, rose, and sandalwood oils. If you like one particular scent more than the others, it's fine to adjust a little bit here and there, but don't go light on the jasmine! Jasmine blooms only at night, making it a powerful ally when working with the moon. Top off the bottle with the carrier oil of your choice.

When you are done blending your oil, place your bottle outside on the night of a full moon to charge.

Refreshing Spritz

This oil blend is designed to be added to water to spray or spritz around your home. To make this spritz you will need:

- 15 drops peppermint oil
- 5 drops rosemary oil
- 5 drops eucalyptus oil
- 3 drops camphor oil or 2 drops lavender oil
- A 2 ounce spray bottle
- Filtered water

Drop your oils directly into your spray bottle and then top off with filtered water. Filtered water is ideal because it's generally free of scents, chemicals, and minerals, all things that have the potential to change the scent and magickal properties of your spritz. If you don't have access to filtered water (or are just in a bind), tap water is fine though not ideal.

To use your spritz, shake the bottle well before using and spray anywhere that needs an energetic recharge. This spray works great to clear a room of negativity or reinvigorate your bedsheets after a night of bad dreams. You can also spray it directly on yourself when you need a pick-me-up or some mental clearly. If you spray it on yourself, be sure to steer clear of your eyes and mouth.

Oil Blend for Creative Inspiration

This oil blend is great for bringing inspiration when you are stuck while working on a creative project. We used it while writing this book! For this oil blend you will need:

- 4 drops bergamot oil
- 4 drops sandalwood oil
- 4 drops lemon oil
- 4 drops clary sage oil
- A 1 dram bottle (optional)
- Filtered water (optional)

You have options when creating this oil blend. The first is to add your drops of bergamot, sandalwood, lemon, and clary sage directly to your oil diffuser and then top with water. The second is to add the four oils to a 1 dram bottle and then top it off with water. If you find yourself really enjoying this blend, mixing a big batch of it in a bottle will make using it easier and more convenient.

Shared Spellcraft: Lilith Strength Oil
by Lilith Dorsey

The earliest surviving record of the name of Lilith the goddess comes from the ancient Sumerian poem *Gilgamesh and the Huluppu-Tree,* which dates back to around 2,000 BCE. In the story we find Lilith first connected with both a sacred serpent and a bird. In later myths and tales she begins to be described as a demon. But is she really just a demon, or is she a goddess, or is she both? Very often she is associated with the owl as her familiar, an animal of night who is also a predator and an unseen warrior of the deep darkness.

This oil is designed to bring out the fierce power of Lilith in you. She has claws and teeth to protect what is hers, and you do too.

Ingredients:

- ½ ounce olive oil
- A glass bottle
- 3 strands of saffron
- 6 drops copal oil
- 6 drops myrrh oil

Assemble all the ingredients on your working altar or shrine. Add the olive oil to your bottle. Then add the saffron and the copal and myrrh oils. Rub the bottle quickly between your hands to charge it with your energy. Now it is ready for use.

Lilith Dorsey is an author, blogger, filmmaker, Voodoo Priestess, and psychic. She's also one of Jason and Ari's favorite people and a fine dining companion when visiting a greasy spoon in New Orleans at 2:00 a.m.

Spring Cleaning Spell

This spell will cleanse, protect, and bring blessings to your home. It can be done any time of year, but the best times are when you celebrate the new year or are doing some spring cleaning. For best results, perform this spell once a year.

For this spell you will need:

- 1 camphor square
- Myrrh resin
- Frankincense resin
- A small bowl
- White candles: one for every room of your home if possible (Tealights are fine.)
- Van Van oil
- Charcoal discs
- A portable censer for incense (or a small cauldron or a small dish full of sand)

Start by mixing your incenses: camphor, myrrh, and frankincense. Camphor squares contain far more camphor than you'll want to use for the creation of your incense. Start by breaking off about a quarter of the square and then crumble that square into smaller pieces in your bowl. Add an equal amount of myrrh and frank-incense and mix together.

Anoint all of your candles with Van Van oil. Dress the candles by starting at the top and moving downward in a counterclockwise motion. Once your candles are dressed, open all the windows in your home, or at least one in each room. As you open each window, invoke the power of air:

Spirits of air, be welcome and help me to clear this space!

Leave one candle in every room. Leave your candles in a spot where they won't be disturbed by wind, animals, or anything else that might knock them over.

Light your charcoal in a portable censer or other container that you can easily carry around your home. Small iron cauldrons work well here. Failing that, a small dish full of sand with the charcoal disc on top will work too. Be careful: charcoal is hot! Sprinkle your incense on the charcoal and begin moving through your house, fanning the incense through each room. It's important to be thorough here, so pay special attention to corners and be sure to get under the beds!

After your entire home has been censed, light the candles in each room. While lighting each candle, say:

I invoke blessings and new beginnings in this space!

Let each candle burn for at least half an hour before blowing it out. A lit candle should always be attended, so it might take a few hours to light every candle. (If your home is especially large, you can light the individual candles over the course of several nights.)

If there are parts of your home that don't feel completely refreshed after doing this spell, you can add a salt scrub and give those areas a bit of individual attention. To make a cleansing scrub, you will need:

- Table salt
- Van Van oil
- A small dish of water
- A rag, paper towel, or sponge

Add a couple pinches of salt and a few drops of Van Van oil to your small dish of water. For extra energy, mix your ingredients together with your athame or other ritual tool (such as a wand). Once everything is blended, apply the water to the most troublesome areas of your home and wipe in a counterclockwise motion to remove unwanted energies.

Tool Cleansing

While Witches don't *need* tools, they do make doing magick easier. When we buy tools, we often find ourselves in a big hurry to use them, but cleansing and blessing your tools before using them will make them more effective. Why cleanse and bless? Cleansing helps remove all the built-up energy on a tool, including the energy it absorbed while being made and shipped. Blessing your tools is a way of dedicating them to your magickal practice, making them more sacred than they might otherwise be.

Using the powers of the four elements (earth, air, fire, and water) is the most basic way of cleansing tools and is what we utilize here. For this exercise you will need:

- Your athame or wand (optional)
- A small bowl of water
- A small dish of salt
- A pentacle (optional)
- A candle
- Frankincense incense
- Lighter or matches

If you have a pentacle, it's customary to place the four elemental items (and later your tools) you will be charging and cleansing upon it. Pentacles are more than just pretty pentagrams; they are doorways to magickal energy. Placing your items on the pentacle will infuse them with positive energy![27]

To begin, you'll want to cleanse your salt and water before mixing them together. Start by placing your athame (or pointer finger on your dominant hand) in the bowl of water and pushing your own energy into it. You are using this energy to cleanse the water of any psychic debris it might contain. Visualize your energy moving through the water, removing anything there that doesn't serve your purpose.

Once the water has been charged by your energy, say:

---

27. Jason spends a lot of time writing about pentacles, including instructions on how to build your own, in *The Witch's Altar*. Sorry for the commercial.

I bless and consecrate thee, O water!
Through my power you are now free of all impurities.
May your powers and energies cleanse and charge all that they touch.
So mote it be!

Cleanse your salt just as you cleansed your water. Push your energy into the salt, removing any negative energy that might be there. Once the salt is cleansed, say:

I bless and consecrate thee, O salt of earth!
Through my power you are now free of all impurities.
May your power and energies cleanse and charge all that they touch.
So mote it be!

Using your athame (or wand or finger), place three measures of salt into the water. While placing the salt in your water, say:

Water and earth become one in this cauldron.

Mix the salt in the water with the athame.

Place whatever kind of incense you are using (and its holder, most likely) on your pentacle or altar. Touch the incense with the tip of your athame just as you touched the water and the salt, sending your own cleansing energy into it. Once the incense has been cleansed, say:

I bless and consecrate thee, O incense of air!
Through my power you are now free of all impurities.
May your power and energies cleanse and charge all that they touch.
So mote it be!

Repeat with the candle, touching it with the athame to cleanse it. As you light the candle say:

I bless and consecrate thee O candle of fire!
Through my power you are now free of all impurities;
May your powers and energies cleanse and charge all that they touch.
So mote it be!

Light your incense with the candle and say:

Air and fire have now joined as one.

Your salted water and incense are now ready to cleanse your tools (and can also be used to cleanse yourself and anyone else you are working magick with). Begin by picking up the first tool to be cleansed. As you hold it in your hand, take a moment to really look at your tool and feel it in your hand. Practice using your tool for its intended purpose. If you are cleansing a wand, draw a banishing or invoking pentagram. If you are cleansing a bell, ring the bell gently. Take a moment to connect with your tool on an energetic level.

Once the connection has been made, place the tool on your altar or pentacle and sprinkle it with the salted water. As you sprinkle the tool, say:

> *I cleanse and consecrate this tool that it may serve me in my practice of Witchcraft.*
> *I remove from it all that is unwanted and leave only that which will serve me.*
> *So mote it be!*

Be sure to flip your tool over so the salted water touches both sides of it.

When you are done with the water, pick up your tool and run it through the incense smoke. Move slowly, letting the smoke touch every inch of the item. As you move the tool through the smoke, say:

> *I cleanse and consecrate this tool that it may serve me in my practice of Witchcraft.*
> *I remove from it all that is unwanted and leave only that which will serve me.*
> *So mote it be!*

Your tool is cleansed and ready for use. If it's made of metal, be sure to wipe the salted water from it so it is not damaged.

Tool Oil Blessing

In Gerald Gardner's 1949 fiction book *High Magic's Aid*, a picture of an athame is shown with a variety of magickal symbols on its hilt. Nearly all the symbols there come from the fifteenth-century grimoire the *Key of Solomon* and make appearances in both Witchcraft and other magickal traditions. Because of Gardner's inclusion of this image, many Witches carve symbols into their tools, especially their athames.

For many of us, carving or drawing permanent symbols on our tools is undesirable. We like our athames as they are, thank you very much. However, symbols and images have power and can help charge a magickal tool. If you'd like to add a little extra power to your tools, you can add nonpermanent sigils and symbols to them using oil.

For this blessing all you'll need is some sort of oil you associate with consecrating items. We suggest basil, allspice, frankincense, or the Egyptian oil at the beginning of this chapter. Whatever you use, just be sure it resonates with you. And if it's an essential oil that's harmful to the skin, be sure to use a carrier oil.

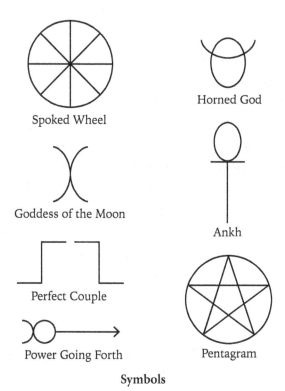

Spoked Wheel

Horned God

Goddess of the Moon

Ankh

Perfect Couple

Power Going Forth

Pentagram

Symbols

There are a variety of different symbols that can be drawn on or carved into your tools, such as the ones pictured here. While certain symbols are more traditional than others, pick the ones you are attracted to. As you trace a symbol onto your tool, imagine that specific power entering the tool and infusing it with that particular energy. Jason, for instance, often draws a Horned God symbol on all his tools and, while doing so, imagines his connections with the god of the wild spaces and his own place in the natural world. While we've included some common symbols here, you can use whatever you wish or even make up your own!

One of the most powerful things you can draw on a tool is your own name or, at the very least, your initials. Drawing your name on your tool marks it as your own and brings that tool more in line with your own personal energies. Try writing your signature with oil on your tool—you'll practically feel your energy rushing into the tool!

While drawing on your tool with oil, verbalize your intention by saying something like this:

> *I infuse this tool with the energy and blessings of the Horned God (or whatever else).*
> *May this tool serve me well in my work and be a valuable ally in my Craft.*
> *So mote it be!*

You can draw as few or as many symbols on your tool as you wish. You can even draw symbols on top of one another; the energy will still enter your tool. All of the symbols included here can be used in the rest of your magickal work, too. They are extremely popular in candle magick, for instance.

Once you have added all the symbols you desire to your tool, either work the oil into your tool or wipe it off, depending on what the oil might do to it. If you are anointing a wooden wand, for instance, rub the oil into the wood to add extra energy to your wand. If you are adding symbols to an athame, you'll probably want to wipe the oil off and then add whatever protective oil you keep on your blade.

While some Witches will do this blessing just once with their tools, we recommend doing it about once a year. Imbolc, with its focus on renewal and preparing for spring, is an excellent time to reanoint your tools and give them a fresh charge of energy.

Shared Spellcraft: Guardian Toy Blessing for Children
by Bader Saab

Once when one of my cousins visited us, the youngest of them all, I wanted to give her a special gift, something that would remind her of me every time she saw it but that would also protect her and call good energies. You wouldn't think it would be easy for an older, gothic cousin like me to find something that a five-year-old girl would like, but it appears that anything is possible!

I asked her if she would like a surprise, and of course she said yes, with excited eyes. When I showed her a Harlequin figure of mine, dressed in wine-purple, green, and gold, she wasn't that enthusiastic, but after assuring her that it was just a different kind of toy, she smiled again.

In an effort to make the figure special, I asked my cousin to pick one of the feathers I had collected (she chose a white one) and an oil with a good aroma (she liked a 30+ herbs mix, the refined little witch) and to give it a name only she could know. "It will be our secret," I told her, and she laughed, excited.

I cleansed the Harlequin figure with the feather, sweeping it from the head to the toes, and she did the same. Finally, she applied just a tiny bit of the oil to the toy's chest, saying, "I name you _____." When I asked if she liked it, she said yes with bright eyes. She left my house with a toy blessed by her and a white feather to cleanse it whenever she wanted to.

Bader Saab is an Arabic witch and journalist with a master's degree about to be finished on digital research. He has worked as a book reviewer and written about pre-Islamic folklore. You can visit him at A Modern Day Sha'ir, *a part of* Patheos Pagan.

Angelica Athame Spell

Magickal spaces attract magickal entities. If you consistently do magickal work in the same place over an extended period of time, it's likely that some otherworldly entities might peek into your circle now and again. Most of the time such entities are benign and are simply attracted to the magick you are creating. But every once in a while, you might end up with an unwanted interloper.

How do you know if you've got a malicious spirit or other unwanted entity in your home? If you feel like something is constantly looking over your shoulder without your permission, you might have a problem. Simply feeling icky energy is another sign that something is wrong. Other signs are unexpected cold spots in otherwise warm rooms and strange and unexplainable sounds. Trust your intuition and how your body feels.

The easiest way to get rid of an unwelcome visitor is to ask it to leave. If that doesn't work, you can beef up your "magickal security" with Witch bottles (see chapter 17) and some of the spells for protection in this book. If you've exhausted all of those options, it's time to break out the angelica oil.

For this spell you will need:

- Angelica oil
- A rag or paper towel
- A tool to project energy, preferably an athame, sword, or wand (If you don't have any of these, a kitchen knife will work, as will the index finger on your dominant hand.)

Place 5–6 drops of angelica oil on a rag or paper towel and wipe down your ritual tool with the oil. Start at the base of the tool and work your way up. If you are anointing an athame, you only have to oil the blade and not the handle. If you plan to use your fingers to apply the angelica oil, we suggest adding the angelica oil to the carrier oil of your choice. A little oil will go a long way, so use sparingly. As you anoint the blade (or other object) with the oil, say:

> *To keep baneful forces at bay,*
> *I shall send evil far away!*

As you anoint your tool, visualize some of your own energy going into it. Between the angelica oil and your own power, the tool should become warm to the touch.

Once the tool is anointed, go to the area of your home with the unwanted entity. Stand in the center of that space, take a deep breath, and feel your own personal energy radiating through you. As you exhale, push that energy out of yourself and through your tool. Visualize it as a blue-white cleansing energy. Imagine its purifying energy burning away all that's unwanted and making your space uninhabitable to undesired forces.

You can say something during this part of the rite, but when we've had to do this, we've generally been too focused on what we were doing to say anything. As the energy spills out of you, it will react with the angelica oil, forming a protective boundary that will repel unwanted spirits and entities. For maximum protection, repeat these steps for three consecutive days, then redo as needed.

If you are in a situation where you feel the unwanted entity near you, it's possible to slash at it with your anointed athame. (I don't recommend using your finger here.) You can't cut a magickal being like you can a mortal one, but the unwanted touch of steel and angelica oil should drive it away. If you find yourself in such a situation, verbalize your intention by saying, "Stay out!" "Keep away from this space!" or "This space belongs to me!" After this, it's unlikely that you'll have further troubles.

Shared Spellcraft: A Spell for Gaining the Home You Desire
by Alura Rose

Buying a home can be challenging. First you have to find the perfect one to fit the needs of you and your family. Then once you've found it, others may want it as well, creating a competition and a race to the finish line. This spell will help you seal the deal, whether you are buying or applying to rent your most perfect home.

Materials needed:

- A green seven-day jar candle
- A picture printed out of the home that you are bidding on or applying for (best if printed on thin paper)
- Scissors

- Glue or Mod Podge
- Decorations for the candle, such as metallic pens or rhinestones (optional)
- A sharp object such as a drill or a wine screw (to drill holes in the wax)
- A small amount of dirt from the property you desire
- Patchouli essential oil
- Small amounts of dried basil, ground cinnamon, and dried peppermint leaves

This spell is best started three days prior to the full moon. Once your candle is prepared for this spell, allow it to burn down completely. You may snuff the candle if you have to leave its presence, but you should burn the candle each day until it can burn no more.

To begin, take the picture of the home you desire and cut it to fit on the outside of your candle. Apply some glue or Mod Podge to the back and press the picture onto the outside of the candle glass. Allow it to dry. Further decorate the outside of the candle however you wish. Each item will add energy to your intention. Try using colored or metallic pens, rhinestones, or other items.

With the top of the candle facing you, use a sharp object to carefully drill three holes in the wax between the wick and the glass. The holes should be about an inch or so deep and about a quarter inch in diameter. Take the dirt that you have collected from your desired home and place some into each of the holes. While you are doing this, visualize your home and what it would feel like to live there. Imagine yourself walking through the front door feeling happy and confident.

Once you have filled the holes with the dirt, place three drops of patchouli essential oil on the top of the candle, being careful not to let it touch the wick. Swirl the drops by moving the candle in a slow clockwise motion. Continue to focus on visualizing your desired home.

Add small amounts (a pinch of each will do) of the basil, cinnamon, and peppermint to the top of the candle. The patchouli essential oil should absorb some of this. In other words, the herbs should look somewhat wet.

Place your candle near a north wall or shelf. Make sure it is in a place where it can safely burn undisturbed.

As you first light your candle, say these words out loud:

> *Goddess, power of three, come and listen to my plea.*
> *As I light this candle so bright, let my intention take flight.*

The home I desire is now near, let the current owners see clear.
This home is mine, I know it true; there is nothing left for me to do.
I light this candle on this day, bring this home to me this way.
An it harm none, so mote it be, this home was made just for me!

Allow the candle to burn over the next three nights at least, remembering to extinguish it whenever you aren't around to watch over it. Allow the candle to burn down completely for best results.

———————————

Alura Rose *is a Witch, professional Tarot and toe reader, herbalist, teacher, and author. Find out more about her and her wares at poisonedapple.org.*

Chapter Fifteen
Knot Magick, Sachets, and Binding

When we were discussing the contents of this book, the chapter that worried us the most was the one you are currently reading. Knot magick? There was even some talk about leaving it out entirely. As we began to outline what exactly we'd be writing about in this chapter, we all slowly came to the realization that knot magick is far more practical and useful than we initially thought. In fact, knot magick applies to a variety of situations and is an especially useful tool in a Witch's cauldron of tricks.

While once a rather popular subject in early Witchcraft books, knot magick is a subject that's rarely untied (sorry!) these days by Witch writers. Much of that is probably because the esthetics of knot magick aren't particularly inspiring. When scrolling through social media, it's common to see pictures of spellwork with candles and herbs laid out on an altar, but a piece of rope with a few knots in it just doesn't have the same visual appeal. Still, knot magick has its own charm, even if it lacks a certain magickal ambience.

What might be most surprising is just how much we use knots in magickal practice without thinking about them. When creating a charm bag or sachet, we tie them shut with a knot. For many Witches, the knot is a throwaway and not something they actively think about as contributing to their magick. But knots are the easy cherry on top of a spell sundae.

We also use knots and cords/rope/ribbon when doing binding spells and often incorporate knots into those types of magick. Herb bundles are also held together by knots and string, and while we generally think of the herbs as being the source of magickal energy in those creations, why not the knots, too? Many of us braid and put knots in our hair on a daily basis, and that's another avenue for knot magick. The magick of knots and cords can be incorporated into all sorts of spellwork.

How Knot Magick Works

Knot magick works differently than many of the other types of magick described in this book. Oils, herbs, and stones all radiate their own natural energies. We often use our own personal power to charge items such as candles to make them more useful in our magickal endeavors. If you charge a candle and then burn it, the candle's energy will be released as it burns down. If you charge a candle and leave it on your altar and never get around to burning it, the energy you've put into it will slowly leak out until it's mostly just a mundane candle again.

By way of contrast, knot magick begins with a mundane cord, a piece of rope, or a length of yarn. Those items all have a bit of their own power, determined by what they are made of and what color they are, but that's not enough energy to create transformative magick. When doing knot magick, we charge the cord or rope with our own power and then begin tying knots into that cord. Knots lock up the energy in a cord. Unlike a candle or other charged object, the knot will retain its energy as long as it remains tied.

The fact that knots retain their energies until they are untied has serious magickal implications. We can access the energy that's contained in a knot by touching it and then absorbing its power. If you want to feel close to a friend or family member, having them tie a few energetic knots will give you access to their personal energy. Many covens work robed, with cords tied around those robes. Having everyone tie a knot in a new convener's cord is a great way to share personal energy.[28]

Knot magick can be done silently, but there's an extra rush of power that comes with tying a knot and speaking aloud your intention. For example, if you were creating a magickal charm to help you study for a big test, you could take a cord and tie knots into it that are representative of the qualities needed to pass your examination. This could be things such as concentration, retention of ideas, focus, energy for the work of studying, and enough time to thoroughly prepare.

You would then take a piece of cord or rope and think about all of those ideas. You would imagine yourself studying and doing well on your test. You'd picture yourself remembering all you need to know in order get the grade you want. And then you'd get into specifics, such as visualizing yourself concentrating intently on your study materials. At this point you would state aloud your desire: "the concentration needed to adequately prepare!" You would tie a knot as you say these words, drawing it tight as you utter "prepare." This traps the energy you need into the knot,

---

28. Jason has written an entire ritual built around a coven tying knots into a cord for a new covener. It shows up in chapter 8 of his book *Transformative Witchcraft*.

where it can then be accessed anytime you touch it. You would then repeat the process, trapping all the energies needed for you to succeed.

A string of knots like the one just described can also be therapeutic and meditative. Before every study session you might go through each knot on your string, repeating the qualities needed for you to do well on your test. Going through your knots in such a way will not only aid your studies but will also add more power to your charm. By touching the knots and reinforcing their meanings, you make them more powerful.

This is similar to praying the rosary in Catholic traditions. The knots reinforce ideas and have certain qualities attributed to them. A similar string of knots can serve as a powerful way to forge relationships with deity or prepare you for magickal work. Examples of this are included in the next chapter.

Knot tying also taps into the magick of numbers. For Christians, the number thirteen is thought to be unlucky. Tying thirteen knots into a magickal charm designed to rid your work environment of a troublesome coworker adds the energy of the number thirteen to your work and makes it that much more likely that your coworker will be dismissed. The number three is related to ideas such as the Triple Goddess (Maiden, Mother, and Crone) and past, present, and future. Finishing a spell and tying a knot for what has been, what is, and what will be connects your spellwork to such larger ideas.

Numbers are believed to have their own meanings and energies. These are some of the more common associations attributed to the numbers 0–9, along with 11 and 13.

0: The absence of everything, a blank slate for a new start

1: The beginning, the eternal source, power, wholeness

2: Duality such as night/day, yin/yang, etc.; also expresses connection to others

3: Representative of creation, new beginnings, the life cycle (birth, life, death), the Triple Goddess

4: The four elements of earth, air, fire, and water; also balance

5: The five points of the pentagram, the five human senses

6: The number of the sun

7: The number of the moon; in folklore, seven was considered an especially important number, with the seventh son of a seventh son believed to have special psychic abilities.

8: The eight sabbats, the Wheel of the Year, the changing of the seasons

9: The number three squared, so all the powers of three magnified; also happiness and manifestation; one of the most common numbers in knot magick

11: Believed by many ceremonial magicians to be the most magickal of numbers

13: Considered unlucky by some, though many Witches believe just the opposite

When working with charm bags and other items tied shut with string or yarn, knots are the final magickal coda. In most cases the bags and other items we close up with knots are designed to stay closed. When tying a bag shut, it's best to fill your final knot with energy designed to keep other people out of your magickal work. If you have no intention of ever opening the bag again, you might tie an espe-cially tight knot and say something like this:

Over and under, up and around, with this knot my charm is now bound!
My knot will keep it free from prying eyes. With that my spell is done.
So mote it be!

Because knots are designed to hold on to energy, the only way to truly release all of their energy is to untie them. If you've used knots in a spell and that spell is now complete, you may find yourself wanting to release the energy contained within those knots back into the universe. When untying knots, it's generally best to untie them in the order in which they were tied (which would be difficult, of course, if you just tied random knots onto a string!). Magick generally builds upward as a spell is being cast, meaning in most instances the most powerful concentrations of energy are in the last knots you tied. Going from first to last keeps you from being overwhelmed by a big blast of energy.

Materials and Techniques for Knot Magick

When selecting material to use in a knot spell, we believe the choice is up to you and your current circumstances. In most cases you'll probably find yourself using whatever you have lying around the house, which is fine! Like many other Witches, we believe that natural fibers work best, but synthetic is fine if that's all you have. Finding yarn made from all-natural materials is pretty easy, but less so with ribbon. If you do have to use synthetic materials, make sure there are no plans to burn your magickal project. An herb bundle tied together with synthetic material is a disaster waiting to happen!

When working with knot magick, most of us will probably be using premade string, yarn, or rope, but there's something satisfying about creating your own cords. If you want to use thicker cords for your magickal work, using yarn to create your own cords will greatly enhance their magickal energy. While weaving a cord, simply visualize yourself doing your magickal work and push that energy into the yarn you are using.

The phrase "cut the cord" is not just an expression for leaving home as a young adult but can also be applied to magick. Magick works best when it neatly symbolizes something we are going through, and nearly all of us have been in situations where it's time to cut something or someone out of our lives. This type of magick can be accomplished rather easily with a length of twine or rope and a pair of scissors or an athame.

To cut someone or something out of your life magickally with a cord, write the name of the person (or thing) you are trying to remove from your life on one end of the cord. If that's not possible (such as with a very slender piece of twine), attach the person's name or picture to one end of the cord. On the other end of the cord, write your own name (or attach your name or picture to it). Think about your need to leave this person behind and then cut the cord with your athame or scissors. Place the two strands of cord on your altar and slowly move them apart over the next few days, further cementing your new disassociation.

This type of magick can be used to cut all sorts of things out your life and doesn't require much in the way of supplies. It's rather simple magick, but it works! A more elaborate version of this technique is included in the "Cut Them Out!" spell in the next chapter.

Not quite knot or cord magick but included here because they, too, utilize cords/yarn/etc., are weaving and braiding. Both weaving and braiding join two or more pieces of fiber together to form one continuous whole, although braids tend to be less permanent structures than pieces that are woven together. When many of us hear the word *braiding*, we think of hair braids, which are usually easy to undo. Trying to take apart a woven shirt would be a much more involved process. What's great about weaving and braiding is that they can both be used for magickal purposes anytime you want to join two different kinds of energy.

Braiding your hair, or having someone else do it for you, is a powerful way to carry a bit of extra magick with no one being the wiser. While the braiding is being done, all you have to do is chant and visualize whatever it is you are trying to accomplish. Before a job interview you might create a few braids while chanting "poise and confidence," qualities that are desirable when seeking a new job. The braids will hold that energy close to you, where it will have a positive impact on what you are doing.

There are other creative things that can be done with hair. You could add colored twine or ribbons to your hair to utilize the energies associated with particular colors. You could also add charms to your hair that are reflective of your magickal goals.

If you are one for kitchen magick, weaving together two strands of bread dough is another way to fuse two different kinds of energy together. To bring joy and goodwill into your home when celebrating the holiday season, dye one strand of dough green and the other red, adding herbs and other ingredients that are reflective of each of these ideas. Before baking, weave the two strands of dough together while chanting "joy and goodwill." Then bake your bread and serve it to your guests. If your skills as a baker match your skills as a Witch, everyone who eats the bread should be full of good cheer when they are done!

Charm Bags

After candles, charm bags (sometimes called mojo bags) might be the most common form of magick in Modern Witchcraft. Valued for how easy they are to put together, charm bags also pack a lot of magickal punch despite their often small size. One of the strengths of the charm bag is that it combines a wide variety of magickal disciplines. Most of our charm bags contain stones or crystals, herbs, essential oil, something written, a few magickal knots, and even candle wax.

Charm bags are also easily portable. The average charm bag is no more than a few inches in either direction and will fit comfortably in a pocket or purse. Charm bags can also be kept in a drawer at work, tucked under a pillow, or stored on a magickal altar. They can also be placed directly on or near the item they are targeting. For example, Jason has a couple of charm bags to help with writing that are taped directly onto his computer. There's really no limit to what you can do with a charm bag or where you can place one.

The more thought you put into your magick, the stronger it becomes. When creating a charm bag, it's tempting sometimes to just grab a ready-made bag, assemble a few random objects, smear everything with oil, and call it a day. And that might just work! But if you really want to get the most out of a charm bag, it's best to carefully consider every aspect of its production.

After figuring out what you are going to build your charm bag for, you should first choose what sort of bag you are going to use. Many Witch shops today sell premade bags (which are readily available online as well), complete with a drawstring around the top. This is great if you are in a hurry or perhaps are building a number of charm bags with some other Witches, but there are drawbacks here, too. Premade bags are often made of synthetic materials, which many Witches frown upon. A premade bag also limits your options magickally. For this reason, we generally prefer to make our own bags.

A charm bag does not need elastic or drawstrings; all it needs to be able to do is hold a few objects. For that reason, a small square of cloth (and some string or thread) is all you need to create a charm bag. The material you use doesn't even have to be new. There's something to be said for using old dish towels, clothes, or even bedsheets to create your magick. Not only will you be doing the earth a favor by recycling something you were probably going to throw away, but you'll also be infusing your charm bag with extra energy.

For instance, if you are trying to create a charm bag to help you sleep, what better fabric to use than an old sheet? (Sheets can also be used for intimacy spells!) If you feel like you do your best magickal work in the kitchen, why not use a dish towel? Your charm bag might be focused on walking away from a difficult situation, so for this you could use an old sock. All of these previously used items are infused with energy directly related to the goal of your magick, which makes them far more powerful than a premade bag. They're also all simmering with your own personal energy!

Another powerful option here is using materials or clothing once owned by a deceased friend or relative. The energy from such items will help facilitate contact with the deceased person or with the spirits of your ancestors. If you associate a certain feeling or emotion with a particular deceased friend or relative, using their items is a way to tap into that energy. If a grandparent had a calming influence on others while living, that influence can be felt from the afterlife, too, and using their clothing and other similar items is an easy way to access it.

When creating a charm bag, you might want to consider the color of the bag. Don't feel like reusing something? That's fine. Using a piece of felt or fabric in a color related to your end goal will help make your magick stronger. (The color correspondences here are the same as the ones listed for candle magick in chapter 7.) The color of any thread, string, or yarn you use to tie your bag applies here, too. For example, a green bag is obvious for a money spell, but how about some purple yarn to tie it shut (the purple being representative of ambition)?

Many Witches overlook the fact that their charm bags are the equivalent of a blank canvas waiting to be drawn upon. You can write the end goal of your spell directly on your charm bag. You can also draw magickal symbols on the bag to attract or repel whatever it is you are seeking. Don't want people to see what you've written? One of the advantages of using a piece of cloth for a charm bag is that it's easy to write or draw on the inside of it! Once you tie the bag shut, no one will know what you drew on the inside of the fabric.

You can put anything you want in a charm bag. If it has meaning for you, that's all that's required. Most Witches use the magickal items they are familiar with, but if there's something out of left field that you want to use, by all means do it! Here are some of the more common items that you might want to consider adding to your own charm bags.

Herbs and Other Natural Materials

When adding herbs to a charm bag, you want those herbs to be dried! Just because something is in a magickal bag doesn't mean it's safe from rotting. You also want to consider whether anything you are adding might overpower someone's olfactory nerves. If you don't want your charm bag to attract attention, it probably shouldn't be filled with so much oregano that it'll make your coworkers sneeze.

Jewelry Charms

There's a bead store not too far from our covenstead that's a "must visit" when we create charm bags as a group. The beads and stones at this shop are useful, but even more beneficial to our magickal endeavors are the various charms for jewelry that are sold there, including little metal money bags, dollar signs, hearts, four-leaf clovers, tiny angels, and acorns! If people will wear it on a charm bracelet, it's probably at this shop.

We love using jewelry charms in our bags because they are a perfect example of "like attracts like." The charms are a constant reminder of what we are trying to achieve when assembling our magick, adding more energy to our charm bags. Jewelry charms can go in your bag or be tied to the outside of the bag to serve as a reminder of the bag's purpose.

Oils

Oil can be used in a charm bag in a variety of ways. You may want to anoint every item you put in your bag with oil, or perhaps anoint the inside or outside of the bag itself. To avoid a mess in your pocket or purse, perhaps the easiest way to use oil in a sachet is by anointing the inside of the cloth.

Instead of just randomly dabbing some oil on your material, try drawing an invoking or banishing pentagram (depending on your magickal objective) on your cloth. This is usually enough to get the magick of the oil in your charm bag without making the fabric too oily.

While adding the oil or drawing a pentagram with oil, you might want to say something like this:

> *With the Witches' sign I anoint this bag with oil*
> *So that it might help bring me what it is that I desire.*

Stones

Stones and crystals are frequent occupants of charm bags and for good reason: they will never rot and are odorless, too. The only downside to putting a stone in your bag is that you are essentially giving up that stone for other magickal uses, as it will remain in the bag until you no longer have use for your magickal bundle.

Written Items

In addition to writing on your own bag, you can also write your intention on a piece of paper (or other item) and place that inside the bag. This is another way to focus your energy and intention on your bag and make your magick stronger. It can also help you better clarify and target your magickal endeavors. What you write might be just one word, or you might include an entire list. Do what works for you. Jason often includes detailed lists of every step needed to arrive at his end goal when creating a charm bag. In addition to magickal words, you might include a rune or a picture in your charm bag.

Other Bits

The sky's the limit for what you can put in a charm bag. If an item's energy resonates with you and your goal, by all means throw it in! Some of the items we've used in the past include pieces of candle wax, dried leaves, acorns, twigs, buttons, a drop of water from a sacred spring, and dirt. Don't let anyone tell you that what you are putting in your bag is "not traditional." It's Witchcraft, so there really aren't a whole lot of rules!

If you have a particular person picked out as the target of your bag's energy, you can add something that belongs to them to the bag. This could be a personal item or a strand of hair. If you are the target of the spell, you can also add a strand of your hair, some spit, or a fingernail. This will better align the bag with your own energies. It's a way of programming your bag so it only works for you! (Be careful, though, not to lose your bag if you add something so personal to it. Items like hair and fingernails connect directly back to you.)

There's no real trick to how you put your items in a charm bag. Some Witches have a set order, such as stones, then herbs, etc., but do what works best for you. Let your intuition be your guide! If you can, state your intention aloud as you place each item in your bag. Don't worry so much about the words. They don't need to rhyme or sound fancy. Simply state the purpose of each item that goes into your bag.

When your bag is full, you'll want to seal it. The easiest way to seal a bag is with a piece of twine or string. Some Witches like to turn their charm bags into small pouches that they sew shut. However you seal your bag, you'll want to do so in a way that adds more magick to it.

The easiest way to seal a charm bag made from a piece of cloth is to gently lift up all four corners of the fabric you are using. The materials in your charm bag should then all be nestled snugly at the bottom of the fabric. The ideal place to tie your bag is right above the spot where those items come together. This will sometimes give your bag a large "tail" of unfilled fabric. You can keep the large tail or trim it with a pair of scissors when you are done creating your sachet.

If you are sealing your bag with a knot, you'll want to state your intention while doing the tying. In addition, you may want to tie more than one knot. Many Witches like to use a number with magickal significance, such as 7, 9, or 13. For example, if you are creating a spell to bring more wealth into your life, you could say:

> *One knot for the money that is to come.*
> *Two knots for my increased income.*
> *Three knots for the money I'll keep.*
> *Four knots for what I'm about to reap.*
> *Five knots for all the work I'll do.*
> *Six knots for all that I'll accrue.*
> *Seven knots for all that is to be won.*
> *So mote it be, my spell is now done!*

If you are sewing your sachet closed, you could use a similar rhyme, but because it's harder to determine just how many stitches you might end up using, another option is to repeat a short incantation like a mantra. Not only can repeating the same words over and over add a lot of energy to a spell, but you also might find your stitching falling into a rhythm that matches your words. Here are some examples of couplets you could use while stitching a charm bag shut:

I am worthy of love, may it come from above.

In peace I will sleep, both restful and deep.

Bother me no more, show yourself the door.

Protected I will be, no danger will I see.

We like to include a charm on the outside of our bags so we can keep track of what the bag is for. If you're using a jewelry charm, your string can easily be threaded through the charm, which should securely tie it to the bag. We usually thread the charm onto our string before we start tying our knots to close up the bag.

After tying your bag, you can also seal it with candle wax. If you're doing your magickal work in a ritual setting, using a candle lit for a deity or a particular element is a fantastic way to add the energy of that deity or power to your charm bag. Another option is to light a fresh candle when you've begun putting your charm bag together, as any residual energy you emit will be picked up by the candle and then dropped back into your charm bag through the wax.

Once your bag is securely tied and the wax has dried (if used), you'll want to charge the bag and attune the energies within it. To start, hold the bag in your dominant hand and envision what you are working on becoming a reality. Feel that energy build in your body, and move it through yourself and into the bag. It's important to put a bit of yourself in your bag so that it's in sync with your specific energies.

Once a bit of your personal power has been added to the bag, while still holding it in your dominant hand, take a moment to feel the various energies moving through it. Everything you've put in the bag should have a type of energy you can feel. Because all of those energies align with your magickal goal, they shouldn't be all that different but they should still be noticeable. As you notice those energies, imagine them like threads that need to be woven together.

Ideally you want to take all of those different threads of energy and get them to "link up" with one another so they will work together as a whole. Picture the threads in your mind's eye and imagine them coming together, each one still unique but all a part of a greater whole. The idea of linking up all the different threads of energy that make up the magick in your charm bag might sound complicated, but you'll find that it comes together easily enough. It just takes a little concentration.

Once your bag has been charged and its energies have been aligned with one another, it's ready for use! You can keep your charm bag on your person or simply nearby. You can also set it in a spot where its energy is most needed. Charm bags are potent magick, easy to put together, and a favorite of many Witches!

Shared Spellcraft: The Magick of Hair
by Martha Kirby Capo

Look up "folk magic" and "hair" and you'll find all kinds of articles about knot spells and Witches' Ladders. Tales of Witches' use of hair in spellcasting go back several hundred if not thousands of years. Diane Purkiss, professor of English literature at Oxford University and fellow and tutor at Keble College, Oxford, writes:

> The main difference between a magician and a witch to Shakespeare's contemporaries was books. Witches do magic with their bodies, or sometimes with other people's bodies, but magicians do magic with words.[29]

Hair is also mentioned in the infamous *Malleus Maleficarum*, a manual published in 1487 that was used in the identification and persecution of alleged witches. In the *Maleficarum*, hair is listed alongside powders, liquors, nails, and toads as magickal implements used by Witches.[30]

In his *Folk-Lore in the Old Testament: Studies in Comparative Religion, Legend, and Law*, Sir James George Frazer writes:

> Here in Europe it used to be thought that the maleficent powers of witches and wizards resided in their hair, and that nothing could make any impression on these miscreants so long as they kept their hair on.[31]

Perhaps one of your parents clipped a lock of your baby hair as a keepsake, or maybe you did this with your own child so you could have a memento of your little one. It's a very old practice to clip a small lock of hair, tie it with a ribbon, and affix it to the back of a photo or in a memory book. Cut hair has been known to keep its

---

29. Diane Purkiss, "Witches in Macbeth," British Library, March 15, 2016, https://www.bl.uk /shakespeare/articles/witches-in-macbeth#.

30. Hans Peter Broedel, *The Malleus Maleficarum and the Construction of Witchcraft* (Manchester, England: Manchester University Press, 2003), 139.

31. Sir James George Frazer, *Folk-Lore in the Old Testament: Studies in Comparative Religion, Legend, and Law, vol. 2* (London: Macmillian and Co., 1918), 485.

color for decades (and sometimes centuries!). While it's unlikely that the majority of the folx doing this expressed any magickal intent while clipping their baby's hair, it's undoubtedly true that they, too, recognized the power our hair evokes.

In Victorian times infant mortality was high, and that's when hair art became widespread. The loved one's hair could be woven or braided (or a combination of both) and incorporated as a border around a family photograph, then placed under glass, framed, and hung on a wall. A family tree might be constructed from the hair of several loved ones, with their photos then placed along the branches of the tree, and the whole thing again placed under glass, framed, and displayed. Just like with the clipped infant's hair, it's highly doubtful that magickal intent was spoken over the hair while these mementos were being constructed. Still, there was a strong awareness of the physical connection with the loved one evoked when working with and viewing art created using their hair.

Hair is powerfully magickal stuff. While the hair shaft (made of the protein keratin) is dead, the subcutaneous hair bulb (in which is anchored the hair follicle—the bit that anchors the shaft to the bulb) contains living cells that divide and grow to build the hair shaft. And, as most of us learned back in our school days, cells contain DNA, that double helix structure that carries genetic instructions for, well, everything. Your DNA is a big part of what makes you *you*.

To work spells using hair, save the hair that collects in your brush so that you'll have a ready supply. If you have short hair, it might take a while to save the necessary amount of hair needed for some spells, but you'll get there eventually.

Martha Kirby Capo is the editor/page manager of The Agora*, a shared blog on Patheos Pagan, where she writes as* The Corner Crone*. You can hear her* Moments for Meditation *on KPPR Pure Pagan Radio. She currently resides in South Florida. Her spell involving hair and knot magick appears on page 248 of this book.*

Binding Magick

After charm bags, spells related to binding are the most popular form of magick involving cords and knots. The most familiar image of binding magick is a Witch wrapping a cord or ribbon around the picture of an antagonist. During the creation of a binding spell, words to the effect of "I bind you from doing harm to yourself and others" are usually spoken. For many Millennials and members of Generation X, such descriptions of binding magick probably conjure up memories the 1996 movie *The Craft*, which vividly brought a binding spell to life.

Traditionally, binding spells are used to halt the actions of other people, which has resulted in many Witches perceiving binding spells as "bad" since they limit the free will of others. However, if someone is purposefully causing harm to themselves or others, don't we have an obligation to step in? The person doing the harm obviously has no concern about how their actions affect other people. Witchcraft is not a passive exercise. If magick works, we shouldn't be afraid to use it!

But we'll also add that many books present a rather limited understanding of binding magick. Binding spells can be used for far more than stopping the actions of a bully; they can also be used to bind ideas and energy to yourself and others. Binding magick is not just about limiting yourself or others; it can also be used to bring new things into your life or reinforce qualities you'd like to be more dominant in your life or the lives of others.

Binding magick is popular because it requires very little in the way of materials and is easy to do. It requires only three things: a connection to the person or thing you are trying to bind; some ribbon, cord, or yarn (some sort of fiber that can be wrapped around an object); and a clear focus on what you are trying to bind. There are a few instances where you might want to add a fourth object, but we'll get to that.

The most important part of a binding spell is figuring out what needs to be bound. Let's say you have a neighbor named Larry who refuses to respect your property and privacy. Just binding Larry is not enough; you want to think through the particular actions that you want to bind Larry from doing. Larry might have kids, so binding Larry from a job seems like a pretty rotten thing to do. In a case like this, you'd probably want to bind Larry from doing things that harm and/or bother you and your property. The words you'd say during your binding spell might read like this: "I bind you, Larry, from causing harm and distress to me and my house. So mote it be!"

Now that you've figured out what your binding spell is for, you'll need to gather some ribbon, cord, or yarn to use in your spell. You most certainly can use anything that's sitting around in your home, but for better results you might want to choose a specific color of ribbon or cord. Black repels negativity, which makes it a popular choice in binding spells, but if Larry is mostly loud and annoying, you might want to a choose a calming color to cool Larry off.

Because like attracts like, the stronger your fiber is, the stronger your binding spell will be. Use yarn or ribbon that is strong and doesn't easily break. If your problem is really serious, rope or even chains are acceptable. Another option is tape. Even something as simple as masking tape will work.

The last thing you'll need in our example here is something that connects your spell to Larry. Pictures are common connecting pieces but also have some drawbacks. A traditional photograph has weight and presence, but an image printed from your computer, less so. Writing someone's name on a slip of paper is a way to connect to them, but it's hard to wrap a cord or piece of yarn around a flimsy piece of paper.

If you do have an image of your target printed on a standard piece of paper, it can be helpful to glue that picture (or name) to something more substantial, like a magazine cover or a heavy page from a book you have no plans to read in the future. If your way to connect is to simply write Larry's name on a piece of paper, why not write it on a popsicle stick instead? It's much easier to wrap ribbon around something solid than a piece of paper.

In addition to pictures and written names, you could also use something that belongs to Larry here. If Larry has left trash or litter in your yard, that would be an excellent way to connect to him, since he's touched those things and perhaps left his DNA on them. Hair or blood works best, of course, but you probably don't want to sneak up on your neighbor with a pair of scissors. (If you do get a lock of hair, we suggest wrapping it around a popsicle stick to make the binding easier.)

Once you have your object connecting your spell to Larry and the cord or yarn you will be using, it's time to start the spell. This is the most important part of the entire process and requires more than just saying, "I bind you, Larry, from causing harm and distress to me and my house!" While the words of the spell are important to say, what's most vital is the energy you send out while working on your spell. In the case of a binding spell, you want to actively visualize your magick doing its work—in this case, binding Larry from bothering you and harming your property.

As you physically wrap your cord around Larry's picture, visualize the energy of your spell winding around Larry. As your cord circles around and around the picture in the physical realm, imagine your energy wrapping around Larry—an energy that will prevent him from acting in ways that harm you or your property. Binding is powerful magick and requires a lot of energy. Wrapping up a small picture and then going on your way is not enough. You need to slowly picture your energy wrapping around Larry, moving slowly up his body, and covering every aspect of his being.

Continue the visualization as you do the binding, repeating the intent of your spell until you've *completely* covered Larry's picture (or whatever other item) with your cord or ribbon. Not adequately covering the object that connects you to Larry will leave room for him to break your binding, so be as thorough as possible. We suggest wrapping at least two or three layers of ribbon around his picture. When you are done, there's no need to charge your item, since you've already charged it while creating your spell. As you wrap your cord around your object, state your goal and do your visualization, and you'll be actively adding all the energy your binding spell needs.

When you are done wrapping your cord around Larry's picture, secure the end of it so your cord doesn't unravel. How you secure the final bit of your magick will vary. One method is to reserve a length of your cord's beginning, which means starting the wrapping of your cord about five inches in from your starting point. When you are done, you can then tie the two ends of the cord together using the magickal knot of your choosing. Another option is to secure the end of your cord with candle wax or a piece of tape (or some glue) or by tucking or tying it into the cord you've already wrapped around your picture or object.

Another way to use binding magick is to bind something to you or someone else. You could bind good luck to yourself by writing your signature on a popsicle stick, drawing symbols of luck on it (like a four-leaf clover, horseshoe, etc.), and then wrapping your cord around it. You could also use an actual four-leaf clover or other lucky item and wrap your cord around that, along with something representing yourself. In this case you'd be binding happiness to yourself and would want to envision luck encircling you while saying, "I bind good luck to myself so that I might have all I need." You could also bind money and wealth to yourself, or even love or self-acceptance. Whatever you envision can be bound to both yourself and others.

It's also possible to use binding magick to keep things away from you and other people. If you are a smoker, you could bind a pack of cigarettes, saying, "I bind this addiction from tempting and harming me." As you wrap your cord around the cigarette pack, you'd want to envision a similar energy encircling you, keeping you far away from the temptation of smoking.

When you've finished your binding spell, you want to keep the bound-up item as safe as possible. Don't leave it out in a place where it might get unwrapped, thereby breaking the spell. If possible, put your bound item in a place that is hard to access. If your spell is directed at someone else, putting your bound item in an inhospitable place will attach the person you have bound to the claustrophobic energy of a dresser drawer or the back of your freezer.

If your spell is meant to benefit you, you'll want to put your bound item in a more hospitable place, perhaps on your magickal altar or the top of a bookshelf. In the case of something like a good luck binding, you might want to keep your bound object in a purse or pocket. If you drive a lot, keeping your charm in the glove box will keep your magick close to you and provide you with good luck in a place where the mistakes of others (bad luck) can have deadly consequences.

If your spell is being done to banish a bad habit, hide your bound object in the bottom of a closet or some other place you rarely visit. The idea here is that you want that bad habit out of sight and out of mind so you'll no longer engage in it! It's tempting to bury pieces of binding magick, but there are dangers there, the biggest one being that decay, a worm, or perhaps a wild animal will eat through or dig up your spellwork, releasing its energy so that it no longer works.

To make your magick stronger, you can add other energetic properties to your binding spell. Essential oils are easy to add to both your cord and your picture or other item. Charged stones and herbs can be attached to pictures and popsicle sticks and then wrapped in ribbon or tape. When you are through with a binding spell, you can place the bound object under a large protective stone, adding that stone's energy to your spell. Burning an appropriate candle and then dripping some of the wax onto your bound object is another easy way to strengthen your binding magick.

Binding magick is a versatile and powerful tool in the Witch's arsenal. It can be used for far more than just binding another person from certain behaviors. It can also be used to bind certain behaviors or attitudes to others and to ourselves.

Chapter Sixteen
Spells by Knot and Rope

Knot magick is for more than tying a bag closed. It can be used in a variety of magickal operations. In addition to the usual spells in this chapter, we've also included information about the Witches' Ladder, along with an alternative look at the process by our friend Thorn Mooney.

Many of the spells here involve nine knots, with nine being perhaps the most often used number in knot magick. If other numbers appeal to you more, by all means use them! Nine is popular, but it doesn't have to be used. If eight knots make more sense to you, use eight knots.

The Witches' Ladder

The first use of the term *Witches' Ladder* occurs in an article from *The Folk-Lore Journal* published in 1887 in England. The author of the article details several recently discovered items that he believes were owned by Witches. The article's author, Dr. Abraham Colles, describes it thus:

> It is composed of a piece of rope about five feet in length, and about half-an-inch in diameter. It is made with three strands, and has at one end a loop, as if for the purpose of suspending it. Inserted into the rope cross-ways are a number of feathers—mostly goose, but some crow or rook—not placed in any determinate order or at any regular intervals, but sticking out on all sides of the rope at (or near) right angles to its axis.[32]

Colles suggests that the Witches' Ladder might have been designed to keep people from entering the house of the Witch who made it. In actuality, the item described by Colles most likely didn't belong to a Witch at all and was simply a

---

32. Dr. Abraham Colles, "A Witches' Ladder," *The Folk-Lore Journal* 5, no. 1 (1887): 1–5. https://www.jstor.org/stable/1252510.

sewel, a string of feathers often hung from a tree and used to scare deer away. No matter its origins, the Witches' Ladder has become a popular item in many Witchcraft circles and can be used for a variety of purposes.

Like many items involving knot magick, the Witches' Ladder is often described as being like a Catholic rosary: a string of knots and items for Witches to pray, meditate, and/or reflect upon. Others use the ladder in binding, healing, and protection spells. While the Witches' Ladder in Colles's article contained forty feathers and no knots (the feathers were worked into the braid), most Witches today make their ladders with nine feathers (or other items) and knots.

In most Witchcraft traditions, the rope used for the ladder is braided by the individual Witch with three lengths of yarn, each one a different color, traditionally red, white, and black. This sounds more daunting than it actually is. To create a Witches' Ladder, you simply tie your three lengths of yarn together at the ends and start braiding. As you braid, tie your feathers or other items into your pieces of yarn, securing each one with a knot. When you're done, you can either create a loop at the end of the ladder so you can hang it, or you can tie the two ends of the rope together to form a circle.

The energy placed into the knots and the cords while creating your Witches' Ladder is the fuel that your ladder will use to draw your desires to you (or, in some cases, repel what you want to keep away). The charms and feathers you add to it will reinforce those energies, adding their unique elements to make your ladder as powerful as possible.

To create your own Witches' Ladder, you'll need:

- 3 lengths of yarn, each approximately three feet long (minimum)
- 9 feathers or other items (The maxim "like attracts like" is in play here, so use items that represent your magickal end goal.)

Begin by tying a knot in your three lengths of yarn. As you braid them, focus on your intent, and feel that energy moving into your yarn. For every four inches of yarn that you braid, you'll want to add some feathers or other items. Feathers are traditionally used in the Witches' Ladder because they are thought to carry the energies of our desires out into the universe. Other common trinkets found on many ladders include charms, beads, and bones. Whatever you use, make sure it has resonance with you and fits into your ultimate end goal. If you use feathers, you can select them by color (red for love, for example) or by bird.

Work your feathers into the braid of your cord and secure them in place with a knot. Amanda uses the following rhymes when tying knots into a Witches' Ladder:

> *By knot of one, the spell's begun.*
> *By knot of two, it cometh true.*
> *By knot of three, so mote it be.*
> *By knot of four, this power I store.*
> *By knot of five, the spell's alive.*
> *By knot of six, this spell I fix.*
> *By knot of seven, events I'll leaven.*
> *By knot of eight, it will be fate.*
> *By knot of nine, what's done is mine.*

Your knots store energy in the Witches' Ladder, so it's important to be focused on your end goal when tying them. Feel the energy of your will and body move into each knot! Draw energy from the earth and place it into the knot. You want each knot to contain as much magickal energy as possible.

When you come to the end of your yarn, you have a choice to make. You can either create a loop at the top of your Witches' Ladder so it can be hung, or you can tie the two ends together to form a circle. If you choose to hang your ladder, you may want to add a tenth charm to the end of your ladder to weigh it down, especially if you've chosen to adorn it only with feathers. This will prevent it from being blown off the wall by a strong breeze.

Alternatively, you can tie the two ends of your ladder together to create a circle. If your magickal goal is related to endings/beginnings, wholeness, eternity, or unity, turning your Witches' Ladder into a circle not only is symbolic of these energies but will further empower it. No matter how you choose to finish up your Witches' Ladder, you'll want to add some extra power to your final knot by saying:

> *Eleven knots encircle thee,*
> *And feathers nine and cord of three.*
> *As I will, so mote it be!*[33]

To give your Witches' Ladder a little extra juice, you can anoint it with an appropriate essential oil or drizzle candle wax on it after tying the final knot.

---

33. I know what some of you are thinking: *but we only used nine knots!* But there are two knots at the top and bottom of the Witches' Ladder.

If you are using your Witches' Ladder for protection, it's customary to place it near the entrance of your home or hang it on your porch. You can also bury it in the ground, ideally under a window or near a doorway. If you've turned your ladder into a loop, you can place it on your altar. If you'd like to turn your loop into something resembling a wreath, you can spread it out into a circle and spray sealant on it, making it stiff and easy to hang (though you'll be adding strange chemicals to it).

Depending on the intent behind your Witches' Ladder, you may want to check in on it periodically and add additional energy to your knots and charms. You can also use your ladder as a meditative device, using the knots as starting points to focus on specific parts of your spell. If you're using your Witches' Ladder to enact a specific goal, then when your magick comes to fruition, you may want to burn or bury your ladder to release its energy back into the universe.

Shared Spellcraft: The Witches' Ladder as a Portable Altar
by Thorn Mooney

By now you've probably figured out that magic can be as elaborate or as simple as you wish. You can acquire a full set of tools right away and use all of them every single time you work a spell or conduct a ritual, or you can focus only on harnessing your own mental faculties, conducting your workings purely in other worlds or perhaps only with the things you have immediately at hand. You could build a complex altar that takes up half of your bedroom, or you could work solely from a corner of a desk or a kitchen counter, and only when you have business to attend to. Some witches enjoy alternating between lots of different tools—each with highly specific functions—and learning elaborate ritual scripts that take hours to perform. Others stick to one thing—like candle magic, or working with crystals, or jar spells—and tend to hoard supplies that pertain to that one style of magic. The variety really is never-ending, and your own practice will likely shift depending on other things that are happening in your life at the moment.

No matter what you prefer, though, at some point you can bet that you'll find yourself in a situation where things just aren't ideal. You'll be traveling and won't have access to your altar, you'll be momentarily (or permanently) closeted, you'll be out of whatever supply you need, or your coven will bail and you'll be left to work on your own. Sometimes it may be as simple as not having the physical or emotional energy to conduct a full ritual in the manner you normally would. In any of these sorts of situations, it's helpful to have something in your pocket that allows you to feel connected and work magic efficiently, with minimal effort. And I do mean *literally* in your pocket.

Witches' ladders are a well-established form of magic. In folk traditions, they may be crafted from hair, strips of torn clothing, thread, or other personal items in order to cast spells. The witch sets the direction and intention of the spell and then knots their power into the ladder, usually while reciting some kind of incantation. In some traditions, the power is released when the knots are untied. In others, the ladder is left knotted, with the witch continuing to imbue it with magic as needed. In recent years, many contemporary witches have come to use the witches' ladder in the same way that rosaries and malas are used in Catholic and Buddhist traditions. Each knot represents a prayer or mantra, which the witch recites in order to bring about an altered state of consciousness, whether casting a spell or praying to a deity.

When I was first taught to use a witches' ladder, it was in this manner. I made different ladders for each of the gods and spirits I worked with, in addition to the cords I would use for simple knot spells. Over time, though, as a result of often finding myself on the road for work or family commitments, I crafted a ladder that sort of does double-duty, functioning as my altar and circle in and of itself, in addition to its more traditional purpose. I can't throw a whole set of tools into my car, especially when I'm couch surfing or sharing a hotel room with non-witches, but I always have room in my purse for my witches' ladder!

I started by collecting charms and tokens that represented aspects of my practice, as well as important tools. I ended up with a pentacle charm to stand in for the altar pentacle, a small sword absconded from a tabletop miniature to serve as an athame, pieces of amber and jet and an antler tine to represent the goddess and god I worship, and other small things unique to my own Craft. Some already had jump rings or holes that made them appropriate for tying onto thread, but others (like the antler tine) I simply wrapped in craft wire. Get creative here. My ladder has a skeleton key that serves as a reminder that, as a witch, I have the power to open doors closed to others. I've also tied in a two-inch piece of oak to serve as a wand, a fox vertebra to maintain a connection to an animal spirit I work closely with, and various runes and other symbols I've carved onto wooden craft disks for personal purposes and reminders. You might choose beads, bones, crystals, twigs, metal charms, and whatever other talismans and tools you can concoct.

Knot each of these into yarn, thread, hair, or strips of cloth as you like. My own ladder is made from a braid of four differently colored strands of yarn, each representing one of the four elements. (I'm a Wiccan witch, so this makes a lot of sense for me—your mileage may vary.) Whisper words of power into your ladder as you braid it, tying your charms in whatever order makes sense to you. Your ladder can be any length you like, too. You could choose a sacred number to determine its length—perhaps thirteen inches for each full moon, or your own height, or the length from your elbow to the tip of your index finger, as is sometimes the custom for cutting wands. If your practice entails the casting of a circle, consider making a ladder that's long enough to form a small circle on your floor or tie around your waist (so you can be "inside" the circle whenever you need).

You decide what each knot, object, and strand represents. With a witches' ladder, you can keep representations of your tools, your spirits, your traditions, your ancestors, and yourself with you at all times. Use it to recite memorized prayers or affirmations or use it almost as an altar itself. It's not the size of a tool that makes it powerful, after all. Challenge yourself to adapt whatever your "full" ritual is so that it can be accomplished by only yourself and what you have woven into your ladder.

Given the choice, I love having a big altar with a spread of tools, extra hands to help me do the work, and plenty of space and privacy. That can't always happen, though. When I'm on the road or short on time or space, or when I need to keep it down or keep out of sight, I have everything I need right in my bag or my pocket. The witches' ladder is a versatile, fully customizable tool available to you, regardless of your tradition or experience level.

Thorn Mooney is a Wiccan priestess and coven leader in North Carolina and the author of The Witch's Path: Advancing Your Craft at Every Level *and* Traditional Wicca: A Seeker's Guide. *Find Thorn on YouTube and Instagram and at www.thornthewitch.com.*

Amanda's Kitchen Charm Bag

As we all know, no matter how well the party is going, everyone always ends up in the kitchen! This room is almost universally recognized as a place of comfort and love and a great place to entertain guests. So why not add a little extra magick by incorporating a charm bag to keep the kitchen a place where everyone feels welcome?

For this bag I recommend using herbs that bring joy and delight. The goal is to bring richness and abundance into your kitchen, which is why I suggest using herbs from a family recipe or a meal that you love serving to your friends and family. You are also welcome to use herbs that traditionally represent abundance, love, family, or whatever vibe you are intending to bring into your kitchen.

When you have decided on what herbs you would like to use in your bag, it is now time to create the charm. You will need the following items:

- Your chosen herbs (dried and finely chopped)
- A small glass bowl
- A wooden spoon
- A kitchen hand towel
- Kitchen scissors
- Kitchen twine (also known as butcher's twine or cooking string)

Chop your herbs if necessary, then place them in your glass bowl. Mix them together with your wooden spoon, envisioning your kitchen as a warm and welcoming place. Imagine it filled with friends and loved ones. Perhaps you see yourself cooking nutritious meals or baking delicious treats for those individuals. While you envision this, recite this chant as you stir the herbs:

Magical herbs of my kitchen,
Fill this place with joy and love
As I cook and bake and do my witchin'.
As below and so above!

Cut your kitchen towel into a 6-by-6-inch square with the scissors. Place your chopped herbs that you have magically charged in the center of the fabric. Gather the edges of the fabric and tie the bag shut with your twine, reciting the chant one more time as you tie. Place the charm bag in a spot in your kitchen where its energy will be most easily felt.

Psychic Power Mini Pillow

This small pillow is the perfect thing to keep around if you are a tarot reader or are in search of prophetic dreams. The herbs in the pillow will increase your psychic powers, making it that much easier to catch glimpses of the future.

For this spell you'll need:

- 2 small pieces of fabric, no larger than 8 by 5 inches each (A small square, just 3 by 3 inches, is more than enough!)
- A needle and thread

- Herbs for the pillow (We recommend mugwort, jasmine flowers, thyme, lavender, juniper berries, basil, and rosemary. You can use all of these herbs or just some of them.)
- Charms (if desired)

Any kind of fabric will work in the creation of your pillow, but if you can reuse and recycle something you already own, all the better. If you have a deteriorating bag you use (or used) to carry tarot cards, then you've found your ideal fabric. An old altar cloth or even an old shirt that you associate with magickal work will make your pillow that much more powerful. Another thing to consider is color. Are there certain colors that make you feel more magickal or psychic? If so, they are the perfect colors for your pillow and/or thread!

Start by sewing your pillow together with the needle and thread. You'll want to sew three of the pillow's four sides, leaving an opening on one side so you can stuff the pillow with things. If you are using two different sizes of fabric, sew the base and the two sides, leaving the top open. If you are a creating a square pillow, it won't really matter what side you leave open.

As you sew the two pieces of fabric together, think about the magick you want to receive from your pillow. You can say the following rhyme as you sew:

> *Magick of needle and thread,*
> *Show me where I soon will tread!*

Once you have three sides sewn up, you can leave the entire "top" open or just a small portion of it. Whatever you choose to do, make sure there's enough room to add your herbs (and charms) through the opening. As you add your herbs to the pillow, visualize their energies empowering your tarot cards and your intuition. Feel their energies empowering your psychic senses and divinatory powers.

In addition to herbs, you can add other items to your pillow. You can add charms that suggest psychic awareness, such as an eye. If you have an old, beloved tarot card from a deck whose cards you've mostly lost, you can add that to your pillow, too. What you add here is up to you, and there's nothing "wrong" that can be added. If the item resonates with you, that's good enough. Just be careful not to overstuff your pillow, because you still need to sew it shut!

Once you've sewn the pillow shut, add a few knots (we recommend three) to seal it while saying:

One knot for what I will see,
One for what will come to be,
Tied now with the power of three.
My will be done, so mote it be!

When your pillow is done, you can keep it on your altar and use it any time you read tarot or oracle cards. If you've created a small enough pillow, you can keep it in a bag with your cards, empowering them (and making them smell amazing!).

If you are in need of prophetic dreams, place this mini pillow under your normal one and say:

With the magick stitched inside these seams,
Bring to me prophetic dreams!

In the morning, be sure to write down anything you remember from your dreams.

Cut Them Out!

There are times when you need to remove a friend, family member, or significant other from your life. This spell is designed to do just that, so you can move on with your life and focus on healthy relationships instead of toxic ones.

For this spell you will need:

- A length of easily cuttable rope, twine, or yarn (at least one foot long)
- Anointing oil, such as Be Gone oil or Road Opener oil
- A pair of scissors or an athame or other type of ritual knife
- Connections to the person you are leaving behind and to yourself (such as your names written on pieces of paper or some hairs from each of you)
- An area where you can tie the rope so it's taut (If you're working at your altar, tying the rope to two candleholders works really well. Don't light the candles in this instance!)

Start by anointing your rope with oil. Start in the middle and anoint the rope in a counterclockwise motion toward each end. Once the rope has been anointed with oil, mark one end of the rope as yours and the other end as belonging to the person you are trying to remove from your life. If your rope is thick, this can be done by writing your names on the rope. If you are using twine or yarn, you could attach a name written on a small piece of paper to each end. You could also tie hairs from each party on the rope. Just make sure you signify which end belongs to which person.

With the sides of your rope marked, tie the end representing the person you are cutting out of your life to the candleholder (or other object) with a loose knot (you want to be able to untie the rope when you are done). As you tie this knot, say:

> *I tie this knot for the person who has done me wrong.*
> *In this parting between us, may I be strong.*
> *What was once shared has been torn apart.*
> *Tonight we move on by the Witch's art!*

Now tie your end of the rope (loosely) to your candleholder (or other object). As you tie this second knot, say:

> *I tie this knot so that I may begin anew.*
> *I bid goodbye to the relationship I once knew.*
> *Tonight I cut the ties that were once between us.*
> *Forevermore now apart, my will be thus!*

Make sure your rope is taut before moving on. You want the rope to be tight enough that it will be easy to cut. Once the rope is situated safely, say:

> *Now the connections between us I will sever.*
> *What was once there is now gone forever.*
> *Where paths once crossed, they from now on are parted.*
> *With this cut, this relationship is now departed!*

Carefully cut your rope in its middle after saying the last words of the spell. As you cut the rope, visualize the connections between you and the person you are removing from your life fall away. Then take the two ends of your rope and place them on your altar (or other safe space), and over the next couple of days or weeks, slowly move the two pieces of rope apart a little more each day.

When the two pieces of rope reach the ends of your altar, burn or bury the part representing the person you cut out of your life. If burning or burying is not possible where you live, loudly and emphatically throw the piece of rope in the garbage. You can either keep the end representing yourself as a reminder of your individual strength or dispose of it however you choose.

Shared Spellcraft: Knotty Hair Spells
by Phoenix LeFae

Knot spells have a long lineage and history, and their potential uses are endless. One simple way to bring knot magick into your spellcasting is through the use of braids.

This spell is for manifestation. The specifics of the spell will need to be modified based on your goal. The only requirement is having hair long enough to braid.

Choose from the following based on your goal and what you have access to.

Type of Braid

First determine how you are going to braid your hair.

- *Full plait:* A braid of all your hair is best for major workings and big goals.
- *French braid:* A French braid works well when you can decorate your hair without it being seen as odd. This choice wouldn't be the best for a job interview.
- *Tiny hidden braid:* A small braid is great for hiding your work and being more stealthy.

Oils

Add oils to your hair that are in alignment with your goal. If you don't usually douse yourself in essential oils or perfumes, keep this light. A few drops of an essential oil rubbed into the palms of your hands and then applied to the hair you are going to braid will work perfectly.

Tokens

Braid items into your hair. These could be colored ribbons, herbs, flowers, trinkets, and more. Choose your items carefully. If it is appropriate, the items can be obvious. If you need to keep the working secret, choose tokens that can be easily hidden in the plaits.

The Knotting/Braiding

When you have gathered all your items and oils together, sit down with these objects in front of you. Take some deep breaths to center yourself and bring you to a place of focus. Speak your goal or intention out loud. Keep breathing with focus, and feel this intention coming to life in your hands.

When you are ready, split your hair into three strands and begin applying the oils, slowly and with intention. Focus on your goal, feeling it coming to fruition.

Next, pick up the items, charms, tokens, etc., that you want to weave into your knots. Begin your braiding and fold in these items. As you fold over each strand of hair, see your goal manifesting and feel your power rising in your hands and flowing into the braid. When you reach the end of your hair, tie off the braid with a rubber band or an appropriately colored ribbon. Visualize or feel this as a period on the sentence of your success. Know that your goal will be achieved.

Undoing the Knot

If possible, leave the braid in until your action has been completed. For example, if you go on a date, keep the braid in until the date is over. If it is for a new job, keep the braid in your hair until you receive the job offer.

Phoenix LeFae is a witch, Priestess, and shopkeeper. She is author of several books, including What Is Remembered Lives, Walking in Beauty, *and* Life Ritualized.

Meditative Rope Spell

This spell is designed to help you forge closer relationships with deity or other higher powers. While this book has been pretty light on deities and spirits, such forces are important to many Witches. If you are trying to grow closer to a goddess, god, angel, fairy, saint, or ancestor, this spell is for you.

For this spell you will need:

- A reasonable length of rope or cord (Choose something more substantial than twine or thread.)
- A candle
- Road Opener oil
- Incense (optional)

Start by anointing both your length of cord and your candle. We suggest using Road Opener oil since you will be forging new bonds and exploring new avenues. Anoint your candle and rope in a clockwise manner, starting at the bottom and moving upward. As you anoint your candle and rope, think of the higher power you are trying to grow closer to. Picture their image in your mind and feel their power around you. If you can, burn incense that you think they would like.

Once everything has been anointed, light your candle and say:

I light this candle so that I may grow closer to you.
May my heart and magick both be true!

Feel free to add words expressing your desire to build a relationship with the power you are calling to. Simply saying the name of the power you are trying to grow closer to can be especially powerful.

In this spell you will be tying eleven knots. Aleister Crowley's famous dictum "Do what thou wilt shall be the whole of the Law" has eleven words and eleven syllables, making the number eleven an especially magickal number. Start by tying a knot in the middle of the rope while saying:

Humbly I begin this petition.
To know you is my mission.

Tie the second knot on the left-hand side of your rope and the third knot on the right, alternating sides with every knot (left, right, left, right, left, right, left, right, left, right). Try to keep at least a small amount of space between each knot. As you tie each knot, say the following rhymes:

Two to acknowledge your mysteries.
Three for knowing all your histories.
Four for the purity of my heart.
Five for the power of our arts.
Six for your continued presence.
Seven for all your lessons.
Eight for insight you may give.
Nine for the life we might live.
Ten that you I will see.
Eleven the spell is done, so mote it be!

When you are done tying your knots, keep the rope in an easily accessible place. For the next eleven days, relight your candle and then revisit the cord and go through each knot, starting with the first knot and moving through the remaining ten. As you touch each knot, say the incantation above, and when done, act on the words in the spell.

Speak to the deity you are trying to grow closer to, and read their mythologies and histories. Practice your magick in their name when appropriate and speak your truth to them. Be open to the presence of the higher powers you have invoked, and be aware when they are around you. Picture them as a part of your life and know that they will walk with you as long as you are sincere in seeking them out. Repeat the incantation any time you need to strengthen your relationship with them.

Shared Spellcraft: Binding Knotted Hair Spell
by Martha Kirby Capo

When I work this binding spell, I use hair that has accumulated in my hairbrush over the past two or so weeks. If it takes you longer to get a good handful of hair to work with, that's perfectly fine. (The hair on your head is already dead; the hair bulb under your skin is where the living cells are that create the hair shaft.) I only use my own hair when doing this work. While binding spells using other people's hair are common, that's not something that has been part of my practice.

Here is what you'll need for this spell:

- Enough hair to twist into a single strand about nine inches long (This part is really important. For this spell you aren't using just one strand of hair; you are using a lot of hair formed into a single strand.)
- A full moon (preferable but not absolutely necessary)
- Some paper and a writing implement
- Fire (such as a cauldron, a campfire or firepit, a hearth fire, or even a match or a candle)

Before your ritual, set your intention. Take your time with this and be as specific as possible. Words are powerful, so it behooves you to use them wisely and well. While my own tendency is to bind the target of my intention so that its power/effect will reduce to nothing as the full moon begins to wane, this binding spell is not necessarily tied to moon phases. Sometimes the target needs to be affected sooner rather than later, so if waiting for the full moon skews the timing of your spell, then by all means proceed at your own pace.

Make some time and space to sit quietly with your twisted hair strands, a blank piece of paper, and a writing implement. Roll your hair strands in the fingers of one hand and think of the words you associate with the target of your binding spell. Don't worry at this point about making it "pretty"; just write down random words or phrases that come to mind when you think about the target you're going to bind. Romantic partner too controlling? You might find yourself writing words like "controlling" or "restrictive" or "clingy." Ex-boss threatening your livelihood? You might be writing "attack" or "evil intent" or "reputation."

After you've spent some time writing several words down and continuing to roll your hair strands in your fingers, look the words over and circle the two or three that resonate most strongly with you. These words form your distillation, the core, of your intention. My personal belief is that the strongest, most effective intentions are quite compactly written; having more words does not mean more magic. Write one short, direct declarative sentence that embodies your intention. An example is "Bind any evil that (name of person) intends against me or my livelihood." When you've got your phrasing worked out to your satisfaction, write your intention on a slip of paper.

During your ritual you'll want to have a fire of some sort to burn your hair and intention. I use a small cast-iron cauldron into which I've poured a very small splash (no more than 2–3 tablespoons) of isopropyl alcohol, but you could certainly use a campfire or outdoor firepit, a hearth fire, or even a match or a candle. Whatever you use, be sure you're taking appropriate safety precautions.

Before you work your binding spell, take a few moments to settle and connect with that which you find holy. If you work with a deity or deities, follow your practice of connection with and petition to them. If you work with earth energies, ground yourself so you're deeply connected with All That Is.

When you're centered and ready, hold your hair strands in one hand, take the slip of paper that has your intention written on it in the other hand, and speak your intention with conviction three times. Lay the strip of paper at a right angle (crosswise) across the center of your hair strands, then tie your first knot tightly around the paper strip using the hair strands.

Firmly speak the nine-knot charm as you set the remaining knots (see below).

When you've finished knotting, throw the binding into the fire and focus on your spell until the hair and slip of paper have burned completely. You may find that your hair doesn't burn down to nothing. Mine often becomes a charred lump instead, which I leave in my cauldron for several days before disposing of it.

Nine-Knot Charm

I use a variation of a nine-knot charm that you can find just about anywhere online. When knotting, I start by making a knot in the center of the hair strand, with knots 2 and 3 worked on either far end of the strand. This gives me a good feel for where to place knots 4–8, which are worked alternately on either side of the center knot going out to the end knots. Knot 9 ties the two ends of the hair strands together to form a circle.

Here is my version of the nine-knot charm:

By knot of one, this spell's begun.
By knot of two, may it come true.
By knot of three, so may it be.
By knot of four, my Will I store.
By knot of five, this spell's alive.
By knot of six, this spell I fix.
By knot of seven, my words to heaven.
By knot of eight, open the Gate.
By knot of nine, I hereby bind.

Personalize the nine-knot charm as suits your practice. For example, one of the aspects of Hekate that I work with is *Rixipyle*, She Who Throws Down the Gates; Hekate Rixipyle is who I'm petitioning as I'm setting knot 8. Tailoring this charm to include elements of your practice will infuse it with even more magical power.

Martha Kirby Capo is the editor/page manager of The Agora, *a shared blog on Patheos Pagan, where she writes as* The Corner Crone. *You can hear her* Moments for Meditation *on KPPR Pure Pagan Radio. She currently resides in South Florida.*

Shared Spellcraft: The Nine Witch-Knots Charm
by Ian Chambers

Oh who has loosed the nine witch knots
That was among that ladie's locks?
—*Willie's Lady*, Child ballad 6 (1783)[34]

---

34. Francis James Child, *The English and Scottish Popular Ballads, Volume 1* (Boston, MA: Houghton, Mifflin and Company, 1882), 87. Accessed December 5, 2021. Available as a Project Gutenberg e-book at https://www.gutenberg.org/files/44969/44969-h/44969-h.htm#Ballad_6. To make this charm more readable, I've changed two words. The original version uses the word *wha* instead of *who* in the first line, and *amo* instead of *among* in the second.

The first three knots are for increase and gain, the fourth being both of boon and of bane.[35] The next knots three are for wane and decline, while the eighth celebrates the light divine.

Knot the First

Take you a hempen cord or else a rope of good length. When Candlemas Bells shew 'pon the frozen ground, those Fair Maids of February dancing the spring, take up the cord. When the north- easterly blows, a Stafford knot[36] fashion and purse thine lips as though to whistle. Through the loop that is formed before tightening the tie, whisper the charm and seal the knot:

> *Out of the mound, serpent queen rose,*
> *Speckled maid, snake of hazel grove.*
> *I will not harm the Queen,*
> *Neither will She harm me.*

Knot the Second

Upon thy compass cord, orient to the east of the dawn's first light. When day and night being equal, fasten again the Stafford knot and afore the loop is sealed upon it, whisper the charm of the east wind:

> *O Morning Star, light of the east,*
> *Eternal shining, sun of righteousness;*
> *Come ye, Lucifer, to illumine the hearts*
> *Of all who in darkness now dwell.*

Knot the Third

When the May blossom blooms its maiden white bouquet and merrymaking abates, take once more your hempen cord and prepare the wind that waits. With pursing lips and half-drawn knot, charge full the loop with breath. Whistle the wind through that knot as it is drawn closed with the following charm:

> *O lusty May with Flora Queen,*
> *The balmy drops from Phoebus sheen*

---

35. Jason's note: This spell is in the style of Traditional Witchcraft, which is the reason for its very different sort of cadence. Some Witches love this type of thing, others not so much. We thought it was important to include this particular spell to illustrate those differences.

36. The Stafford or Staffordshire knot is a three-looped knot that appears on the heraldic device of Staffordshire, England.

Prelucent beam before the day;
By thee Diana groweth green,
Through gladness of this lusty May.[37]

Knot the Fourth

As Sol climbs higher in the noonday sky, Apollo's empyreal journey reaches the welkin summit. This is the time when the cord should be taken from its place of safekeeping and knotted upon summer's southern wind, Tubiel's blessing to fasten fast:

At topmost peak of heaven's hill,
Bold Summer King, honour to thee,
Dark shadow looms as sun stands still,
Lord of Death must soon come to be.

Knot the Fifth

The knotted cord now past its midpoint, the waning tide doth hold the sway. To the winds of waning now we move as the reaper stalks the corn with his sickle blade. When the harvest has commenced, the Stafford knot shalt thee tie. Between the ends of the knot, breathe the charm and make it tight:

In the ripening of the seed,
Its quickening is received,
But by the stalk that holds the crown,
Shall summer's lord be cleaved.

Knot the Sixth

When the nights have been made equal to day, when the scales are upturned by Her will, 'tis time to hold the knotted cord once more. Under the squalls of the western wind, with moon high and sun low, show thou the open knot which you will seal upon this eve. As the wind passes through the hollow loop, chant the spell and close the cord upon the zephyr:

Day and night, sun and moon,
Old and young, bane and boon,
Start and end, light and dark,
Summer, winter, owl and lark,

---

37. John Ross, *The Book of Scottish Poems: Ancient and Modern* (Edinburgh: Edinburgh Publishing, 1884), 318.

> *Now the balance of scales must tip,*
> *And close this wind in fated grip.*

Knot the Seventh

Now is the time when the birds have flown and the Winter King is in the woods, stripping naked the trees and bringing slumber to the beasts. The northwest brings a clearing wind, opening the way to the crisp, cool night. Before the gaping maw of the mound, fashion thou the seventh sacred knot and whistle the spell as the cord is bound:

> *To the High Sabbat, of masters four,*
> *Cometh the huntsman from mound's open maw,*
> *Gatherer of souls, to his hame does he drave,*
> *From the east to the north, escort of grave.*
> *Hoarder of souls, night's cold breath,*
> *From south to the west, stalker of death.*

Knot the Eighth

The eighth knot is sealed upon the winds of chaos and change, the mystery out of time. Take up your cord and prepare for when the cold hollow tomb has become the birthing womb to capture the vagitus wind of the newborn light and the crowning of the year.

> *Dark and dismal cavernous night,*
> *Death's abode, secreting light,*
> *Star-studded cloth of heaven's high bower,*
> *Venus heralding dawn's coming hour,*
> *Bind now this, the eternal knot,*
> *Which compasses round this divel's plot.*

The Nameless Knot

Now thou hast walked the wheel of the year, binding the winds in the knotted cord. Eight are they all as a compass rose, bound in a circlet of hempen thread worn about the waist or the neck. When girt at the waist, the wearer becomes the centre, the axial spirit which commands the airts. At the heart of the compass, betwixt heaven and hell, wear thou the airs tied in each knot. Whenever the need should arise, a wind may be loosed and its spirit unleashed. When the cord is unbalanced, its knots out of kilter, so too will its gait be uneven. Ever mind, this should be remedied lest the compass become precarious and unwieldy.

The final knot, standing out of time, should be secured when the winds are in equipoise. When a wind blows that hath no direction, which flurries and blusters from all and none, you may lock the knot which binds the lot. Take you the cord and recall ye this charm as the loose end is fastened upon a slipknot—for the Nameless Knot is most surely a noose, whose meaning and use is yet to be told.

> *Tie a knot to catch a wind,*
> *The devil in a bind,*
> *Take it with you e'ery day,*
> *Nine knots of fate entwined.*

Ian Chambers is a journeyman upon the path of folk sorcery, traditional witchery, and cunning art. He lives in the countryside of leafy Surrey, England, with his wife.

Chapter Seventeen
Poppets, Witch Bottles, and Container Spells

By Witchcraft standards, this is a long book, but it still doesn't include *every* magickal technique and trick used by Modern Witches. In this final chapter we wanted to share a few more advanced techniques. Most of these are magickal practices that combine the various things we've already written about here. This chapter also includes a deep dive into one particular root that has a special story to tell.

Some of the things outlined here are among the more "exciting" kinds of magick used by Witches. Poppets and Witch bottles feel evocative and are often what many of us think of when we imagine magick. But they truly are more advanced types of magick, not only because of the variety of disciplines that go into creating them but also because their magick is often highly targeted at ourselves or specific individuals.

Poppet Magick

In Great Britain, the term *poppet* is a term of endearment, most often directed at children. If the word *poppet* seems similar to *puppet*, that's not a coincidence. Poppet is a Middle English term for puppet, and when not being used as a term of endearment, poppet pops up most exclusively in magickal settings.

To put it simply, a poppet is a puppet used for magickal purposes. Poppets don't have moving mouths, but they are usually made to appear vaguely humanlike. Poppets are almost exclusively used to represent a specific individual (including oneself) or ideal. Poppets are often associated with negative forms of magick. The ubiquitous "Voodoo doll" is a type of poppet because it's easy to direct one's wrath into a doll that represents a specific person. But poppets can also be used for healing and other more benign practices.

In magickal practice, the most common form of poppet is one that resembles a stuffed animal. A pattern is drawn on two pieces of cloth, then the pieces of cloth are cut out and sewn together and the poppet is stuffed with a variety of magickal materials. This is the image most of us think of when we hear the word *poppet*, but a poppet can really be anything that represents a specific person (or thing). A piece of wood with a hand-drawn face and some glued-on yarn for hair is a poppet too. So if you don't like sewing, you could make poppet corn dollies or poppets from sticks. Heck, you could even use a toy doll as your poppet if you really wanted to.

For a poppet to work in the way it's intended, there needs to be a connection between the poppet and the target of the magick. The most effective forms of connection are physical items, such as nail clippings, hair, blood, spit, or sexual secretions. If these aren't available, an item touched by the person being represented by the poppet is a powerful second choice, as is a signature written by the target. Lastly, the old standbys—a name written on a piece of paper or a picture of the person—are also acceptable.

Making your poppet resemble the target in some way strengthens the bond between poppet and person. If you aren't an artist, you could always choose a color of cloth that has energies that resonate with the poppet's purpose. Don't want to sew? A poppet made from natural materials that will rot and fade away is a great way to do banishing magick. As the poppet decays, the target will fade away from the spellcaster's life.

Poppets also benefit magickally from the time it takes to assemble them. Yes, you could make a cheap and simple poppet by gluing some googly eyes on a stick, but the magick is always stronger when we take time to build a spell.

Much of the magick within a poppet is the result of what's stuffed into it. We suggest using the various things written about in this book: stones, dried herbs, used candle wax, oils, charms, and incense resins. If you've chosen not to create your poppet from fabric, you can glue or attach various magickal implements onto it for the same effect.

Sympathetic magick plays a role here, too, as you might want to stuff your poppet with things representative of your end goal. If you are trying to remove someone from your life or keep them from bothering you, fill your poppet with undesirable things that are symbolic of how the person's presence is not wanted in your life. Sawdust comes immediately to mind as a cheap, light, and easy way to fill a poppet. If your poppet is about healing, you could stuff it with some moss (cooling) or cotton (comfort).

Because it takes a significant amount of time to construct and fill up a poppet, poppets contain a lot of energy from the Witch who creates them. If you were to create a poppet to get revenge against someone who has wronged you, you'd fill your poppet with all of your justifiable rage and anger while visualizing the end result of the magick you want to manifest. As you stuff the poppet, you would also add your specific energies to it. Chanting or stating your desires out loud while filling the poppet are other ways to fill your poppet with its specific purpose.

Every inch and fiber of a poppet has the potential to be magickal. Something as simple as thread color can add more of your energy to a poppet's magick. Stitching a poppet together can be a meditative exercise, easily accompanied by a chant to infuse the poppet with even more energy. Not surprisingly, the final knots used to finish a poppet's creation are one more chance to infuse the poppet with more magickal energy.

Poppets, because of their close relationship to specific individuals, are traditionally "breathed into" to awaken their power. Breath is sacred and contains within it the power of life. Many practitioners use a straw to breathe into their poppet in an attempt to push their breath deep into the poppet. If this technique appeals to you, then you should most certainly use it. However, simply moving close to your poppet's mouth and whispering, "I now awaken you and your magick, my will be done!" while pushing your breath into its mouth should be more than enough to awaken the energy inside the poppet.

After the poppet has received your breath, it's important to verbalize your intention so the magick within the poppet can be properly projected out into the universe. Saying something like this will work: "May this poppet bring justice to me and rectify the wrongs of (name of person)!" If you follow the Wiccan Rede, you might want to add some sort of caveat to the declaration, like this: "May this poppet bring justice to me against (name of person) while harming none."

In most cases, the act of creating a poppet and then directing that poppet toward its specific goal will be enough to accomplish your magickal work. But poppets are also active conduits of magick, and continuing to interact with your poppet after its creation will strengthen your spellcraft. For instance, if you are doing a healing spell for a sick friend, picking up the poppet, whispering words of encouragement into it, and cradling it in your arms will transfer energy to your sick friend.

On the other hand, can you drive a pin or nail into a poppet in an attempt to hurt somebody? Yes, that's a valid form of magick. We don't expect the person you built the poppet for to writhe in pain the moment you jab the pin into their side, but the pin will most likely cause some sort of damage, either mental or physical. Of course it's more effective to have a specific end goal in mind than to simply cause hurt. Laying your poppet on a piece of wood and then driving your pin through the poppet and into the wood while saying "I bind you from moving against me!" will yield better results.

When working a spell to curse, punish, or rid yourself of someone, you can do more than just stick pins and needles into your poppet. Lighting a red candle for justice and then dripping the hot wax on your poppet will unleash the powers of truth upon your target. Burying a cloth poppet (or throwing one into a compost bin) and allowing it to rot and decay will remove a negative person from your life. If your poppet is targeting a well-known liar, you might want to cover the poppet's mouth with duct tape or wrap a cord or piece of fabric around the poppet's mouth to stop them from talking.

If you are trying to separate a person who is a negative influence from a group of friends or coworkers, you could hang the poppet from a doorknob, symbolizing how that person will soon be twisting in the wind, isolated and alone. Some of these suggestions look and sound quite sinister but are largely symbolic. The over-the-top symbolism is used to drive home the point of the magick and to make the end goal clear. Before hanging a poppet, though, you might want to verbalize your intention to prevent anything too nefarious from happening.

Creating a Poppet in a Few Easy Steps

Follow these steps to create your own poppets.

1. *Create a figure to represent the magick's target.* Traditionally poppets are made out of cloth and sewn together, but if that's not possible, other options are available. As the poppet is assembled, infuse it with your personal energy.

2. *Gather items to stuff into (or add to) the poppet.* Everything added to the poppet should be symbolic of your end goal or resonate with its energy.

3. *Stuff the poppet.* There's no right or wrong way to stuff a poppet. You can save your most important magickal "goodies" for the end or sprinkle them throughout. As you stuff your poppet, continually add your personal energy to it and verbalize or project your intention into it.

4. *Stitch up and/or finish the poppet.* As you near the end of the poppet's creation, state again your intention for making it. When it's done, you may want to hold and push your own personal energy and will into the poppet.

5. *Breathe life into the poppet.* Activate the poppet's energy by breathing into it and awakening its power.

6. *Use the poppet.* Simply stating your intention one final time and directing the poppet to work your will is all that is needed to activate the spell. However, handling your poppet, whether that involves sticking it with jagged glass or giving it loving hugs, will add more power to it and more accurately direct its magick.

7. *Dispose of the poppet.* When your spell has come to pass, you should dispose of the poppet. You can simply bury the poppet or throw it in the trash, but a more ethical way of disposing of a poppet is by disassembling it (and this is an absolute must if your poppet was for healing or encouragement—what if the poppet falls into the wrong hands?). The most important parts to remove are the ones that connect your poppet to its target. If you added a stone or crystal to your poppet that you want to keep, be sure to cleanse that stone before using it again.

Jason's "Shut Your Lying Mouth!" Poppet

Ever find yourself in a situation where a former friend or coworker is actively lying about you and trying to ruin your reputation? That happened to Jason a few years ago, and when all his other attempts to rectify the situation didn't work, he created this poppet. This poppet is designed to target a specific individual, which fit Jason's moral code, but it's a type of magick some Witches might be uncomfortable with.

For this spell you will need:

- A black pillar candle (Avoid dripless candles. You'll want the drips!)
- Copal resin incense (or a copal incense stick)
- A charcoal disc (to burn the incense)
- An incense burner
- A stencil for a poppet (These are easily found online and have a generic human-looking shape.)
- Markers to draw on the poppet (most notably red and/or black for the mouth and a marker the color of your target's eyes)
- Two pieces of light-colored cloth for the poppet (White and tan both work well. You will be drawing on the poppet, and what you draw should be easily seen, hence the light color.)

- Fabric scissors
- Buttons the color of your target's eyes (if you don't use a marker)
- Some blue thread and a needle
- Pine shavings (generally available at pet stores)
- Something to represent the target of your poppet
- A piece of jet (stone)
- Be Gone oil (or the equivalent)
- Colorful tape (Electrical tape and duct tape work great; transparent tape does not.)
- Pins

Start by lighting your black candle while saying:

> *Lies have been told, the facts concealed. But tonight I will put an end to the lies*
> *and shut the mouth of the person who has told them.*
> *May the light of truth shine*
> *in the darkness of deceit! Now that the spell is begun,*
> *tonight my will shall be done.*
> *So mote it be!*

Say the opening words here with all the malice and anger you truly feel, and let those emotions pour out of you. A black candle is used here because the color black absorbs everything around it, and you want all of your emotional energy to be stored someplace so you can add it to your poppet.

Using the black candle, light your charcoal disc and set it on your incense burner (or light an incense stick). As you sprinkle the copal upon the disc, say:

> *This space shall be one of protection as I work my spellcraft.*
> *Let no harm come to me,*
> *but let my wrath fall upon the one who has harmed me.*
> *The copal incense smoke shall*
> *keep me safe but provide no shelter to the one who has wronged me.*
> *So mote it be!*

Using your stencil, draw a poppet outline on your two pieces of cloth. As you draw on the fabric, visualize your target. Picture their face, hear their duplicitous voice, and smell whatever you associate with them. Pour all of your understanding of them into your poppet as you trace its form on the cloth and cut it out with a pair of scissors.

If you are using buttons for eyes, you will want to sew those onto your fabric before sewing the two pieces together. We prefer button eyes because of how haunting they look, but eyes drawn with marker are also acceptable. Using buttons or a marker the color of your target's eyes will strengthen the connection between them and your poppet (but don't worry if this is not possible).

After adding the eyes, draw the mouth. You'll want to draw your target with an open mouth to represent their lies and slander. Giving them lips (with a red marker) is a nice artistic touch. Make sure the mouth is reasonably large and easily seen. As you draw the mouth, verbalize that the mouth is a cesspool of diarrhea and untruths and that tonight you will be shutting it.

With the face of your poppet decorated and the fabric cut, it's time to sew the two sides of the poppet together with your blue thread. Start stitching near a shoulder and proceed downward and then back up, leaving a large unsewn space at the head so you can add things to your poppet. Blue is symbolic of truth, so as you sew the poppet, chant:

> *Your lies shall stop! The truth will reign!*

Visualize your tormentor shutting their mouth and the truth of the situation being revealed to all who know you.

Begin stuffing your poppet with the pine shavings, being sure to work them into the bottom of your poppet, filling up the legs. We chose pine shavings here because they are dry and generally unpleasant, and we want the mouth of the poppet's target to dry up and stop spreading lies. Sawdust is another option here, but the larger pine shavings are less likely to leak through the seams of your poppet. As you add the pine shavings, say:

> *Your mouth shall be dry! To your lies, goodbye!*

Once the legs are full of shavings, add whatever it is you are using to link your poppet to its target. In Jason's case, he had a letter written by his foe, complete with signature. Whatever you are using, place it inside the poppet. As you do so, say:

> *Great deceiver, emperor of lies, I link you and this poppet!*
> *I control and limit what you will say.*
> *Your mouth will no longer gush forth deceit.*

Let all see your lies for what they are,
and may you return to the silence of the shadows!

If you are comfortable with it, say the name of the person you are targeting here, building the psychic link between your poppet and the individual it represents.

Pick up your piece of jet and hold it in your hand. Think of how you've been wronged, and let that energy flow into the jet. Jet is a powerful stone for holding energy, and black absorbs energy and emotion, and here you want to let the jet absorb as much of your anger as possible. By the time all of your rage and frustration have been poured into your piece of jet, it should be quite warm.

Anoint the piece of jet with your Be Gone oil (or other appropriate oil). As you anoint the jet, chant repeatedly:

Lies be gone! Lies be gone!

Work the oil deep into the stone so the power of the Be Gone oil mixes with your angry energy in the jet. When you feel that the stone has been properly anointed, say:

Feel my anger, feel my rage,
Your words locked up in this cage!

Add the jet to your poppet, along with more of your pine shavings.

By this point you should have some dried candle wax from your candle. Gather up that wax and add a few pieces of it to your poppet. As you crumble the wax and place it in your poppet, say:

Righteous indignation fallen from the light of truth.
Let your voice be silenced and the lies cast out.
May you feel my pain and may the reality
of the situation be revealed for all to see!

Finish filling up your poppet, making sure that the arms are full of shavings. At this point you can also add whatever else you feel is necessary.

Finish sewing up the head of your poppet. As you tie the poppet shut, make three knots as you say:

One knot for the lies you will no longer say.
Two knots for the truth that all shall see.

Three knots to tie this poppet to the master of lies.
The poppet nearly done, my power and will set free!

Now breathe into your poppet and say:

(Name of target), connected now to this poppet you shall be!

Hold the poppet in your hand. It should now pulse with energy. If the energy is uncomfortable, you've succeeded, because the poppet should be transferring your righteous anger to your target.

Tear a piece of tape large enough to cover the poppet's mouth and gather up your pins. Say this incantation while placing the tape over the poppet's mouth and the pins into the appropriate body parts:

I silence you and I bind you
From the lies you so blissfully spew. (Tape mouth.)
No focus or time for your slander,
May your mind now only know candor. (Stick pin in top of head.)
I pierce your heart to cleanse your bile,
We have now come to the end of my trial. (Stick pin into heart area.)
May you not know pleasure, comfort, or rest
Until the truth is known and your lies are professed.
This is my will and tonight it shall be done,
Your untruths will end and justice be won!

As the days go on, add more tape and needles to your poppet as needed until your target is silenced or has been forced to move on. (You might find that your magick makes them change jobs, towns, or situations.) If you think the individual will be a problem going forward, heavily tape the mouth and place the poppet in a discreet place to keep your target's lying mouth shut!

Shared Spellcraft: Poppet Spell for Friendship
by Astrea Taylor

Friends are so important. They help us develop into our best selves, share our sense of humor, and stick with us through good times and bad. However, if you've moved around, it can be hard to make new friends. You can use this long spell to help you make a friend whenever you need one.

Materials needed:

- Paper and pencil
- A poppet with your likeness to represent you
- Another poppet to represent a friend (any likeness)
- An altar for your working for the next fourteen days

With the pencil and paper, write down the qualities you desire in a friend. Roll up the paper and place it into the poppet that represents the friend.

Hold the friend poppet and close your eyes. Feel the energy of the friendship you want in your body, almost as if you're sharing a special moment with them. For a minute or two, exchange energy with the poppet as if they were your friend.

Place the two poppets on opposite sides of the altar so they don't face each other directly. Every day for the next fourteen days, move the poppets a little bit closer together and have them face each other a little more. Spend a minute gazing at the poppets with love and trust. If possible, go out every day to a place where you can meet people, such as a coffeehouse, a bar, or a meetup.

On the fourteenth day, move the poppets together so their hands touch. If you've met anyone during this time, think about how you'd like to meet up again. If possible, contact them and ask them if they'd like to hang out. Leave the altar up until the friendship has gelled.

Astrea Taylor is the author of Intuitive Witchcraft: How to Use Intuition to Elevate Your Craft. *She leads workshops and rituals at festivals across the United States. She also blogs about strange experiences with the otherworld and pagan pop culture on the Patheos Pagan platform as* Starlight Witch.

Witch Bottles

Every year a sensational story will circulate online documenting the discovery of a "Witch bottle." Despite what the name implies, Witch bottles were most commonly used *against* Witches and witchery. It's worth noting that no one targeted by a Witch bottle was likely a Witch during the bottle's heyday from the seventeenth through the nineteenth century, and individuals who crafted Witch bottles most likely thought of themselves as pious Christians (despite using magick). Witch bottles and their contents could be directed at specific individuals thought to be Witches but were more generally seen as a form of protection against an unknown magickal assailant.

The idea behind a Witch bottle is simple sympathetic magick. Nasty and hurtful things such as pins, thorns, broken glass, needles, and nails were added to a glass jar, along with something identifying the caster of the spell, usually urine, blood, and/or nail trimmings. The urine was especially important, because in the classic version of the Witch bottle, the bottle was meant to simulate the bladder of the Witch in question and cause harm to that person. A Londoner claimed to have heard the voice of the Witch who was tormenting him while boiling the bottle directed at her. He claimed that she "Screimed [*sic*] out as if she were Murdered" and appeared the next day with a swollen face.[38]

In addition to Witch bottles being used against specific threats, they were also made to protect the homestead. Bottles of nails, urine, and other materials were often buried under the hearth, porch, or front door. There the bottles would quietly go about their work, protecting all the inhabitants inside against negativity and baneful magick. In the United States the practice of using Witch bottles was adopted by a diverse range of magickal practitioners. By the nineteenth century, the bottles were being used in Conjure and Hoodoo traditions.

Though Witch bottles don't turn up all that often in the archaeological record, they were probably rather common in the United States and Britain up until the start of World War I. It's likely that over the years, many unearthed Witch bottles were simply mistaken for trash and ignored or discarded. Outside of Modern Witchcraft, most people are unaware of Witch bottles, despite their one-time popularity.

Modern Witches generally use Witch bottles today for protection of the home and its habitants. All of the "painful stuff" within the bottle is thought to break apart any negative magick being directed at the home or those who live there. Shiny items such as dimes are sometimes added to Witch bottles to deflect negative energy back to the sender. The tradition of burying Witch bottles near the entrance to the home is one that has continued to the present, and that is where we advise you to bury your own. Jason and Ari have four Witch bottles buried around their home: back door, front door, side window (where the coven meets), and bedroom window.

When a Witch bottle is used for protection, you should add something to it that identifies you as the one to be shielded from negative energy. Nail clippings are a good (and easy) option here. They also have the added benefit of being able to cause

---

38. Owen Davies, *Popular Magic: Cunning-Folk in English History* (London: Hambledon Continuum, 2003), 108.

pain, which adds to the power of the nails and broken glass. Blood and urine are other options, but urine's real power lies in being an unpleasant deterrent.

For those who don't want to use a bodily fluid, any liquid that is unpalatable will work. When creating Witch bottles with the coven, we top off our bottles with vinegar. Any liquid that causes thirst will add to the power of your Witch bottle. Another alternative is cheap alcohol. Not only does an unpleasant spirit work as a deterrent, but alcohol's intoxicating properties will confuse the negative energies attempting to get into your home. You can also use sour wine or beer that has gone bad.

The energy within a Witch bottle does not last forever, and when a Witch bottle is unearthed by weather, animals, or humans, it's a sign that the bottle's energy is largely spent. A fellow covener of ours was forced to move out his house after a steep increase in rent. Upon cleaning up the grounds, he noticed that several Witch bottles had surfaced around the perimeter of his yard, bottles he and his wife had not even buried! Before he moved out, his own bottles had found their way to the surface, and the house had sagged a little bit deeper into the ground. It was definitely time to go!

Witch bottles can be used for more than protection; they can also be used to magickally target a specific individual who might be causing you or a loved one harm. In such instances, we suggest adding something to your Witch bottle that targets that individual, such as their name, something belonging to them, a picture of them, etc. We also recommend that you refrain from burying the bottle in the ground, and perhaps place it on your altar instead, where you can monitor the progress and deterioration of the item representing your target. When that item becomes completely eroded and unidentifiable, the Witch bottle has done its job, and its contents should be disposed of.

The items you want to add to a Witch bottle that is directed at a specific individual are the same as in the traditional version. You want to include all the painful things, such as thorns and nails, along with reflective items if you believe you are being attacked magickally. Personal materials, such as nails or blood, should be left out of this version of the Witch bottle (you don't want your bottle attacking you by accident), but urine can still be used.

If something can be used to harm, it can also be used to heal. To use a Witch bottle for healing, you want something in the bottle identifying the bottle's target as well as items of a positive nature. Instead of pins and needles, add crystals, stones, herbs, and any other item you associate with healing energies. You could also add items suggestive of power, strength, and endurance to assist the immune system.

Instead of urine, the bottle should be topped off with spring water or, even better, water from a sacred spot, such as a local spring or a place renowned for healing energies, like the water from the Chalice Well in Glastonbury, England.

An alternative method of using a Witch bottle to heal would be to use the contents of the bottle to attack a specific disease in the body. To accomplish this, you'd want to use thorns, nails, and pins to target and attack cancers and viruses magickally in the body. While magick can't cure a disease, we believe that the energies raised by magick strengthen both the body and one's resolve. When using a Witch bottle in this way, you could still top it off with urine, but vinegar is a better alternative.

Make Your Own Witch Bottle

This spell follows the traditional model of using a Witch bottle for protection. However, Witch bottles are an extremely flexible and powerful magickal accessory. Within a Witch bottle you can also combine dozens of magickal disciplines. This spell contains traditional items, such as nails and other items to cut and hurt, but it also includes hot foods that typically irritate the mouth and body. You could also add essential oils, stones, or wax drippings from a candle burned for protection. Note that in the nineteenth century it was traditional to add nine of any item to your Witch bottle, such as nine nails or nine dimes. You don't have to do this, but if it appeals to you, feel free to do so.

Materials needed:

- A Mason or other type of jar (A spaghetti sauce or jelly jar will work here.)
- Items to pierce and cut (such as nails, razor blades, broken glass, bottle-caps, pins, and screws—If the items are rusty, even better. Be careful when handling them.)
- Edibles to cause thirst, burning, and blistering (such as hot peppers and other spicy foods, ginger, cinnamon, salt, vinegar and/or spoiled wine, or anything else you personally don't like)
- Reflective materials/items (such as aluminum foil, reflective glass, or several shiny dimes)
- Something from yourself (such as urine, fingernail or toenail clippings, hair, or blood)

Start by putting all of the sharp and hurtful items into your jar. As you add them to your jar, envision them slicing, pricking, and hurting any negative energy sent your way. Once they've all been added, say:

Sharp and pointy,
Metal and mighty.
No one shall hex or curse,
So says this Witch's verse.

Now add whatever liquid you are using and your "hot" food items. The idea here is that the fiery and caustic foodstuffs will burn away any negativity directed at you. Hold that image in your mind as you add the ingredients. Once your burning ingredients are all added to the bottle, say:

Blister, thirst, and burn,
To this spell we turn.
Taste failure, taste despair,
So says this Witch's prayer.

Your third step here is to add things that are reflective in order to deflect the negative energy away from you and back to its user. The easiest items to use here are dimes (or other reflective coins), which are used in Conjure to deflect curses. Alternatives here include reflective pieces of glass or even a couple of strips of aluminum foil. As you add the reflective materials, say:

Silver dime (or name of other reflective item), protect me from harm,
Be a part of this Witch's charm.

The last step involves using something from your own body. By adding a nail clipping or a bit of your saliva, blood, or urine, you are telling the Witch bottle whom to protect. If putting some of yourself in the bottle makes you uncomfortable, simply write your name on a piece of paper and add that to your bottle. For maximum results, a little nail clipping or some urine goes a long way. As you add this last ingredient, say:

I give this bottle a bit of me,
From evil and darkness free.
Witch bottle, I have conjured thee.
The spell is now cast, so mote it be!

Feel free to add more vinegar at this point if you want your bottle to be completely full.

Before you bury the bottle, you can also seal it with candle wax or tie a string around the bottle's mouth. If burying your Witch bottle is not possible where you live, your bottle will still be effective. Just stick it in an out-of-the-way place, such as under the kitchen sink or in the back of a closet. If you do have to keep your bottle indoors, make sure it is sealed tight and is in a spot where it won't be disturbed.

Container Magick

Similar to a Witch bottle is what we call "container magick." This type of magick involves a container of some sort, the most common being a glass jar, along with some magickal items placed inside of it. As with a Witch bottle, common items to put inside one of these containers include stones, crystals, herbs, oils, and whatever else feels right to the Witch putting together the container. While these two magickal techniques are similar in appearance, they don't work in the same way.

When we build a Witch bottle, we add ingredients to the bottle, charge it up, and then bury it in the yard or place it in an inconspicuous spot in the house. There the Witch bottle operates much like a battery, radiating its energy until it needs to be replaced. Container spells, on the other hand, require that you keep them "active." This means you are working with them continually, at least once a week though preferably more often. Instead of limiting your magick to a certain place, like a home with a Witch bottle, a container spell is constantly sending energy out into the greater universe. Container spells are for ongoing magickal operations, such as having money to pay the rent, and not for one-offs, such as finding a job or a place to live.

Container spells are also useful because they don't require an altar or much in the way of elaborate ingredients. After they've been created, they can be tucked into a drawer or some other inconspicuous place. If you are living in a household where Witchcraft and spellwork are frowned upon, container spells are a great way to utilize the various magicks found in this book without anyone else being the wiser.

To use container magick, all you need is a container and some items to fill that container with. We recommend using a glass jar. This can be rather small, like a jelly or spaghetti sauce jar, but you can also use a container that will only hold a few ounces of stuff; just make sure it has a mouth that is wide enough for you to place things in it. The only other things you need are a specific goal, something to connect your container to the target of the spell, and some magickal ingredients related to your goal.

Because a container spell represents something ongoing, it's generally related to a specific objective. If you own a small business, your container spell could be related to making a healthy profit. To that end, you'd use magickal ingredients associated with attracting wealth and money. For instance, you might anoint a small piece of aventurine with Road Opener oil and add that to your jar, along with some cloves, vervain, and frankincense resin.

Before sealing your container, you want to "mark" the delivery point of your spell's magick. If you were doing something to keep yourself or a loved one safe, you could add a nail clipping from the person, an item that contains your (or their) energy, a picture of the person, or even just a slip of paper with their name on it. If you were doing a spell for a business, you could add the store's business card or perhaps a receipt from the cash register.

Unlike a Witch bottle, which usually doesn't contain a written petition within it, we recommend adding a written intention to your spell container. All that's required is a small piece of paper with your intention written on it as clearly and concisely as possible. In the case of a spell for a business, the intention might be something like "To operate a successful business in a sustainable way that treats both employees and customers with respect." For this part of the spell, you could also reuse that receipt, business card, or slip of paper with your name on it; just write down your intention on the other side of whatever you've already used.

Unlike a Witch bottle, to which liquids are traditionally added, a container spell doesn't need any vinegar (or urine), making it that much easier to store. Of course, you can add such ingredients, but because a container spell represents something ongoing, you may find yourself wanting to add to it over the coming weeks and months, and filling a jar up with vinegar would make that more challenging. Unlike a Witch bottle, a container spell doesn't have to be buried or even hidden. Just place it in a spot where you can easily access it and it won't be disturbed.

Witch bottles are used mostly for protection, hence the inclusion of razor blades and rusty nails, but a container spell can be used for anything, including love, money, health, and prosperity. One of the things that container spells are most often used for is sweetening up a coworker, friend, or lover. For this reason, container spells are sometimes referred to as honey jars, especially when honey is used as one of the ingredients. Honey has great magickal properties, but it's also messy and crystallizes over time. Regular sugar is a much less messy choice.

Keeping a container spell active might sound rather daunting, but the amount of work required to do so does not have to be overwhelming. Simple acts such as routinely shaking your jar and stating your intention again will keep its energies flowing. Matt suggests shaking it every day, either first thing in the morning or right before bed. Ideally you want to make it a part of your general routine so it's easy for you to remember to shake the jar.

Another way to keep the energy of a container spell flowing is to burn a candle on top of your container once a week (or month, depending on your circumstances). Burning a properly prepared candle on top of your container not only will keep the energy moving but will add even more energy to your jar. Even if you shake your jar daily, we recommend burning a candle on top of it, or near it, periodically. While burning a taper candle on top of a jar certainly sounds witchy, burning a simple tealight candle will work too, and it's a lot less messy!

Sweetener Spell

Have you ever worked with someone who just refused to get along with you and made your work life miserable? Have we got a spell for you! This spell is designed to sweeten a toxic relationship you can't escape from, usually someone at work or school or a relative or in-law.

This spell doesn't require much in the way of materials, but you will need a small stone (or sliver of stone) that is in some way connected to your tormentor. The connection doesn't have to be especially strong. For example, the stone might resemble the person in some way or perhaps share an energy signature with them. (When Ari originally did this spell, it was focused on a person named Ruby, so she used a small piece of ruby.)

In addition to your stone, you will need:

- Anointing oil for your stone, such as rosemary, grapefruit, or lavender (optional)
- A tiny jar large enough to hold your stone
- Something to connect the jar to your antagonist (such as a picture of them, their name written on a piece of paper, a strand of their hair, or a piece of their fingernail)
- Sugared water or honey

If you are using anointing oil, start by anointing your stone with the oil of your choice. As you place the oil on your stone, imagine your antagonist being nice to you. Picture them as a pleasant person who doesn't bother you or get involved in your business. Once the stone has been anointed, place it in your bottle, then add whatever you are using to connect the jar to your target. As you add these items to your bottle, say:

> *(Name of person), be pleasant and sweet.*
> *Do this every time we must meet.*

Carefully pour the sugared water or honey into your bottle. As you do this, imagine your antagonist being kind and pleasant to be around. Picture them with a smile instead of a perpetual frown. Place your bottle in an inconspicuous place that your antagonist is likely to be near, such as a desk drawer. Within a few weeks, your tormenter will "sweeten up" and in some instances find a different job that better suits their disposition.

Matt's Put You in a Jar Spell

This spell is a combination of a container spell, a traditional Witch bottle, and a binding spell. It's designed to stop an enemy from causing harm either to you specifically or to your loved ones. In addition to binding your opponent, you magickally place them in a jar where they will no longer be able to harm anyone.

For this spell you will need:

- A jar with a metal lid
- Some purifying incense (such as frankincense, benzoin, sandalwood, or copal)
- A picture of your enemy or a small doll symbolizing them
- Twine or ribbon
- Slippery elm (to stop gossip and conceal your work)
- Black mustard seed (to confuse the thoughts of your enemy)
- A chime candle

Clean your jar and cleanse it with the purifying incense of your choice. Once the bottle has been prepared, speak your intention into the jar. In this case you'd want to say something like this:

> *With this bottle, I bind you and lock you away so you may not harm me or*
> *those I love!*

Pick up the picture or doll representing your adversary, and begin the binding by using your twine or ribbon. If you are using a picture, simply start at the bottom of the picture and move upward. If you are using a doll, start at the legs and move up the body. As you bind, verbalize your magickal intentions:

> *I bind your legs so you cannot walk to harm me.*
> *I bind your arms so you cannot reach out and hurt me.*
> *I bind your hands so you may not touch me.*
> *I bind your mouth so you may not slander me.*
> *I bind your eyes so you may not see me.*
> *I bind your ears so you may not hear me.*
> *I bind your spirit so you may not be near me.*

Before placing the doll or picture in the jar, add your herbs to the jar, saying aloud the purpose of each item. For this spell we recommend slippery elm and black mustard seed, but you can add other herbs you feel are appropriate or simply use whatever you have on hand. You don't have to bury the doll or picture in the jar with the herbs; a handful of herbs is all that is needed here.

Place your doll or picture in the jar, whispering into it once more to set your intention:

> *Bound from doing harm to me or others, I now place you in this jar.*
> *Alone in this space, all will be free from your lies.*

Secure the lid to your jar and place a candle on top of it. While lighting the candle, say:

> *I trap and bind you in this space!*
> *You shall not escape except by my decree.*
> *Here you will pay for your evil and lies.*
> *My will be done, so mote it be!*

The burning candle flame will help seal the energies of your target in the jar, where they will be unable to hurt anyone else. You can drip some of the candle wax onto the lid of your jar to strengthen the seal of your container and keep your target from breaking free.

When the candle has burned down completely, the spell has been cast. To reinforce the spell, shake the jar and speak your intention into it at least once a day for the next week. After a week has passed, shake the jar at least once a week to keep the magick moving. To repower the jar, burn another candle on top of the lid.

When you have no need for the jar anymore, dispose of the doll or picture in a trash can located outside your home or work. The jar can be disposed of in a similar manner or buried in a place where it won't be disturbed.

High John the Conqueror Root

Ask a botanist about High John the Conqueror root and you are likely to get a blank stare. Ask a magickal practitioner about it and you are likely to get a knowing nod and a smile. High John is a magickal powerhouse, but it's also a root with a tangled and mysterious past. Because it's so unlike anything else magickally, we thought it deserved its own section in this book. It's also one of our favorite magickal plants, with Matt and Jason particularly obsessed with it.

Part of what makes High John the Conqueror root so fascinating is that no one is exactly sure what it is. The original High John was an African root, most likely one that looked like a phallus or testicle. The most likely candidate for the original High John was the root of spiral ginger (*Costus lucanusianus*), which was used by the Kongo people. To access the power of the root, people would chew on it and then spit. The ginger-infused spittle was thought to provide protection. The Kongo people also believed that the spirit of former tribal chieftains was in some way tied to the root, making it an honored and revered magickal ally.[39]

High John's primary magickal uses are protection, luck, and sexual potency, meaning both the look and the energy of High John today are consistent with those of spiral ginger. The High John root is also revered and often "fed" in a way unlike the methods used with most other herbs and roots in magickal practice. From experience we can say there is a spirit in the roots identified as High John the Conqueror that is absent from other plants.

When Africans were forcibly removed from their homes and brought to the United States as slaves, they brought their magickal traditions with them. But the flora and fauna of the American Southeast were not the same as in those parts of Africa, so a substitute was sought for the original African precursor of today's High John. Adding to the confusion, the specific name High John the Conqueror is rather modern, first appearing in print in 1899. Before that there were a couple of variations in the historical record of "John" being used in reference to a magickal root, and it's likely that what we today call John the Conqueror had a variety of different names throughout the American South in the nineteenth century.

---

39. Carolyn Morrow Long, *Spiritual Merchants: Religion, Magic, and Commerce* (Knoxville, TN: University of Tennessee Press, 2001), 222.

References to a magickal root used by people of color for protection in the American South are plentiful. No less than the great abolitionist and writer Frederick Douglass (c. 1818–95) mentions a magickal root much like High John. Writing in *Narrative of the Life of Frederick Douglass, an American Slave* in 1845, Douglass recounts how he came upon the root, its uses, and his success with it.

In Douglass's account, a fellow slave named Sandy advises him to find the root to protect himself from being beaten by Edward Covey, the man who claimed ownership over Douglass:

> I must go with him into another part of the woods, where there was a certain *root*, which, if I would take some of it with me, carrying it *always on my right side*, would render it impossible for Mr. Covey, or any other white man, to whip me. He said he had carried it for years; and since he had done so, he had never received a blow, and never expected to while he carried it.[40]

Douglass ends his account by describing a physical altercation with Covey that ends with Covey erroneously believing he had hurt or beaten Douglass. Douglass writes that "he [Covey] had drawn no blood from me, but I had from him."[41]

Most magickal practitioners believe that a person or spirit lies behind the name High John the Conqueror, but who (or what) High John refers to is an open question. The story we hear most often involves an African prince named John whose spirit was never broken after being captured and sold into slavery. John the Prince is described as a trickster, playing pranks on his masters. Because he loved his people so much, he transferred much of his magickal power into a particular root to be used as a form of protection. The root thus takes its name from Prince John. This is a great story, but there's not a lot of textual evidence to back it up.

High John could get its name from Prester John, a legendary African (or sometimes Asian) king thought to be descended from the Three Wise Men of the Bible. Prester John stories became popular in the twelfth century, when Europeans were seeking Christian allies in the Middle East in their wars against Islam. Prester John was thought to rule over an earthly paradise free of poverty and hunger, and tales of his realm continued to be told for hundreds of years after the Crusades. This sounds

---

40. Frederick Douglass, *Narrative of the Life of Frederick Douglass, an American Slave* (Boston, MA: The Anti-Slavery Office, 1845), 70.

41. Douglass, *Narrative of the Life of Frederick Douglass, an American Slave*, 72.

like the type of figure who could inspire enslaved and mistreated individuals, but Prester John was more a presence in European mythology than in African folklore.[42]

It's also been suggested that High John could be a term of endearment for one of the loa (or lwa) of New Orleans Voodoo.[43] This would connect the figure of High John back to deities in Africa worshipped by the Fon and Yoruba peoples. There's another possible New Orleans connection. High John the Conqueror root might be named for Dr. John Montanee (c. 1815–85), one of the most famous practitioners of New Orleans Voodoo in the nineteenth century.[44]

What's most important about all of these origin points for the name High John the Conqueror root is that they all reference people of color (or, in the case of the loa, higher powers traditionally honored by people of color). Today High John the Conqueror root can be found in botanicas and metaphysical stores, but its origins lie in the traditions of Hoodoo and Voodoo, paths with unquestionable African roots. If you choose to work with High John, honoring its African origins is imperative.

Beginning in the 1900s, High John was commodified and was more likely to be picked up in a Hoodoo drugstore than gathered by practitioners in the swamps of Louisiana or North Carolina. Since no one knew exactly what High John the Conqueror root was, manufacturers of *curios* (magickal Hoodoo items) chose the roots that are most often used as High John the Conqueror today. At one point there were probably dozens of different roots used, but today there are three that are particularly common.

The first type of root that is often sold today as High John is jalap root, which looks a lot like a dried testicle. Jalap root is a type of morning glory flower, and Witches such as Scott Cunningham (1956–93) recommend using the roots of the morning glory as a substitute for High John.[45] In no way is jalap likely to be related to the original African precursor of today's High John. Jalap root hails from Mexico, which means it would have been unavailable for use by African slaves living in the American South. Jalap is also poisonous, and in some instances High John is chewed.

---

42. Carolyn Morrow Long, *Spiritual Merchants*, 231.

43. Not familiar with the loa? The loa are intermediary spirits who interact with an unknowable higher power on behalf of human beings. Loa are sort of like deities, but mortal people such as Marie Laveau can rise to the status of a loa.

44. Carolyn Morrow Long, *Spiritual Merchants*, 231.

45. Scott Cunningham, *Cunningham's Encyclopedia of Magical Herbs* (1985; reprint, St. Paul, MN: Llewellyn, 1987), 156.

Galangal is another type of root often sold as High John. Galangal is a type of ginger, and its root sometimes resembles a phallus. Galangal is not native to North America, which means there's no way it could be the root written about by Frederick Douglass. Beginning in the 1920s, galangal was often sold under the name Chewing John and was used in ways similar to how the Kongo people used spiral ginger. My favorite stories involving Chewing John mention it being spit out in courtrooms for protection and to ensure justice would be served.

Beth root (the red trillium flower) is the third most common root sold today as High John, and it's the most unique-looking. Like jalap root, Beth root kind of resembles a testicle, but this time it's a testicle covered in hair. Beth root is native to the eastern United States and can be ingested (though we don't recommend you do this!), so it could be one of the original roots to go by the name of High John in the United States.

Calling upon the power of High John the Conqueror taps into a unique energy unrelated to the specific plant, one that has offered hope and protection for over two hundred years in North America. When you call upon High John the Conqueror, you aren't just awakening plant energies, you are awakening the power of High John himself. To get High John to work for you, it's imperative to honor the energy of the protective and conquering John and to reflect on the oppression, enslavement, and mistreatment of people of color since their arrival in the North Americas centuries ago.

The energy attached to the name High John is so powerful that you might find magickal items for sale under this name that contain no roots at all. These items are generally infused with the essence of John and contain properties similar to the roots sold under that name. What's in a name? In the case of High John the Conqueror, quite a bit!

According to tradition, High John the Conqueror root should never be used for "bad work." It's antithetical to use High John to harm or hurt, since this root is a charm used primarily for protection. If High John is used incorrectly, there will be a negative backlash against the practitioner.

High John the Conqueror can be utilized in a variety of ways but is typically placed in charm bags or carried in the pocket as a protective talisman. It can also be boiled in water, with that water then used for cleansing or added to a bath or shower. You can also soak High John in perfume (such as Florida Water), whisky, or an essential oil and then use that perfume, alcohol, or oil to anoint yourself or your magickal tools.

Today High John the Conqueror root is sold under several other names. Joan the Conqueror adds a bit of feminine mystique to the power of High John. In Spanish, High John the Conqueror is sold as *Juan el Conquistador*. Products sold as Juan the Conquistador often depict European royalty on them, an image similar to what is found on the packaging of many High John products sold to the Hoodoo community. Despite the white man often depicted on the box or bottle of High John products, the powers of both John and Juan stem from Africa and the people who came from there.

Using High John the Conqueror Root

This particular spell does not specify what you will be using your High John the Conqueror root for. No matter what you choose to do with the root, whether it's for protection, sexual potency, luck, money, or just to remove psychic blockages, we recommend using the following approach.

You will need:

- A piece of High John the Conqueror root
- A small bowl of whisky or other alcoholic spirit (As an alternative to whisky, you could also use Florida Water or some other type of aromatic perfume/cologne.)
- An anointing oil compatible with your magickal goal
- A bag or piece of cloth to hold your High John the Conqueror root
- Anything else you might want to add to your bag (such as stones/crystals, other herbs, charms, etc.)
- Thread/yarn to tie the bag closed

The use of High John the Conqueror root is unlike that of any other herb, so it requires a few extra steps to reach maximum magickal efficiency. We suggest that you start by giving an offering to the souls of the people first brought to the Americas against their will and enslaved. Alternatively, you could make a small donation to a civil rights organization such as the NAACP or Black Lives Matter as a thank-you to the people who were most instrumental in providing this powerful form of magick.

After making your offering, start by waking up the root. To do this, dip your High John root in an alcoholic spirit such as whisky. In Southern Conjure traditions, whisky serves a variety of purposes. It's an offering to spirit. Here you are offering it to the power of High John. Whisky is sometimes called the "waters of life," for the joy and feeling of escape it can bring when used in moderation. It's important to dip, not soak, your root in the alcohol. You aren't trying to drown the root; you are honoring it and tapping into its energies.

Once the magick in your root has been awakened, work your favorite anointing oil into the root. As you anoint your root, focus on your magickal intent, infusing it into the root. Make sure your intent does not violate the edict against using High John for "bad work." Whatever you choose to use your High John for should be focused on gain and shouldn't do lasting harm to others. If your piece of root is more than two inches long, you might want to anoint the root by starting at whatever you deem to be the root's bottom and working your way up.

Because of the alcohol and oil now in and on the root, we think the best way to work with High John is in a charm bag. When picking out the bag that you want to house your root, pick a color that complements your magickal goal. You can also add additional materials to the bag that might assist you in obtaining your desires.

When we work with High John in a coven setting, we close our bags with nine knots. Keep in mind that there are many people who believe that the High John the Conqueror root should be continually cared for and fed. This means that to keep the magickal energy of your High John flowing, you will want to resoak it in whisky and add additional oils to it. If you go this route, be sure to use a heavier cord to tie your bag shut, because you'll want to be able to untie it later. Whatever you use to tie your bag shut, make sure the color of the material is compatible with your magickal objective.

As you tie your bag shut, say the following words:

By knot of one, this spell's begun.
By knot of two, this spell comes true.
By knot of three, so mote it be.
By knot of four, this power I store.
By knot of five, this spell's alive.
By knot of six, this spell I fix.
By knot of seven, this spell I'll leaven.
By knot of eight, I'll cast the fate.
By knot of nine, what's done is fine!

Your bag is now ready for use. Keep it in a secure place or carry it in your pocket or purse. Add more alcohol and oil to your High John root every few months to keep it fully charged.

A Final Charm for Protection

This final spell is designed to keep your home safe from all threats magickal and mundane. Unlike with a Witch bottle, you continually add to this charm bag to keep the magick flowing strong. This is an ideal charm to use when you find yourself in a particularly thorny situation.

We use blood in this spell, which is something many Witches are uncomfortable with. If that is the case for you, simply omit that step. Blood is used here both as an offering (you are giving up a bit of yourself to be protected) and to mark the charm bag's magick as your own.

For this spell you will need:

- Parchment paper or a brown paper bag to write on
- A writing utensil
- A lancet
- Disinfectant
- A sterile bandage
- A bowl or small cauldron
- Dirt from your home
- Angelica root
- Boldo leaves (Boldo is a tree.)
- A cloth bag, either red or black
- Thread to tie your bag shut
- Protection oil or whisky/rum (optional)

Write your intention on your parchment paper (or piece of brown paper bag), being as specific as possible. Then gently prick the index finger of your nondominant hand. The easiest way to do this is by applying pressure to the tip of your finger with the thumb and index finger of your dominant hand and then quickly pricking your finger with a lancet with the intention of protection. Smear the blood on your piece of paper. When working with blood in magick, we highly recommend using a lancet because it is guaranteed to be sterile. After getting the small amount of blood needed for this spell, disinfect the wound and apply a sterile bandage.

In your bowl or cauldron, mix the dirt, your spell paper, and the angelica root and boldo leaves. As you mix them, chant, "I am safe, I am protected," along with any other words you feel are appropriate. As you mix your magickal ingredients, visualize a protective energy and force in front of you. Picture the energies of the herbs entering the soil in your bowl or cauldron and then moving through that and into the earth outside your home.

When you feel that your ingredients have been properly mixed and charged, add them to your bag. Before tying the bag shut, speak into it, stating your intention one final time, breathing life and meaning into your magick. Then use the thread to tie your bag shut with three knots while saying:

> *One knot for the magick I have begun.*
> *Two knots for the spell I have spun.*
> *Three knots my work will not be undone.*
> *So mote it be, my will be done!*

Place your bag in a safe place. Once a week, anoint the bag with protection oil or spill a small bit of whisky or rum onto it to feed your charm and keep its energy moving.

Some Final Thoughts
Cast Your Own Spell

Spell books are more popular than ever. They often top the Witchcraft best-seller lists on websites like Amazon, and our local Witch shops carry dozens of them. Matt, who works in a local Witch shop, is often asked by customers not only to recommend spell ingredients but also to write spells for those customers. (We won't even get to into how many people think that kind of work should be free.)

There is a lot of thought that goes into the spells we find in books. Authors will spend hours crafting rhyming couplets and compiling impressive lists of charms and ingredients for books. But in the real world, away from the printed page or the shining screens of social media, magick tends to be messier. In the heat of the magickal moment, flowery words dissipate and suddenly you find yourself substituting parsley for a far more exotic ingredient. Spellwork doesn't have to be as pretty as a picture, and it often isn't. Don't worry about making your spellcraft match up exactly with what you see in books like this one.

There are dozens of spells in this book and we hope you use them, but we truly believe that the strongest spells are the ones we write for ourselves. This book was written to give Witches the tools necessary to develop their own unique magickal practice, and the spells here are provided as examples to help you do just that. More importantly, we hope you make the spells in this book *your own* by adding your own words to them and being as imaginative with the ingredients as you see fit.

Writing your own spells can be daunting, and if you have any doubt about your ability to do this, start by tweaking existing spells and adding your own spin to them. You'll find that your spellwork is stronger when there's more of you in it. It's your magick, so take charge of it! Writing spells is a big task, but Witches thrive on big tasks.

There is no one way to write a spell, and while the best course of action is to trust your own intuition, we can offer some guidance. What follows is a simple step-by-step guide to writing your own spells. This book has all the ingredients and tricks for putting together effective spellwork. This last bit ties it all together.

Identify the Problem and the Possible Solutions

Most of us use magick for a specific purpose, so the first thing we need to do is identify the problem in our life that we want to solve. Our problems can often be stated in simple, broad terms, but our magick will be more effective if we have a specific, concise goal. For example, if you're doing a job spell, there are almost always jobs available, but what about a job that will pay your bills? Will just any job give you a degree of personal satisfaction? Is it possible that some jobs might make your current situation worse rather than better?

Use creative visualization to analyze the problem from as many angles as possible. Take all the variables into account when visualizing possible solutions. Do you need a new place to live or just a new roommate? Those are two very different problems and spells, so this is a good illustration of why it's so important to take some time to determine what you really need magick for.

When writing ritual, we often begin our rites with a statement of intent. This statement outlines what we'll be doing in ritual and why we've gathered as a coven. A statement of intent works well for casting spells, too. Once you've truly identified your problem and the best solutions for it, distill it down to its essence. Write down or commit to memory the purpose of your spellcraft, and as you assemble your spell, discard anything that doesn't serve that greater purpose. The end result of this process should be a thorough understanding of the issue you need to resolve and how you see it coming to that resolution.

Big or Small Magick?

The bigger the magick, the bigger your spell should be! This doesn't mean that a spell to buy a new house requires thirty different stones but only that you should probably plan to spend a bit more time raising serious energy for it. Instead of saying a quick incantation and raising a bit of personal power, big magick might require a large candle lit over several days or even weeks. The more energy you can gather up for your spell, the greater your chance of success.

When deciding how to put together a spell, time is a factor. Sometimes the magick can be done slowly, over a period of weeks or months. At other moments, time is of the essence, and the spell has to be cast tonight! Big magick can be done in a night; just spend some time thinking about what will best send your energy and intention out into the universe in a hurry. For example, perhaps the spell calls for a votive candle that will burn down in four hours instead of a seven-day candle.

We think that the location of the sun and moon can be beneficial in magickal practice, but sometimes there's no time to wait for a full moon, and that's okay. When Jason was hexed by a local Witch once, he broke the hex under a waning sun (that daily cycle is useful!) instead of waiting for the new moon. Take advantage of all the energies around you, but do the work you need to do, and do it as quickly and as simply as needed.

Gather Your Ingredients and Tools

Books like this one often include long lists of magickal ingredients, but the most effective magickal items are the ones you most strongly resonate with. If you feel like you need to track down an exotic flower to use in a particular spell, then by all means track it down! But if that kind of thing just frustrates you, find something in your backyard; it should work just as well. When working on a major piece of spellwork, we'll all go out and buy some extra magickal stuff, but generally we use what we've already got on hand.

When we conjure up as much energy as possible, our magick tends to be more effective. That's why magick involving candles, charm bags, and poppets is so popular: all of those magickal techniques involve lots of "stuff." A charm bag, for instance, utilizes stones, crystals, knots, color, herbs, and sympathetic magick in its creation. But if you aren't in a position to use eight different magickal disciplines, your spellwork isn't doomed to failure. As long as you put your heart and will into what you are doing, things should turn out just fine.

As you gather the ingredients for your spell, make sure they resonate with you. Don't just consult books; consult your intuition—trust that voice inside of yourself! And if your spell starts to feel needlessly complicated, pare down the number of items you are using.

Write Your Incantation

When writing a spell, the most important thing to focus on is your intention. Rhymes and flowery words are nice, but none of that matters nearly as much as your intention. If you don't like poetry, don't write spells that utilize rhymes. If spells that sound like they came from a Shakespeare play feel more magickal to you, write your spells that way. If you are using someone else's spell as a starting point and you don't like how they worded something, change it!

People tend to worry far too much about the words they use in spells. When in doubt, keep it as simple as possible. Chanting "heal my cat, heal my cat, heal my cat" when that sentiment comes straight from your heart is stronger than reciting a perfectly rhymed sonnet that is more of an English class assignment than a heartfelt sentiment.

Words can also be overrated, especially when doing magick alone. As long as you are focused on what you are doing, the words don't matter as much.

Prepare for the Spell

Before casting your spell, make sure you are in the right state of mind to do so. If that isn't the case, wait an hour, a day, or even a week. We all have bad days, and if you are having a rough one, the magick can wait.

When you are ready, make sure both you and the place where you are working your magick have been properly cleansed. Cleansing isn't an especially involved process, and if you've spent a few days crafting just the right spell, what's another ten minutes of effort to make sure you get the best results possible?

Finally, spend some time focusing on your spell long before you cast it. The more time you spend assembling and thinking about a spell, the more energy you'll raise and the stronger your magick will be. In the days and hours before doing an especially important piece of spellwork, go over your creative visualizations again and again to make sure you are focusing on exactly what you want to achieve.

Cast the Spell

As you cast your spell, do so with confidence and authority. Be sure about your work and the reality of magick in your life. If you have doubts about your spellwork or your life as a Witch, set those aside so they don't pollute your spellwork. You are a Witch! You've been working hard at this! You will succeed!

As you approach the end of your spell and light your candle or tie the final string around your charm bag, you should feel at least a thread of the energy that your magick is sending out into the universe. It most likely won't be an overwhelming sensation, but if you've stayed true to yourself and raised real energy, you'll notice it. If you don't feel anything, take a few minutes to add a little extra power to your spell. The work is never truly done until you say it is.

Follow Up on the Spell

The larger spells we've worked on over the years have most often been focused on ongoing concerns. If your spell requires you to light a candle every night for the next ten days, do it! Don't just pay lip service to the idea, but actually finish the spell as you intended. And if you've done a big piece of magick, you might need to reinforce it periodically. Shake that poppet, add some extra oil to your charm bag, and keep that magick moving!

Following up on a spell also requires action in the mundane world. For magick to work, we have to put ourselves in situations where it can find us. When looking for a romantic partner, you can't just sit on the couch and wait for that person to come to you; you have to put yourself in a position to meet new people. Sometimes it feels like the "magick didn't work" simply because we didn't do the work that's required after a spell has been cast. Your magick will get you closer to your goal, but in order to get across the finish line, you will need to take action in the real world.

Going Forward

The more you work with magick, the easier it will be to practice it. Eventually you'll be able to cast really big spells without having to think too much about it. Through trial and error, you'll discover what works and what doesn't work for you. For many of us, magick is a bit intimidating when we first start working with it, but over time it becomes second nature.

And there will be error involved. Not all of your spells will work out exactly as you intended them to, and some may simply fail. Even the most accomplished Witches can tell you tales of when their magick didn't work for whatever reason. It's easy to get discouraged when you don't get the results you want immediately, but that's what second chances are for.

When a spell doesn't work, or it works in an unintended way, take some time to go over what might have gone wrong. We learn through trial and error, and often our biggest mistakes provide the most insight into the magickal process. Maybe you used the wrong ingredient, or were in the wrong headspace, or were focused on the wrong issue. Keep track of both your successes and your failures. It will make your magick stronger and more precise.

The magick and tools of the Witch have brought both meaning and success into our lives. Spellcraft has kept the four of us moving forward, picking us up when we are low and lifting us up even higher when things are great. As Witches, we can transform our lives and control our circumstances through the power of magick. We hope you find the practice of magick to be as powerful as we do.

So mote it be!
Matt, Amanda, Ari, and Jason
March 2021

Appendix I
Types of Spells & Magickal Correspondences

The list of magickal correspondences in the second part of this appendix breaks down the stones, oils, herbs, and other spell ingredients written about in this book into twenty-two separate categories. Most of us don't have dozens of stones and herbs readily available at all times, so this list will help you substitute items so you can use what you already have on hand to get the magickal results you desire, based on the purpose of your spell. The twenty-two categories of spells included here are rather broad and can be applied to a wide variety of magickal practices.

But first we've included a list of spell goals and their possible uses in magick.

Types of Spells and Their Potential Uses

Here is a list of the various types of spells, divided into twenty-two separate categories, along with suggestions for how they can be applied to your spellcraft.

Abundance: Abundance is about growth. It could be about growing something internally or getting the best yield ever in your garden.

Banishing: Banishing helps us get rid of things that are unwanted in our lives. Those things can include people, ideas, habits, and debts.

Blessing: To bless something is to dedicate it to your practice of Witchcraft and add a bit of your magickal energy to it.

Cleansing: Cleansing removes negative energy but also helps us facilitate fresh starts.

Divination: Items associated with divination make us stronger tarot readers (or whatever other divinatory tools you might use).

Dreams: Enhance the energy of your dreams to catch a glimpse of the future or put your unconscious mind to work solving a personal problem.

Friendship: Enhance relationships with people, pets, and even the earth.

Happiness: Create your own happy place and share that feeling with others.

Healing: Send healing energy to others or yourself. As Witches we can also work to heal the environment or a relationship.

Love: Love spells can be used to bring a new romantic partner or lover into your life. They can also be used to attract new (close) friends and animal companions.

Luck: Luck increases the probability that something positive will happen in our lives. Luck magick can be used to enhance the likelihood of anything you desire.

Money: Money spells help make cash appear when we need it, and grow our bank accounts.

Passion: Passion is most associated with physical desire, but passions fuel our work and our Craft as Witches. Reignite your love for a profession or hobby with passion magick.

Power: Power is the strength to overcome obstacles; it's not necessarily about power over others.

Prosperity: Prosperity is about more than money, and will be a bit different for everybody depending on personal needs. To prosper, all we might need is a good job, a roof over our head, and a handful of good friends.

Protection: Protection magick keeps unwanted people and energies out of our lives.

Psychic Development: Many Witches actively work on developing their psychic skills and abilities, and magick can help with that work.

Purification: Purification spells can remove a hex or curse, or negativity in a space or person. They can also help us prepare for new beginnings.

Self-Esteem: When we feel good about ourselves, good things usually follow. You are more likely to be successful at nearly any endeavor if you have confidence in yourself.

Success: Success can mean a job, but it can also be obtaining something, preserving a relationship, or even just creating the perfect dinner.

Travel: Ensure safe travels wherever you go and that you reach your intended destination. Witchcraft itself is a journey, and when we practice magick or engage in ritual, we are in a sense traveling.

Uncrossing: Uncrossing spells can remove a curse or hex. An uncrossing spell can also act as a "magickal reset button," restoring circumstances to a previous state.

Magickal Correspondences

Here is a list of magickal goals divided into twenty-two categories, along with the stones, oils, herbs, and other spell ingredients written about in this book that correspond to each goal.

Abundance: Allspice, flour, grapeseed oil, grapes, lemon, olive oil, olives, patchouli, peppermint, wine

Banishing: Basil, Be Gone oil, black, blue, clove, hyssop, onion, peppermint, thorn

Blessing: Cedar, rain, rose, salt

Cleansing: Birch, cedar, clary sage, copal, dragon's blood, frankincense, hyssop, lavender, lemon, lemongrass, pine, rice, sage, thyme, Van Van, water, white, ylang-ylang

Divination: Anise, apple, coffee, cypress, hibiscus, juniper, mugwort, purple, silver, thyme, vervain

Dreams: Anise, eucalyptus, hibiscus, jasmine, moonstone, rosemary, yarrow, yellow

Friendship: Amethyst, pink, rose quartz

Happiness: Catnip, citrine, lemon, neroli, orange, quartz

Healing: Amethyst, apple, aventurine, blood, bloodstone, blue, chamomile, copal, elder, fluorite, hematite, jojoba, lavender, myrrh, palo santo, rowan, thorn, thyme, white

Love: Adam and Eve, apple, apricot, banana, basil, Bewitching oil, carnelian, catnip, cherry, chocolate, cinnamon, damiana, dragon's blood, garnet, ginger root, hibiscus, hot pepper, jasmine, juniper, malachite, maple, neroli, patchouli, pink, red, rhodochrosite, rose, rose hips, rose quartz, sapphire, Van Van, vervain, willow, ylang-ylang

Luck: Bayberry, Black Cat, catnip, chamomile, cherry, cinnamon, damiana, dragon's blood, four-leaf clover, ginger root, green, High John the Conqueror, rose bud, vervain, vetiver

Money: Aventurine, basil, bayberry, blue, cedar, cottonwood, four-leaf clover, gold, green, pine, pyramid, silver, vervain

Passion: Cinnamon, damiana, hibiscus, juniper berries, quartz, red, rhodochrosite, rose, sapphire

Power: Cedar, cinnamon, coffee, gold, hematite, High John the Conqueror, juniper berries, rowan, sunflower

Prosperity: Ash, aventurine, basil, benzoin, cinnamon, citrine, clove, green, patchouli, peppermint, pyrite, sweet almond

Protection: Amber, amethyst, angelica, anise, ash, benzoin, birch, Black Cat, burdock, camphor, carnelian, cinnamon, citrine, clove, coconut, copal, cypress, dill, dragon's blood, fluorite, frankincense, garlic, gum arabic, hot pepper, jet, lapis lazuli, lavender, Lucky Prophet, malachite, marjoram, mugwort, myrrh, nag champa, oak, olive oil, oregano, quartz, rose, rosemary, rue, sage, Saint Michael, sandalwood, sapphire, sunflower, topaz, vervain

Psychic Development: Basil, benzoin, cedar, coffee, cypress, gum arabic, hematite, hyssop, juniper berries, lapis lazuli, lavender, mugwort, peppermint, silver

Purification: Chamomile, cinnamon, copal, eucalyptus, myrrh, salt, thyme, water

Self-Esteem: Clary sage, rose

Success: Angelica, aventurine, basil, bayberry, cinnamon, clove, Crown of Success, four-leaf clover, green, Lucky Prophet, malachite, pyrite, rowan, yellow

Travel: Malachite, mugwort

Uncrossing: Clove, lemon, pine

Appendix II
General Properties of Herbs, Oils, Colors, Stones, and Crystals

Here is a list of the various magickal items written about in this book and their most common correspondences. This list is meant to be a quick guide for the Witch doing some magick in a hurry. Every item listed here has a far more detailed entry elsewhere in this book.

Adam and Eve: Love

Allspice: Abundance, prosperity

Amber: Protection

Amethyst: Friendship, healing, protection

Angelica: Protection, success

Anise: Divination, dreams, protection

Apple: Divination, healing, love

Apricot: Love

Ash: Prosperity, protection

Aventurine: Healing, money, prosperity, success

Banana: Love, passion

Basil: Banishing, love, money, prosperity, psychic development, success

Bayberry: Luck, money, success

Be Gone Oil: Banishing

Benzoin: Prosperity, protection, psychic development

Bergamot: Inspiration

Bewitching Oil: Love

Birch: Banishing, protection

Black: Banishing, protection

Black Cat Oil: Healing, protection

Blood: Healing, protection

Bloodstone: Healing

Blue: Healing, money

Brown: Banishing, cleansing

Burdock: Protection

Camphor: Protection

Carnelian: Love, protection

Catnip: Love, luck

Cedar: Blessing, cleansing, money, power, psychic development

Chamomile: Healing, luck, purification

Cherry: Love, luck

Chocolate: Love, prosperity

Cinnamon: Love, luck, prosperity, protection, purification, success

Citrine: Happiness, prosperity, protection

Clary Sage: Cleansing, inspiration, self-esteem

Clove: Banishing, prosperity, protection, success, uncrossing

Coconut: Protection

Coffee: Divination, power, psychic development

Copal: Cleansing, healing, protection, purification

Cottonwood (Poplar): Money

Crown of Success: Success

Cypress: Divination, protection, psychic development

Damiana: Love, luck, passion

Dill: Protection

Dragon's Blood: Cleansing, love, luck, protection

Elder: Healing

Eucalyptus: Dreams, purification

Fire: Power

Flour: Abundance

Fluorite: Healing, protection

Four-Leaf Clover: Luck, money, success

Frankincense: Cleansing, protection

Garlic: Protection

Garnet: Love

Ginger Root: Love, luck

Gold: Money, power

Grapes (also Wine and Grapeseed Oil): Abundance, healing, prosperity

Green: Luck, money, prosperity, success

Gum Arabic: Protection, psychic development

Hagstone: Divination, psychic powers

Hair: Healing, power, protection

Hematite: Healing, power, psychic development

Hibiscus: Divination, dreams, love, passion

High John the Conqueror: Luck, power

Hot Peppers: Love, protection

Hyssop: Cleansing, psychic development

Jasmine: Dreams, love

Jasper: Healing, protection

Jet: Protection

Juniper: Passion, power, psychic development

Lapis Lazuli: Protection, psychic development

Lavender: Cleansing, healing, protection, psychic development

Lemon: Abundance, cleansing, happiness, inspiration, uncrossing

Lemongrass: Cleansing

Lucky Prophet: Protection, success

Malachite: Love, protection, success, travel

Maple: Love, money, protection

Marjoram: Protection

Moonstone: Dreams, intuition, psychic development

Mugwort: Divination, protection, psychic development, travel

Myrrh: Healing, protection, purification

Nag Champa: Protection, purification

Neroli: Happiness, love

Oak: Power, protection

Olives/Olive Oil: Abundance, protection

Onion: Banishing

Orange: Happiness, success, travel

Oregano: Luck, protection

Palo Santo: Healing, luck, success

Patchouli: Abundance, love, prosperity

Peppermint: Abundance, banishing, prosperity, psychic development

Pine: Cleansing, money, uncrossing

Pink: Friendship, love

Poplar: *See* Cottonwood

Purple: Divination, prosperity, success

Pyrite: Prosperity, success

Quartz: Happiness, passion, protection

Rainwater: Blessing, prosperity, protection

Red: Love, passion

Rhodochrosite: Love, passion

Rice: Cleansing

Rose: Blessing, love, passion, protection, self-esteem

Rose Bud: Luck

Rose Hips: Love

Rose Quartz: Friendship, love

Rosemary: Dreams, protection

Rowan: Power, success

Rue: Protection

Sage: Cleansing, protection

Saint Michael: Protection

Salt: Blessing, purification

Sandalwood: Inspiration, protection

Silver: Divination, money, psychic development

Sunflower: Power, protection

Sweet Almond: Prosperity

Thorn: Banishing, healing

Thyme: Divination, healing

Topaz: Protection

Van Van: Cleansing, love

Vervain: Divination, love, luck, money, protection

Vetiver: Luck

Water: Cleansing, purification

White: Cleansing, healing

Willow: Love

Yarrow: Dreams

Yellow: Dreams, inspiration, success

Ylang-Ylang: Love, cleansing

Master List of Spells

There are nearly a hundred spells in this book, and magickal ideas for a hundred more. This list includes all the major spells found in the spell chapters, along with a few spells that were sneakily included in other chapters. Most descriptions of magickal items in this book include a spell idea, and some of those are well developed enough that they are included here as a specific spell. Spells that show up in an entry for an herb or a stone include the name of the section in which the spell can be found.

You'll notice that many of the spells included in this book appear in multiple categories, and that's by design. Depending on your individual needs and spell design, a Witch bottle could be used for personal blessings or protection. A breakup spell is a type of banishment, but when we let someone go, we also experience a degree of self-healing. In other words, one spell can inhabit several different worlds. How you choose to cast the spell, along with your specific end goal, will ultimately determine the category a spell can be slotted into. For more information on the various categories of spells, refer to appendix I.

The Spells

Absorb Your Sadness with Jet (Jet entry), 164: Blessing, cleansing, happiness, self-esteem

Angelica Athame Spell, 213: Banishing, cleansing, purification, uncrossing

Animal Companion Bonding Spell, 173: Blessing, friendship, happiness

Apple Spell for Health and Protection, 148: Banishing, blessing, healing, prosperity, protection

Attract Customers to Your Business, 169: Abundance, happiness, prosperity, success

Protection Oil, 203: Banishing, cleansing, protection

Psychic Power Mini Pillow, 241: Divination, dreams, psychic development

Put It on Ice!, 72: Banishing, cleansing, protection

Put You in a Jar Spell, 272: Banishing, protection, uncrossing

Putting Down Roots: A Spell for Moving to a New Location, 143: Abundance, blessing, happiness, success, travel

Refreshing Spritz, 204: Blessing, cleansing, friendship

Remembrance Spell with Peppermint (Peppermint entry), 185: Success

Reveal a Future Lover (Apple entry), 126: Divination, passion

Self-Esteem Rose Water, 145: Blessing, cleansing, healing, self-esteem

Shields Up! A Quick Protection Spell, 43: Protection

Shower for Spiritual Cleansing, 136: Cleansing, healing, self-esteem, uncrossing

"Shut Your Lying Mouth!" Poppet, 259: Banishing, protection, uncrossing

Simple Spell for Solstice (or Any Time You Need to Remember Your Personal Brightness), 96: Blessing, friendship, happiness, healing, prosperity, success

Spell for Patience, 174: Cleansing, healing, success

Spring Cleaning Spell, 206: Banishing, cleansing, protection

Stop (Being) Lazy Sigil, 41: Banishing, cleansing, power, prosperity, self-esteem

Sweetener Spell, 271: Abundance, blessing, friendship, protection, uncrossing

Tealight Love Candle Spell, 100: Abundance, friendship, passion, self-esteem

Throw Out the Trash with the Coffee Grounds (Coffee and Coffee Beans entry), 127: Banishing, protection, uncrossing

Throwing Out the Trash: A Protective Potato Spell, 146: Banishing, power, protection, uncrossing

Tool Cleansing, 208: Blessing, cleansing

Tool Oil Blessing, 210: Blessing

Traveler's Spell (for People and Luggage), 175: Protection, success, travel

Truth Spell, 108: Banishing, power, protection, success

Turn Your Tea into a Magic Potion, 141: Abundance, banishing, blessing, cleansing, divination, dreams, friendship, happiness, healing, luck, passion, power, prosperity, psychic development, self-esteem, success, uncrossing

Van Van Oil, 202: Banishing, cleansing, protection, uncrossing

Witches' Ladder, 235: Abundance, blessing, healing, luck, prosperity, protection, success

Witches' Ladder as a Portable Altar, 238: Blessing

Witches' Mill, 70: Banishing, cleansing, divination, healing, luck, power, prosperity, protection, psychic development, self-esteem, success, uncrossing

Appendix IV
Spells by Category

Here is a list of every major spell in this book indexed by category. As in the previous appendix, one spell will often appear in several different categories. For more information on the different categories of spells, refer to appendix I.

Abundance: Attract Customers to Your Business, 169; Bewitch Yourself, 102; Building the Cone of Power, 68; Candle and Pins Spell for Sending Blessings, 98; Good Luck Gambling (Vetiver entry), 186; Earth Energy, 60; Egyptian Ritual Anointing Oil, 201; Exercise Sigil (Create Your Own Sigil entry), 37; Find My Community Spell, 93; Finding the Possibilities Spell, 171; Gaining the Home You Desire, 214; Garden Sigil, 41; High John the Conqueror Root Charm Bag (Using High John the Conqueror Root entry), 278; Increase Your Sense of Self-Love and Self-Worth, 170; Kitchen Charm Bag, 240; Knotty Hair Spells, 245; Luck Envelope Spell (Envelope Spells entry), 50; Money Pyramid Spell, 47; Nine Witch-Knots Charm, 250; Knob Candles for Luck, 106; Open Sesame (Sesame Seeds entry), 129; Paid in Full, 51; Personalize Your Seven-Day Candle, 104; Putting Down Roots: A Spell for Moving to a New Location, 143; Sweetener Spell, 271; Tealight Love Candle Spell, 100; Turn Your Tea into a Magic Potion, 141; Witches' Ladder, 235

Banishing: Angelica Athame Spell, 213; Apple Spell for Health and Protection, 148; Bad Neighbor Onion Spell (Onions entry), 128; Binding Knotted Hair Spell, 248; Blessing Bowl, 25; Breaking Up with a Person Spell, 103; Building the Cone of Power, 68; Charm for Protection, 280; Citrus for Justice, 139; Cut Them Out!, 243; Drive Away Enemies, 101; Ending Harassment with a Banana (Banana entry), 126; Get Out of My House (Spit Magick entry), 73; Get Out of My Parking Spot (Spit Magick entry), 73; Herbal Charm Bag for Protection, 135; Home and Yard Protection Spell with Sunflower Seeds, 138; Invisibility Spell, 95; Letter to the Dead, 50; Make Your Own Witch Bottle, 267; Manage Your

Glossary

altar: The focal point of most Witch rituals and is where a great deal of spellwork is performed. At its simplest, an altar is simply where Witches put their stuff.

asperge: The process of sprinkling blessed and consecrated (salted) water around the circle for purification purposes. If an object other than the fingers is used to sprinkle the water (such as a mini broom or a feather), that object is called an *asperger.*

athame: A ceremonial knife or dagger used to project magickal energy. Athames are most commonly used to cast magick circles and for the ceremonies of cakes and ale and the Great Rite. Traditionally the athame is a double-sided steel blade about five inches long, with a wooden handle. Athames are rarely used for physical cutting.

bell: The energy of a rung bell can be used to clear a space of negative energy.

Beltane: A holiday celebrating the fullness of life, generally celebrated on May 1.

besom: A fancy name for a ritual broom. Besoms in ritual are generally used to sweep away negative energy.

boline: A knife exclusively used to tend to a Witch's magickal garden. Bolines are used to harvest vegetables, fruits, and herbs. The boline is often confused with the white-handled knife, and because of that confusion, many bolines have a white handle. The blade of a boline can be either straight or curved like a sickle.

Book of Shadows (BoS): A book containing the spellwork, rituals, thoughts, and dreams of a Witch. If it's sacred and important to you, it can go into a Book of Shadows. The earliest version of the BoS was reserved exclusively for Witch ritual and instruction. Since then, many Witches have begun keeping their own personal Book of Shadows.

chalice (or cup): A cup or wine glass reserved for Witchcraft ritual. The chalice is generally used during the ceremonies of cakes and ale and the (symbolic) Great Rite.

charge: To "charge" an item is to infuse it with your own magickal energy. In ritual, a charge is a firsthand written revelation from deity itself (such as the Charge of the Goddess). The term *charge* in this context is originally Masonic and indicated a set of instructions.

circle: A Witch's working space, generally created with personal and natural energies. A circle exists between the mundane world and that of higher powers. Circles can be cast anywhere. The term *circle* often indicates an open ritual group that performs Witch rites. The term *circled* is used by many Witches to indicate the people they practice ritual with, as in "I circled with Phoenix and Gwion."

coven: A Witch ritual group that acts in perfect love and perfect trust. Some Traditional Witch groups use the term *cuveen* as an alternative.

covenstead: The territory of a Witch coven. A coven's covenstead is their base of operations.

Cowan: A term for a non-Witch. This word was originally Masonic and referred to non-Masons.

Craft, the: An abbreviation of *Witchcraft*. The term *the Craft* originally referred to Freemasonry.

creative visualization (CV): A mental picture used in magickal work in order to apply intent to energy. Creative visualization (or CV) is one of the building blocks of magickal practice.

degree: A symbol of rank and/or accomplishment in many initiatory Witchcraft traditions.

deosil: To walk or move clockwise. Clockwise is the default direction that energy moves in and is how most Witches operate in sacred space.

drawing down: The willful surrendering of consciousness to a higher power (generally a deity) so that higher power can interact with the people around them.

elements: The powers of air, fire, water, and earth. Most substances on Earth can be broken down into these four broad categories and contain attributes generally associated with one of these powers.

esbat: A Witch ritual performed on or near a full or new moon. Alternatively, an esbat might be used as shorthand for "Witch ritual not connected to a sabbat."

fey: A name used for the unseen folk who share this world with us. They are sometimes also known as the fair folk and as fairies. Despite Disney's claims to the contrary, the fey aren't always nice.

greater sabbats: This term refers to the cross-quarter sabbats of Samhain, Imbolc, Beltane, and Lughnasadh (or Lammas). The greater sabbats were all originally celebrated by the Celts of Ireland. Most Witches today celebrate an eight-spoked Wheel of the Year, with the sabbats on the equinoxes and solstices given equal standing with the cross-quarter holidays; but the first modern public Witches originally celebrated the solstices and equinoxes on the full moon closest to those events. Because the cross-quarter sabbats were celebrated on a traditional date instead of a full moon, they were seen as the "greater" sabbats.

intent: The specific, desired outcome of a magickal working.

invoke: An invitation to a higher power to be present at a ritual or magickal working. In some instances, *invoke* is used as a synonym for drawing down the moon.

Lammas: Another name for Lughnasadh, originally used by Anglo-Saxon Pagans and later by Christians.

lesser sabbats: The sabbats celebrated at the solstices and equinoxes: Yule, Ostara, Midsummer, and Mabon.

Like attracts like: A magickal philosophy that encourages the use of items and ideas that are similar to the magician's end goal. For instance, to attract love, you'd want to use ideas and items associated with love instead of the opposite. It also suggests that Witches will attract and find Witches similar to them because "like attracts like."

Lughnasadh: The celebration of the first harvest, generally observed between July 31 and August 2. Spellings of Lughnasadh will vary, and the sabbat is also called Lammas by some Witches.

Mabon: A name used by many Witches to indicate the Autumn Equinox. The term Mabon was first used by the Witch Aidan Kelly in the early 1970s and means "son of the mother." It's essentially a Modern Witch holiday, as there were no ancient Mabon celebrations, though harvest celebrations were common enough.

magick: Energy that is given a specific intention. Many Witches spell magick with a *k* to differentiate it from stage magic.

Midsummer: A sabbat celebrating the Summer Solstice, usually around June 21. Some Witches also call this sabbat Litha, which was first suggested by Aidan Kelly in the early 1970s.

Mighty Ones: A phrase used to indicate divine beings, generally deities. Some Witches also use the term *Mighty Ones* to indicate the watchtowers that are invoked at the quarters.

Pagan: Someone who practices a spiritual tradition that emphasizes the sacredness of the earth and calls upon pre-Christian deities. Because most Pagan traditions today utilize both modern and ancient ideas, practitioners are sometimes called Neo-Pagans.

pentacle: A round disc inscribed with a magickal symbol that is traditionally used to invoke spirits, angels, or demons. In most Modern Witchcraft traditions, the pentacle is viewed as a tool of earth and inscribed with a pentagram. It's generally used to bless the elements and serves as a gateway for both deity and magickal energy.

pentagram: A five-pointed star. The pentagram is most often depicted with one point facing upward, which represents the triumph of the spiritual over the material. Many left-hand-path traditions use the star with two points facing upward. In certain Wiccan traditions, the upside-down pentagram (with two points facing upward) is used to indicate the second degree.

perfect love and perfect trust: The ideal coven is said to operate in a state of "perfect love and perfect trust." Because of this, "perfect love and perfect trust" is often used as a password in Witchcraft rituals.

poppet: A doll constructed by a Witch to represent a specific person or idea. Whatever is done to the doll will affect the specific person or idea connected to the poppet.

sacred space: The interior of a magick circle. Alternatively, a room set aside specifically for ritual or magickal workings or an extremely powerful place in the natural world.

sabbat: A Witch holiday, most often associated with the solstices and equinoxes and the cross-quarter days that occur between them.

sachet: A small sewn-up magickal bag, generally stuffed with herbs, stones, and other items.

Samhain: A sabbat commemorating the year's final harvest, celebrated on October 31. Many Witches celebrate Samhain as the Witches' New Year. The modern Halloween is a descendent of the Samhain celebrations of the Irish Celts.

stang: A wooden stick, pole, or pitchfork used in many rituals by Traditional Witches. Stangs often function as the focal point of ritual, acting much like an altar, and can be decorated to represent the change of the seasons.

Summerlands: A place where souls go after death before reincarnating in this world. The term Summerlands comes to us from the Theosophical Society.

sword: A tool generally used to cast a magick circle. Anything a person can do with a sword, they can also do with an athame, and vice versa.

tradition: A specific Witchcraft subgroup that generally requires an initiation. Traditions often have their own Book of Shadows, and members can trace their lineage to a specific individual, such as Gerald Gardner (Gardnerian Wicca) or Cora Anderson (Feri Tradition).

Traditional Witchcraft: A Modern Witchcraft tradition most often focused on ideas found in magickal traditions such as cunning-craft. Oftentimes any Witch group not related to Wiccan-Witchcraft is included in this category.

watchtowers: Four powers that are invoked at the compass points of east, south, west, and north. The watchtowers are associated with the elemental energies of air, fire, water, and earth. In the grimoire tradition, the term *watchtowers* referred to the angels Raphael (east), Michael (south), Gabriel (west), and Uriel (north). The energy provided by the watchtowers is generally thought to be protective.

white-handled knife: A knife with a white handle that is commonly used for cutting or inscribing candles while in ritual space. It's sometimes known as a *kirfane* or a *kerfan*. The traditional white-handled knife is often confused with the boline.

Wicca: A Modern Witchcraft tradition that utilizes some form of the ritual structure first revealed by Gerald Gardner in the early 1950s. Wicca is probably best defined by its ritual structure and not by theological ideas.

widdershins: To walk or move counterclockwise. Widdershins energy is most often used for banishing or aggressive magickal workings.

Yule: The name for the holiday celebrated at the Winter Solstice. Many Christmas traditions actually stem from ancient pagan holidays celebrated near the winter solstice. Some Pagans call the holiday Midwinter, as it falls between Samhain and Imbolc (which are seen by some as the start dates of winter and spring, respectively).

Bibliography and Additional Resources

Most bibliographies are a list of sources cited in a book, but not this one. Sure, we are including the titles included in the footnotes, but it's also a list of supplementary material for those interested in additional titles on magick (mostly from a Witchcraft perspective). Attempting to write a book about a wide range of magickal practices meant that we were unable to devote large amounts of space to topics that deserve a book of their own. Luckily, a lot of those books have already been written, so we've included them here. Most people ignore the bibliographies in books, but we hope you'll take some time to dig into this one.

Many of the books included in this bibliography were written by friends and acquaintances of ours. No disrespect is meant or implied when Jason refers to them by their first names in this bibliography. It's simply how he knows them.

American Geosciences Institute. "How Can We Tell How Old Rocks Are?" Accessed December 4, 2021. https://www.americangeosciences.org/education /k5geosource/content/fossils/how-can-we-tell-how-old-rocks-are.

Atkin, Emily. "Do You Know Where Your Healing Crystals Come From?" The New Republic, May 11, 2018. https://newrepublic.com/article/148190/know-healing -crystals-come-from. This might be the best (and most up-to-date at the time of this writing) article on the ethical conundrums we face when it comes to buying stones and crystals.

Auryn, Mat. *Psychic Witch: A Metaphysical Guide to Meditation, Magick & Manifestation.* Woodbury, MN: Llewellyn, 2020. Early Modern Witches were quite focused on growing and harnessing their psychic powers. This is an aspect of Witchcraft that's often overlooked, making Mat's book a welcome remedy.

Beckett, John. *The Path of Paganism: An Experience-Based Guide to Modern Pagan Practice.* Woodbury, MN: Llewellyn, 2017. Interested in magick but Witchcraft isn't quite the right fit? Then dive into John's book on Paganism, which still presents a magickal worldview, just minus the cauldrons and pointy hats. And if you are a full-fledged Witch, this is still a great book for anyone who practices polytheism or works with a variety of higher powers.

Bird, Stephanie Rose. *Sticks, Stones, Roots & Bones: Hoodoo, Mojo & Conjuring with Herbs.* St. Paul, MN: Llewellyn, 2004. One of the best books on magickal herbs you'll ever read! Stephanie is terrific and you should read everything she writes.

Blackthorn, Amy. *Sacred Smoke: Clear Away Negative Energies and Purify Body, Mind, and Spirit.* Newburyport, MA: Weiser Books, 2019. Everything Amy writes is amazing. In addition to this book on incenses and other burnables, she also has books on essential oils and herbal potions.

Bogan, Chas. *The Secret Keys of Conjure: Unlocking the Mysteries of American Folk Magic.* Woodbury, MN: Llewellyn, 2018. Interested in learning more about Conjure and other forms of American magic? This is the place to start. Conjure, though, is not Witchcraft, and often utilizes the Christian Bible in some of its spellcraft.

Boxer, Alexander. *A Scheme of Heaven: The History of Astrology and the Search for Our Destiny in Data.* New York: W. W. Norton and Company, 2020. Boxer is an atheist, but his enthusiasm for casting astrological charts, alongside his lucid history of astrology's development, will have you interested in how the stars affect your life (or don't).

Boyer, Corinne. *Under the Witching Tree: A Folk Grimoire of Tree Lore and Practicum.* London: Troy Books, 2016. The best book on tree magick and folklore we've ever come across. If you love trees (and who doesn't?), you should track down this book!

Broedel, Hans Peter. *The Malleus Maleficarum and the Construction of Witchcraft.* Manchester: Manchester University Press, 2003. *The Malleus Maleficarum* translates as "Hammer of the Witches" and was a guide for hunting Witches originally published in 1487. We are not fans.

Buckland, Raymond. *Practical Candleburning Rituals: Spells & Rituals for Every Purpose.* 3rd ed. St. Paul, MN: Llewellyn, 1993. Many of the spells in Buckland's book call for multiple candles, which often cuts down on their practicality. Still, this is a heavily influential book and one of the earliest books dedicated strictly to candle magick. Buckland offers two versions of each spell here, one for Witches and one for Christians. Very interesting. Also by Buckland is *Advanced Candle Magick: More Spells and Rituals for Every Purpose*. St. Paul, MN: Llewellyn, 1996. Just in case you didn't get enough spells the first time!

Cabot, Laurie, with Tom Cowan. *Power of the Witch: The Earth, the Moon, and the Magical Path to Enlightenment*. New York: Delacorte Press, 1989. Laurie Cabot was one of the first public American Witches. Her influence on the Craft is enormous.

Francis James Child, ed. *The English and Scottish Popular Ballads, Volume 1*. Boston, MA: Houghton, Mifflin and Company, 1882. Accessed December 5, 2021. Available as a Project Gutenberg e-book at https://www.gutenberg.org /files/44969/44969-h/44969-h.htm#Ballad_6.

Colles, Dr. Abraham. "A Witches' Ladder." *The Folk-Lore Journal* 5, no. 1 (1887): 1–5. https://www.jstor.org/stable/1252510. Essential reading if you are interested in the history of the Witches' Ladder.

Cunningham, Scott. *The Complete Book of Incense, Oils & Brews*. St. Paul, MN: Llewellyn, 1989. (We have 2000's 21st printing.) Is this book truly complete? Probably not, but it does contain a lot of information and dozens of oil and incense blends and recipes.

———. *Cunningham's Encyclopedia of Crystal, Gem & Metal Magic*. St. Paul, MN: Llewellyn, 1988. (We have 1997's 18th printing.) Because of this book's age, there are a few stones missing and it dives into New Age territory now and again, but it's still a great resource.

———. *Cunningham's Encyclopedia of Magical Herbs*. St. Paul, MN: Llewellyn, 1985. (We have 1997's 23rd printing.) It's hard to imagine a complete Witch library without all three of the Cunningham books listed here. Some of the material feels a little dated (Do plants really have "masculine" and "feminine" energies? We don't think so), but there's so much information in all of these books. Out of all three volumes, it's probably *Magical Herbs* that has aged the best, which explains in part why it's still a best seller.

Darcey, Cheralyn. *The Book of Herb Spells*. NSW, Australia: Rockpool Publishing, 2018. I thought I had a lot of magickal books until Amanda shared her contributions to the bibliography with me!

Davies, Owen. *Popular Magic: Cunning-Folk in English History*. London: Hambledon Continuum, 2003. Davies has written extensively about the history of magickal practice over the last twenty years or so. Also recommended, though not cited in this book, is Davies's *Grimoires: A History of Magic Books*, published in 2009 by Oxford University Press.

De Greef, Kimon. "The White Sage Black Market," Vice, August 24, 2020. https:// www.vice.com/en_us/article/m7jkma/the-white-sage-black-market-v27n3. If you are curious to know why buying white sage can be extremely problematic, read this article.

D'Este, Sorita, and David Rankine. *Wicca: Magickal Beginnings*. London: Avalonia, 2008. This is one of the absolute best books ever written on Wiccan history. I love it so much! Also, I (Jason) have a little bit of a crush on Sorita. She's just so brilliant!

Douglass, Frederick. *Narrative of the Life of Frederick Douglass, an American Slave*. Boston, MA: The Anti-Slavery Office, 1845. There's something thrilling about getting to quote Douglass, a true American hero.

Drysdale, Christopher. In Jason Mankey's *The Witch's Book of Shadows*, 85–88. Woodbury, MN: Llewellyn, 2017.

DuQuette, Lon Milo, and David Shoemaker, eds. *Llewellyn's Complete Book of Ceremonial Magick: A Comprehensive Guide to the Western Mystery Tradition*. Woodbury, MN: Llewellyn, 2020. The magick here is very different from that in the book you currently hold in your hands, but it's worth a look if you're interested in history and the practice of ceremonial magick. There are dozens of authors in the pages of this massive tome, including our own Jason, who writes about five hundred words on Modern Witchcraft. Also, we wholeheartedly recommend anything written by both Shoemaker and DuQuette.

Einhorn, Aliza. *The Little Book of Saturn: Astrological Gifts, Challenges, and Returns*. Newburyport, MA: Weiser Books, 2018. The primary focus of this book is on the planet Saturn's role in astrology, but Aliza's introduction to astrology in the book's first third is so approachable that even if you aren't interested in Saturn, you still might love this book.

Farrar, Janet and Stewart. *A Witches' Bible: The Complete Witches' Handbook*. Custer, WA: Phoenix Publishing, 1996. Originally published in 1984 as *The Witches' Way*. This book is the best look yet at early Wiccan-Witchcraft, and is one of the most thumbed-through and consistently used books in our Witchcraft libraries.

Frazer, Sir James George. *The Golden Bough: The Roots of Religion and Folklore.* Two volumes. 1890. Reprint, New York: Crown, 1981. Frazer's magnum opus has been incredibly influential in the Witch and Pagan worlds.

———. *Folk-Lore in the Old Testament: Studies in Comparative Religion, Legend, and Law.* Two volumes. London: Macmillan and Co., 1918.

Freuler, Kate. *Of Blood and Bones: Working with Shadow Magic & the Dark Moon.* Woodbury, MN: Llewellyn, 2020. Freuler's book was released as we were finishing up what you now hold in your hands, but it's so good that we rushed to put it in this bibliography!

Maggie Fox. "Mystery of Exotic Infectious Disease Traced to Aromatherapy Room Spray." CNN, updated October 24, 2021. https://www.cnn.com/2021/10/23/health/aromatherapy-melioidosis-mystery/index.html. Think putting random stones in your water is fine? It's not.

Gardner, Gerald. *Witchcraft Today.* London: Rider and Company, 1954. Jason owns the edition published by IHO in 1999 (which contains inaccurate page numbers). There's a lot of stuff in Gardner's work that is not very applicable to today, but there are a few ritual moments here and there that are probably of interest to history nerds. Gardner's second Witchcraft book was *The Meaning of Witchcraft* (London: Aquarian Press, 1959), which wasn't much better. Also cited here is Gardner's 1949 fiction book *High Magic's Aid* (London: Michael Houghton, 1949).

Guiley, Rosemary Ellen. *The Encyclopedia of Witches & Witchcraft.* New York: Facts On File, 1999. This book was originally published in 1989, so some of the historical entries have some issues. But if you ever need to look up a word like *binding*, you'll find a clear and concise definition, along with a lot of historical context. Super useful book!

Hall, Judy. *The Crystal Bible: A Definitive Guide to Crystals.* Cincinnati, OH: Walking Stick Press, 2004. This is one of Amanda's favorites and is a great resource on the metaphysical properties of stones and crystals.

Harrison, Karen. *The Herbal Alchemist's Handbook: A Grimoire of Philtres, Elixirs, Oils, Incense, and Formulas for Ritual Use.* San Francisco, CA: Weiser Books, 2011.

Heldstab, Celeste Rayne. *Llewellyn's Complete Formulary of Magical Oils: Over 1200 Recipes, Potions & Tinctures for Everyday Use.* Woodbury, MN: Llewellyn, 2012. All of Llewellyn's "Complete" books are treasure troves of information!

Holland, Eileen. *The Wicca Handbook.* York Beach, ME: Samuel Weiser, 2000. One of the handiest and most complete books of magickal correspondences ever. This book is a virtual treasure trove of information. Fantastic! We also recommend Holland's *The Spellcrafter's Reference: Magical Timing for the Wheel of the Year* (San Francisco, CA: Red Wheel/Weiser, 2009).

Illes, Judika. *Pure Magic: A Complete Course in Spellcasting.* San Francisco, CA: Weiser Books, 2007. Everything Judika writes is amazing! Also, she sometimes does workshops with our wonderful editor Elysia Gallo at Pagan events. Those classes are always a must-see!

John of Monmouth, with Gillian Spraggs and Shani Oates. *Genuine Witchcraft Is Explained: The Secret History of the Royal Windsor Coven & the Regency.* Somerset, UK: Capall Bann, 2012. This is the most complete (and exhaustive) text ever dedicated to Robert Cochrane (the architect of what has come to be known as Traditional Witchcraft) and his original coven, and is one of Jason's absolute favorite books! Just three years after this book was published, Jon Day, the cofounder of Capall Bann, passed away, and with Day, his publishing house. Day's death meant that *Genuine Witchcraft* never got a second printing, and copies today go for several hundred dollars online. If you are a history nerd, this book is still worth tracking down (or borrowing if you have a friend who will part with it for a few weeks!).

K, Amber. *True Magick: A Beginner's Guide.* St. Paul, MN: Llewellyn, 1990. We had the original version of what many call "the little green book," which was published as a mass-market paperback. A revised and extended second edition was published in 2006, also by Llewellyn. K's writing is terrific and her spellcraft strong. This is another great starting point!

Kelden. *The Crooked Path: An Introduction to Traditional Witchcraft.* Woodbury, MN: Llewellyn, 2020. Most books in the Traditional Witchcraft category are hard to follow, often intentionally so, but that's not the case with Kelden. This is one of the two books to pick up if you are interested in non-Wiccan-style Witch rites. (The other book is below—keep reading!)

King, Graham. *The British Book of Spells & Charms.* London: Troy Books, 2019. For many years King was the proprietor of the Museum of Witchcraft and Magic in Boscastle, England. If you ever find yourself in Cornwall, you should stop by the museum.

Kynes, Sandra. *Llewellyn's Complete Book of Correspondences: A Comprehensive & Cross-Referenced Resource for Pagans & Wiccans.* Woodbury, MN: Llewellyn, 2013. This is a book that lives up to its title. There's more information here than most Witches will ever need.

———. *Llewellyn's Complete Book of Essential Oils: How to Blend, Diffuse, Create Remedies, and Use in Everyday Life.* Woodbury, MN: Llewellyn, 2019. This book is 336 pages long. We spend 36 pages discussing oils, so there's more here for those looking to expand their knowledge.

LeFae, Phoenix. *What Is Remembered Lives: Developing Relationships with Deities, Ancestors & the Fae,* Woodbury, MN: Llewellyn, 2019. Looking to build relationships with deity and other higher powers? This is the best place to start. We are big fans of Phoenix. All of her books are awesome.

Lightfoot, Najah. *Good Juju: Mojos, Rites & Practices for the Magical Soul.* Woodbury, MN: Llewellyn, 2019. This book is both an excellent introduction to spellcraft and something for experienced practitioners.

Long, Carolyn Morrow. *Spiritual Merchants: Religion, Magic, and Commerce.* Knoxville, TN: University of Tennessee Press, 2001. This book is a history of magickal stores and botanicas, especially ones focused on Conjure and Hoodoo. It's as fun to read as it is enlightening.

Mankey, Jason. *Transformative Witchcraft: The Greater Mysteries.* Woodbury, MN: Llewellyn, 2019. Jason spends a lot of time (and we mean *a lot* of time) on cleansing, circle casting, and building the cone of power in this book.

———. *The Witch's Athame.* Woodbury, MN: Llewellyn, 2016. My first book, which I'm immensely proud of. I think the rituals in this book have held up especially well!

———. *The Witch's Book of Shadows.* Woodbury, MN: Llewellyn, 2017. We are including this book mostly because of the bit written by Christopher Drysdale on the Emerald Tablet.

———. *Witch's Wheel of the Year: Circles, Solitaries & Covens.* Woodbury, MN: Llewellyn, 2019. This is on the list because it contains twenty-four different ways to set up sacred space, including versions from both Wicca and Traditional Witchcraft.

Mankey, Jason, and Laura Tempest Zakroff. *The Witch's Altar.* Woodbury, MN: Llewellyn, 2018. Perhaps the most useful book I've ever helped write (until this one). Not every Witch has an athame, but just about everyone has an altar!

Miller, Jason. *Protection & Reversal Magick: A Witch's Defense Manual.* Franklin Lakes, NJ: New Page Books, 2006. Looking for more magickal defense techniques? This is the book. Also, another Jason!

Mooney, Thorn. *Traditional Wicca: A Seeker's Guide.* Woodbury, MN: Llewellyn, 2018. Designed specifically for Witches interested in initiatory Craft, this is the best introduction to Gardnerian and Alexandrian-style Witchcraft on the market. Thorn is also a terrific writer and one of our favorite people.

Morrison, Dorothy. *Bud, Blossom, & Leaf: The Magical Herb Gardener's Handbook.* St. Paul, MN: Llewellyn, 2001. Did you know that Jason sometimes sends Dorothy private messages about professional football? They might be the only two Witches who are about such things.

Nelson, Bryan. "The World's Ten Oldest Living Trees." Treehugger, updated October 19, 2020. https://www.treehugger.com/the-worlds-oldest-living-trees-4869356.

Orapello, Christopher, and Tara-Love Maguire. *Besom, Stang & Sword: A Guide to Traditional Witchcraft, the Six-Fold Path & the Hidden Landscape.* Newburyport, MA: Weiser Books, 2018. A thorough and easily digestible look at Witchcraft from a non-Wiccan perspective.

Pearson, Nicholas. *Stones of the Goddess: Crystals for the Divine Feminine.* Rochester, VT: Inner Traditions, 2019. We didn't think anything would ever replace *Cunningham's Encyclopedia of Crystal, Gem & Metal Magic*, but this book probably does. Not only is it comprehensive, bit it also features full-color pictures of every stone written about in the book. Nicholas's follow-up, *Crystal Basics: The Energetic, Healing & Spiritual Power of 200 Gemstones*, published in 2020, is just as good!

Purkis, Diane. "Witches in Macbeth." British Library, March 15, 2016. https://www.bl.uk/shakespeare/articles/witches-in-macbeth#.

Randolph, Vance. *Ozark Magic and Folklore.* New York: Dover Publications, 1967. Originally published in 1947. What makes this book interesting is that it contains a lot of indigenous folk magick native to the Ozarks (and before that, most likely Germany and Scotland). Over the years, some people have used it to argue that there was a genuine self-identifying Witch tradition in the American Ozarks, but a critical reading of the book argues against that.

Raven, Gwion. *The Magick of Food: Rituals, Offerings & Why We Eat Together.* Woodbury, MN: Llewellyn, 2020. Curious about all the magickal stuff in your kitchen? Gwion has you covered. Also, Gwion is a coven brother. We run around with some really cool Witches.

RavenWolf, Silver. *To Ride a Silver Broomstick.* St. Paul, MN: Llewellyn, 1990. All of RavenWolf's books are full of practical magickal advice and easy-to-do spells. She's also like the "book mother" to Witches of both Generation X and Millennials.

Riske, Kris Brandt. *Llewellyn's Complete Book of Astrology: The Easy Way to Learn Astrology.* Woodbury, MN: Llewellyn, 2007. There are a lot of these "Llewellyn's Complete" books in this bibliography because they are great books!

Ross, John, ed. *The Book of Scottish Poems: Ancient and Modern.* Edinburgh: Edinburgh Publishing, 1884. Books like this are great sources of inspiration when trying to come up with words for a spell or ritual!

Smith, Steven R. *Wylundt's Book of Incense.* York Beach, ME: Samuel Weiser, 1989. Both Amanda and Matt are big fans of this book, and think it's one of the best introductions to those who walk the magickal path. There are formulas for some very unique incense blends, too!

Starhawk. *The Spiral Dance: A Rebirth of the Ancient Religion of the Goddess.* 20th anniversary ed. New York: HarperCollins, 1999. Originally published in 1979. This might be the most important Witchcraft book ever written. Starhawk is a tremendous writer and her influence is enormous.

Taylor, Astrea. *Intuitive Witchcraft: How to Use Intuition to Elevate Your Craft.* Woodbury, MN: Llewellyn, 2020. We talk a little about intuition and its use in magick in these pages, but Astrea wrote an entire book about it. An absolutely beautiful book about magickal practice in Modern Witchcraft.

Tyson, Donald. *Ritual Magic: What It Is & How to Do It.* St. Paul, MN: Llewellyn, 1992. A concise history of magickal practice, along with some great how-to material and peeks into magick as practiced in a variety of spiritual and religious traditions. This was one of Jason's first books about magick, and it helped shape his practice tremendously.

Valiente, Doreen. *Natural Magic.* Custer, WA: Phoenix Publishing, 1986. Doreen has been hailed as the "mother of Modern Witchcraft," and the title is apt. Also, she and Jason share a birth date, something he points out in every one of his bibliographies.

Webster, Richard. *Llewellyn's Complete Book of Divination: Your Definitive Source for Learning Predictive & Prophetic Techniques.* Woodbury, MN: Llewellyn, 2017.

We aren't sure if divination falls under the "magickal" umbrella, which is why it's not included in this book, but if you want to learn more about divination techniques, this is a great place to start!

Zakroff, Laura Tempest. *Sigil Witchery: A Witch's Guide to Crafting Magick Symbols.* Woodbury MN: Llewellyn, 2018. Our book has two thousand words about sigil magick in it; Tempest wrote an entire book on sigils. This is an absolutely amazing book that will take your sigil making to a higher level. Yeah, Jason wrote a book with Tempest, but even if he hadn't, we would still be recommending this book wholeheartedly. While writing the book in your hands, Jason started reading Tempest's *Anatomy of a Witch*, published by Llewellyn in 2021. WOW! Destined to be another classic, *Anatomy* is recommended for anyone who wants to fully embody their magickal practice.

Acknowledgments

The idea for this book first came to me (Jason) in the place where all my ideas for books come from: the shower. After finishing up *The Horned God of the Witches*, I spent some time daydreaming in the bathroom and came up with the basic outline for what you now hold in your hands. After putting on a pair of underwear (or did I?), I excitedly sent Matt a few messages about the idea, wondering if he would be interested in coming aboard to help with the spellcraft. Ari, credited or uncredited, is a part of everything I write and was quickly added to the project as well. As one of the best Witches we all know, Amanda was the final piece in the puzzle.

This book was written during COVID-19, which presented a lot of challenges. The initial plan was to meet every couple of weeks, discuss magick, and then spend time in our ritual room crafting spells together. We did get to do that a few times, but as the crisis escalated, we found that most of our magickal evenings were now limited to Zoom calls and much of our shared spellcraft was now being done in a Facebook group instead of face-to-face.

Despite the obstacles, I still feel like this book was a group effort, and if a few sentences here or there seem contradictory, it's because of that. Why are there so many magick books on the market? Because everyone interprets magick just a little bit differently, and that goes for the four people (and several outside contributors) who put this book together.

I want to thank Amanda and Matt for their invaluable contributions to this book. With your input, knowledge, and wisdom, it all came together. You two are truly among the finest Witches I know. Ari is my rock and my magickal compass: your name belongs on this book even if you aren't sure of that.

Special thanks to those who contributed their time and expertise to this work: Martha Kirby Capo, Ian Chambers, Lilith Dorsey, Katie Gerrard, Gwyn, Phoenix LeFae, Irisanaya Moon, Thorn Mooney, Jessica Ripley, Alura Rose, Bader Saab, and

Astrea Taylor. I have so much respect and love for all of you. Your contributions made this book that much better. Thank you for letting us show people that there are many approaches to magick. A special shout-out to Lisa Jade, who contributed an amazing piece on poppet magick for this book that sadly ended up on the cutting room floor due to space limitations. Every person thanked here is a fellow writer, and their works are all amazing and worth picking up!

A special shout-out to our friends Callie and Firman for entertaining Ari and me during the shelter-in-place orders. Those nights of socially distanced wine not only kept our spirits up but also helped keep us sane during a difficult time.

Ari wants to thank her family, most especially the Kuchta clan: Brian, Allison, Tim, Christy, Mary, Nick, Mike, and most especially Kevin (dad) and Monica. Jason also sends a special shout-out to the Big Kev and Monica, who have been amazingly supportive the last eight years or whatever. Ari wants to thank her mom, too, but her mother would be horrified that her daughter wrote a Witchcraft book, so we'll leave her name out.

Amanda wishes to thank her magickal kin who have helped shape her into the Witch she is today: Alisa, Nikki, Didi, Susan, Melissa, the Midnight Margaritas, Community Seed, OS, and her dearest Uncle Rabbit. And to her family, Corrinne, Stuart, and Rebecca, for their support.

Matt wishes to thank his Serpent's Kiss family, Ile Ire, his mother Carol, his grandmother Joyce, and her mother and his great-grandmother Margret, and also Kitt, his Reindeer King, for his endless encouragement and support!

I've thanked a lot of people over the course of eight books, so it feels redundant to share most of those names again, so I won't. But make no mistake, I'm so very appreciative of my friends in the Pagan writing community and the amazing folks at Llewellyn who keep publishing my scribbles. I'm even more appreciative of those of you who buy these books and say mostly nice things about them, you are the folks ~~I am writing for~~ we are writing for.

Blessed be!

Jason Mankey, with Matt Cavalli, Amanda Lynn, and Ari Mankey

To Write to the Author

If you wish to contact the author or would like more information about this book, please write to the author in care of Llewellyn Worldwide Ltd. and we will forward your request. Both the author and the publisher appreciate hearing from you and learning of your enjoyment of this book and how it has helped you. Llewellyn Worldwide Ltd. cannot guarantee that every letter written to the author can be answered, but all will be forwarded. Please write to:

Jason Mankey
℅ Llewellyn Worldwide
2143 Wooddale Drive
Woodbury, MN 55125-2989
Please enclose a self-addressed stamped envelope for reply,
or $1.00 to cover costs. If outside the U.S.A., enclose
an international postal reply coupon.
Many of Llewellyn's authors have websites with additional information and resources. For more information, please visit our website at
http://www.llewellyn.com.